Privatization, Corporate Governance and the
Emergence of Markets

## Studies in Economic Transition

*General Editors*: **Jens Hölscher**, Professor of Economics, University of Brighton; and **Horst Tomann**, Professor of Economics, Free University Berlin

This series has been established in response to a growing demand for a greater understanding of the transformation of economic systems. It brings together theoretical and empirical studies on economic transition and economic development. The post-communist transition from planned to market economies is one of the main areas of applied theory, as it is in this field that the most dramatic examples of change and economic dynamics can be found. The series aims to contribute to the understanding of specific major economic changes as well as to advance the theory of economic development. The implications of economic policy are a major point of focus.

*Titles include*:

Irwin Collier, Herwig Roggemann, Oliver Scholz and Horst Tomann (*editors*)
WELFARE STATES IN TRANSITION
East and West

Hubert Gabrisch and Rüdiger Pohl (*editors*)
EU ENLARGEMENT AND ITS MACROECONOMIC EFFECTS IN
EASTERN EUROPE
Currencies, Prices, Investment and Competitiveness

Jens Hölscher (*editor*)
FINANCIAL TURBULENCES AND CAPITAL MARKETS IN TRANSITION
COUNTRIES

Jens Hölscher and Anja Hochberg (*editors*)
EAST GERMANY'S ECONOMIC DEVELOPMENT SINCE UNIFICATION
Domestic and Global Aspects

Emil J. Kirchner (*editor*)
DECENTRALIZATION AND TRANSITION IN THE VISEGRAD
Poland, Hungary, the Czech Republic and Slovakia

Gregg S. Robins
BANKING IN TRANSITION
East Germany after Unification

Johannes Stephan
ECONOMIC TRANSITION IN HUNGARY AND EAST GERMANY
Gradualism and Shock Therapy in Catch-up Development

---

**Studies in Economic Transition**
**Series Standing Order ISBN 0–333–73353–3**
(*outside North America only*)

You can receive future titles in this series as they are published by placing a standing order. Please contact your bookseller or, in case of difficulty, write to us at the address below with your name and address, the title of the series and the ISBN quoted above.

Customer Services Department, Macmillan Distribution Ltd, Houndmills, Basingstoke, Hampshire RG21 6XS, England

---

# Privatization, Corporate Governance and the Emergence of Markets

Edited by

Eckehard F. Rosenbaum
*Senior Economist*
*Federal Ministry of Economics and Technology*
*Berlin*
*Germany*

Frank Bönker
*Lecturer in Economics*
*European University Viadrina*
*Frankfurt (Oder)*
*Germany*

and

Hans-Jürgen Wagener
*Professor of Economics*
*European University Viadrina*
*Frankfurt (Oder)*
*Germany*

First published in Great Britain 2000 by
**MACMILLAN PRESS LTD**
Houndmills, Basingstoke, Hampshire RG21 6XS and London
Companies and representatives throughout the world

A catalogue record for this book is available from the British Library.

ISBN 0–333–77892–8

First published in the United States of America 2000 by
**ST. MARTIN'S PRESS, INC.,**
Scholarly and Reference Division,
175 Fifth Avenue, New York, N.Y. 10010

ISBN 0–312–23034–6

Library of Congress Cataloging-in-Publication Data
Privatization, corporate governance and the emergence of markets / edited by
Eckehard F. Rosenbaum, Frank Bönker, and Hans-Jürgen Wagener.
p.   cm. (Studies in economic transition)
Includes bibliographical references and index.
ISBN 0–312–23034–6 (cloth)
1. Privatization—Europe, Eastern.   2. Corporate governance—Europe, Eastern. I.
Rosenbaum, Eckehard F., 1967–   II, Bönker, Frank.   III. Wagener,
Hans-Jürgen.   IV. Series

HD4140.7 .P723   1999
338.947'05—dc21

99–047836

# Contents

v

# Foreword

The general line of argument within this collaborative work is that markets cannot be assumed as given but rather, are emerging. This message is supported within the context of privatization on the political and theoretical levels. The theoretical dimension combines the analysis of the transformation of corporate governance structures and the transformation of supplier, sales and communication network – issues usually treated separately. To this extent a guide to what institutional economics has to offer is provided. For applied economic policy privatization policy during transition from planned to market economies might by now be of historical interest. However, for corporate governance within its institutional 'embeddedness' experiences of transition economies might guide the future economic policy of market economies.

JENS HÖLSCHER, *Chemnitz*
HORST TOMANN, *Berlin*

# Acknowledgements

The papers which are collected in the present volume were presented at a conference held in Berlin on 22 and 23 May, 1998. We would like to thank first of all the Deutsche Forschungsgemeinschaft for generously supporting this event as part of its funding for the Frankfurt Institute for Transformation Studies, the centre of transformation research at the European University Viadrina in Frankfurt (Oder). And we would also like to thank Andreas Paul for his help in organizing the event, and Bożena Jankowska and Marcin Kowalewski for editorial assistance.

E. F. R.
F. B.
H.-J. W.

# List of Contributors

**Wladimir Andreff**
*Université de Paris I Panthéon – Sorbonne*

**Frank Bönker**
*European University Viadrina, Frankfurt (Oder)*

**Wendy Carlin**
*University College London*

**Robert Chudzik**
*European University Viadrina, Frankfurt (Oder)*

**Stijn Claessens**
*World Bank, Washington, DC*

**Simeon Djankov**
*World Bank, Washington, DC*

**Rainer Gesell**
*European University Viadrina, Frankfurt (Oder)*

**Ralph Heinrich**
*Institute of World Economics, Kiel*

**Gábor Hunya**
*Vienna Institute for International Economic Studies (WIIW)*

**Michael Keren**
*Hebrew University, Jerusalem*

**Klaus Meyer**
*Copenhagen Business School*

**Péter Mihályi**
*Central European University, Budapest*

**Pieter W. Moerland**
*Tilburg University*

**Eckehard F. Rosenbaum**
*Federal Ministry of Economics and Technology, Berlin*

**Uwe Siegmund**
*Institute of World Economics, Kiel*

**Dirck Süß**
*European University Viadrina, Frankfurt (Oder)*

**Hans-Jürgen Wagener**
*European University Viadrina, Frankfurt (Oder)*

# 1
# Privatization in Context: an Introduction

*Eckehard F. Rosenbaum, Frank Bönker and Hans-Jürgen Wagener*

Privatization is a major building block of transformation. At the same time, there are no precedents in Western countries for a privatization programme of the size and scope currently under way in Central and Eastern Europe. These peculiarities of privatization in Central and Eastern European countries and its long-term character have sparked and sustained the continuing interest of economists and other social scientists in the issue. Moreover the hitherto accumulated empirical evidence provides an unequalled opportunity to address issues, pertaining for instance to corporate governance and to the relationship between privatization and the emergence of markets, which not only play a central role in transformation countries but which are also relevant in established market economies, highlighting as they do questions which are of paramount importance for the understanding of market economies themselves.

For obvious reasons, the literature on post-communist privatization was, at the beginning of transformation, essentially normative. On the basis of first principles and some, rather meagre, experience from privatization in Organization for Economic Cooperation and Development (OECD) and developing countries, a flood of papers tried to categorize the available options and discussed the pros and cons of different ways to privatize state-owned enterprises. In the course of transition, however, this picture has changed and an increasing number of studies has begun to develop a modified and in many respects more elaborate perspective on privatization.

To understand this shift of perspective, it needs to be emphasized first that privatization cannot be seen as a genuine economic objective. Rather, if the ultimate objective of the economic transformation is the improvement of economic welfare through increased competition and an efficient division of labour, the implementation of competitive markets is what matters most, and the role of privatization must be seen in the light of its relationship to this goal. That is, the relevant question is now whether markets emerge more or less spontaneously and automatically and whether the transfer of property rights to private hands is a necessary if not sufficient condition for the efficient working of the economic system. Moreover, to what extent does privatization contribute to the emergence of economic actors, and to the development of constraints and incentives which are conducive to market-related behaviour?

Two observations indicate that these questions are far from trivial. For one thing, the transformational recession which has hit all transformation countries much more severely than originally expected attests to the fact that the abolishment of one coordination mechanism, the plan, does not result in the automatic emergence of another, the market. Rather, abolishing the plan means first of all that there is no coordination mechanism whatsoever. At least in part, the transformational recession has therefore to be explained by a *lack* of coordination (Kornai, 1994). For another, not least the Chinese experience suggests (cf. Weitzman, 1993; Herrmann-Pillath, 1994; Krug, 1997) that privatization is not evidently necessary for the implementation of a market economy and hence the emergence of markets as *the* central element of such an economic order. Apparently, decentralized coordination via the price mechanism as well as competition among economic agents can emerge even if the structure and allocation of property rights is neither well specified nor individualized.

Indeed, that the transfer of public property to private hands does not suffice for the implementation of a *functioning* market economy is underlined by the continuing debate in both established market economies and transition economies on the relative merits of different systems of corporate governance as exemplified by the commonplace contrast between the Anglo-Saxon capital market-based system, on the one hand, and the Germanic bank-based system on the other (cf. Edwards and Fischer, 1994; Wagener, 1996, 1997) and by the concerns this debate has raised regarding the fear of short-termism and excessive insider power, respectively.

A second reason which explains the aforementioned shift of perspective is that, 10 years into privatization, there can be no doubt that privatization is a *political* project, as is the implementation of a market economy in general. Indeed markets and their accompanying institutions are, and have always been, the (by-)products of political processes and decisions (Polanyi, 1944). Both are the outcomes of decisions in which political means are used in order to achieve extra-economic objectives. However the specific conditions of transformation make political influence over, and political repercussions from, privatization even more likely than in established market economies because the creation of a market economy was explicitly formulated as an objective of economic policy in transition countries. Hence it should not come as a surprise that the design of privatization programmes in transformation countries is heavily influenced by extra-economic considerations and forces, the more so as privatization has by definition profound distributional consequences which invite rent seeking and coalition building among those most affected by the outcomes of the privatization process.

Both the political nature of privatization and its instrumental function as regards the creation of markets suggest that privatization has to be examined from a much broader perspective. This broader perspective encompasses three dimensions. The first consists of a positive analysis of privatization which blends economic and political aspects with a view to identifying the determinants of privatization choices as well as cross-country differences and similarities of methods and outcomes. A second dimension includes the interrelationship of privatization, corporate control and enterprise restructuring in an attempt to investigate the preconditions and the progress of enterprise restructuring. A third strand, finally, looks at the development of markets and the emergence of market actors *vis-à-vis* different privatization methods and large-scale institutional changes.

The present volume is divided into three parts which correspond to the aforementioned dimensions. The first part contains contributions which focus on the policies and politics of privatization; the chapters of the second part address the connexion between privatization, corporate governance and enterprise restructuring; the pieces in the third part, finally, elaborate upon privatization and the emergence of markets. In this introduction, we shall give a brief overview of the subsequent chapters and relate them to some themes in the general literature.

## The political and fiscal dimension of privatization

Post-communist privatization has essentially been a political project. While spontaneous processes of privatization 'from below' have arguably played a greater role than originally expected, government decisions and programmes have remained at the very heart of the privatization process. Paradoxical as it may sound, the destatization and depoliticization at which privatization has aimed have presupposed political decisions and government programmes. Unlike the situation in the West, 'original endowments' in the East have not 'emerged', but have been deliberately 'created'.

It is thus owing to the political nature of post-communist privatization that initial attention largely concentrated on the optimal design of privatization policies. Only gradually, complementary evolutionary processes, ranging from the substantial privatization 'from below' in Poland to the more or less spontaneous emergence of investment funds in Czechoslovakia, have come into focus. In the course of the transition, the focus has thus shifted somewhat from *privatization as a programme* to *privatization as a process*. With privatization approaching its completion in the frontrunner countries, the analysis of privatization programmes, as it has dominated the early literature on post-communist privatization, will further decline in the future.

Its essentially political character has also meant that privatization has served political as well as economic goals. Privatization has been used to buy off opposition and to build up a constituency for reform (Roland, 1994). This is most visible in the case of mass privatization. While some economic arguments for the giving away of state-owned assets, such as the overcoming of absorption problems, can be formulated, most advocates of mass privatization have put emphasis on its political rationale and have embraced it as a means to make capitalism popular and privatization irreversible. This political use of privatization has stirred the interest in positive theories of privatization, in trade-offs between economic and political goals of privatization and in a privatization design less prone to political instrumentalization.

The first part of the present volume contains three chapters which concentrate on the policies and politics of privatization. The chapters by Rainer Gesell and Uwe Siegmund deal with privatization policies in two countries which have attracted considerable attention within the literature, namely Poland and the former German Democratic Republic (GDR). In contrast, the complementary chapter by Dirck Süß takes a comparative approach. Based on evidence from Hungary, Poland and the Czech Republic, it dwells upon the often mentioned, but rarely analysed, fiscal dimension of post-communist privatization.

In Poland, the privatization of state-owned enterprises has progressed rather slowly. While a mass privatization scheme was drawn up relatively early, political quarrels delayed its implementation until 1994. The scheme eventually adopted has differed strongly from the

Czech and Russian varieties of mass privatization. In line with the re-commendations of many economists, it assigned a central role to newly created National Investment Funds as a means to ensure strong outside ownership. Chapter 2 provides an in-depth analysis of the Polish mass privatization programme. Using a set of political and economic criteria, Gesell identifies a number of flaws in, and weaknesses of, this programme. He argues in particular that its limited size and slow implementation have prevented the forging of a strong pro-reform constituency, and voices concerns that the strong role of the state, the centralist design and the lack of clear-cut incentives for the funds threaten to infringe upon restructuring.

The former GDR represents a special case of a sales-oriented privat-ization. In privatizing the East German economy, the Treuhandanstalt, the German privatization agency, predominantly relied on negotiated sales. Chapter 3 provides an evaluation of East German privatization. In contrast to the bulk of the literature on the Treuhandanstalt, the author adopts a politicoeconomic approach. He shows how politicians have tried to exert influence on the Treuhandanstalt's activities and have burdened the Treuhandanstalt with a set of contradictory goals. Siegmund argues that the assignment of additional distributive goals to the Treuhandanstalt and the concomitant use of negotiations instead of auctions came at high efficiency costs. Accordingly, the large deficit incurred by the Treuhandanstalt was not caused by absorption prob-lems or the wage hike, but largely reflected the instrumentalization of the Treuhandanstalt for purposes of social and regional policy.

As evidence from OECD and developing countries shows, privatiz-ation can also serve fiscal goals. While this fiscal dimension of privat-ization featured prominently in early papers on post-communist privatization, it has yet to be studied more thoroughly. In Chapter 4, Dirck Süß attempts to close this gap by identifying and comparing the state revenues earned from privatization in Hungary, Poland and the Czech Republic. Süß draws attention to what he calls 'the paradox of privatization revenues', namely the fact that the Czech government, in spite of the famous voucher privatization and a generous restitution programme, has achieved rather high privatization revenues. Examining possible explanations, he argues that the buoyant privatiz-ation revenues in the Czech Republic did not simply stem from a greater stock of privatized assets, but reflected a clever privatization design and a smaller political risk. In pointing at some revenue-enhancing effects of voucher privatization, Süß's chapter echoes arguments made in a paper by Schmidt (1997).

## Privatization, corporate governance and economic restructuring

One of the most important economic goals of post-communist privatization has been the improvement of corporate governance. It is a truism, although a sometimes forgotten one, that private ownership can come in different forms and that for the benefits of private ownership to materialize the 'right' structures of corporate governance must prevail. At the same time, we still know surprisingly little about the actual functioning and the performance of these structures. While a lot has been written about the contrast between capital market and bank-based systems of corporate governance, issues such as the genesis of these systems, the particular relationships between the different system elements, the threshold values for effective corporate governance or the impact of different corporate governance systems on national patterns of economic specialization are far from being resolved.

The privatization process in Eastern Europe has created a unique opportunity to address these issues. As a result of differences in both privatization strategies and the regulatory framework, patterns of ownership and control have differed widely over time, between countries and within countries. The remaining state-owned enterprises have co-existed with quite different forms of private and privatized enterprises. Against this backdrop, the literature has focused on the connexion between privatization, corporate governance and enterprise restructuring. At the outset of transformation, the debate largely concentrated on the models of corporate governance the transition countries should strive for (Corbett and Mayer, 1991; Stiglitz, 1992) and the expected effects of different privatization strategies on corporate governance. In the course of the transition, empirical analyses of the relationship between privatization, corporate governance and economic restructuring at the macro and micro level have gained ground. It goes without saying that these empirical studies arrive at different results. However it clearly emerges from this literature that the simple dichotomy of private and public ownership is not very helpful in understanding the outcomes of privatization and the patterns of economic restructuring. Instead additional distinctions between inside and outside owners, concentrated and dispersed ownership, as well as different types of inside and outside owners (foreign investors, banks, other enterprises, managers, workers, the state), need to be made. In spite of the mushrooming literature, however, the jury on the relative performance of the different ownership forms, as well as on the principal–agent model explicitly or implicitly underlying most of the literature, is still out (Earle and Estrin, 1997).

The second part of the volume assembles a number of contributions that address the relationship between privatization, corporate governance and enterprise restructuring. The eight chapters fall into three subgroups. The chapters by Pieter Moerland and Ralph Heinrich elaborate upon the characteristics and coherence of different systems of corporate governance; Chapters 7 and 8 confront the available theories of corporate governance with the empirical findings on privatization, corporate governance and enterprise restructuring in the transition countries; finally, the chapters by Péter Mihályi, Robert Chudzik, Stijn Claessens and Simeon Djankov, and Gábor Hunya focus on individual countries and/or particular aspects of corporate governance.

Chapter 5 surveys different models of corporate governance prevailing in OECD countries. Drawing on a host of data on ownership and control structures, Moerland distinguishes between what he calls market- and network-oriented corporate systems and contrasts the distinct features and the particular merits and drawbacks of these two systems. He concludes by drawing attention to some tendencies towards convergence which are fuelled by the current globalization.

In Chapter 6, Ralph Heinrich takes up these issues by elaborating upon complementarities in corporate governance. Pointing at strong complementarities between different features of corporate governance at both the enterprise and the policy level, Heinrich argues that the different instruments and institutions of corporate governance should be studied, not in isolation, but as elements of broader systems. Likewise any reform of corporate governance should bear the internal coherence of the relevant set of institutions in mind. Heinrich illustrates his case with the Czech experience. Contrary to conventional wisdom, which puts the blame on mass privatization as such and the subscription to a market-based system of corporate governance per se, he maintains that the recent economic problems in the Czech Republic have ultimately resulted from a policy mix suffering from a lack of internal coherence.

The chapters by Wendy Carlin and Wladimir Andreff are complementary, too. Both seek to confront available theories of corporate governance with the East European experience. In Chapter 7, Wendy Carlin begins by outlining unresolved issues within the recent literature on corporate governance in market economies. Updating her well-known earlier surveys, she then goes on to carefully review a handful of new econometric studies on enterprise restructuring. In doing so, she pays special attention to the hitherto neglected question as to what extent characteristics of privatized enterprises have differed and as to what extent differently privatized enterprises have differed, an issue which is highly relevant for interpreting the available findings on the impact of ownership structures on enterprise performance. Carlin concludes by calling for a broader perspective on corporate governance which links firm-level studies with the analysis of corporate governance systems at the country level and national patterns of economic specialization.

Chapter 8, by Wladimir Andreff, starts by contrasting the quantitative and qualitative dimensions of post-communist privatization. Andreff acknowledges the far-reaching shedding of state-owned assets and the rise of the private sector in most transition countries, but takes a rather critical stance towards the corporate governance structures that have emerged. His reading of the empirical evidence on corporate governance and enterprise restructuring in the transition countries leads him to challenge the dominating principle–agent model of corporate governance as it has been codified in the seminal article by Shleifer and Vishny (1997). Questioning the simple dichotomy of outside and inside owners, Andreff argues for more complex investigations of ownership structures, which pay more attention to the identity of owners and the coalitions and alliances inside and outside firms.

The following four chapters deal with individual countries and/or particular aspects of corporate governance. Chapter 9 traces the evolution of corporate governance structures in Hungary over the last 10 years. Mihályi documents the changing composition of owners in the course of the transition, pointing at developments such as the drastic reduction in cross-ownership after 1992 and the increasing importance of financial investors since 1994. He then deals with the behaviour of state-owned enterprises. In this regard, he stresses the deteriorating state control resulting from frequent changes in privatization policy and the political staffing of enterprise boards, as well as the differentiation among state-owned enterprises arising from variance in size, market and financial situation.

Robert Chudzik addresses the role of banks as owners. Reviewing the burgeoning literature on banks as shareholders, Chapter 10 discusses the general pros and cons of bank equity holdings, as well as the particular role banks might play in the context of transition. His reservations regarding large bank shareholding, as recommended by Steinherr (1993), van Wijnbergen (1994) and others, are confirmed by an empirical analysis of enterprise restructuring in the wake of the Polish Bank Conciliation Programme. In the two enterprise samples

Chudzik examines, no impact of bank equity holding on enterprise performance and restructuring can be identified.

The following chapter, by Stijn Claessens and Simeon Djankov, also deals with a particular aspect of corporate governance. Using a cross-section of 706 Czech firms over the period 1993–7, it studies the effect of changes in management and the use of equity incentives on firm performance and market valuation. The authors find that several measures of enterprise performance are positively related with the entry of new managers, whereas equity holdings by managers appear to have no effect on corporate performance. These results suggest that, in transition economies, changes in human capital are more important than equity incentives in bringing about improvements in corporate governance.

Finally, Chapter 12 addresses the relationship between foreign direct investment (FDI), privatization and economic restructuring. On the basis of a rich set of data for the Central and Eastern European countries, Hunya shows that, in the transition countries, privatization has served as a main engine of FDI and that the degree of foreign penetration has thus strongly depended on the pace and method of privatization. In line with conventional wisdom, the chapter also presents massive evidence that the concentrated outside ownership associated with FDI has been conducive to economic restructuring. In stark contrast to most survey results on FDI motives, however, Hunya finds a strong export orientation of most foreign investment enterprises. He concludes by discussing future opportunities for FDI in different categories of Central and Eastern European countries.

## Privatization and the emergence of markets

The core question of privatization, in our eyes, is the interrelationship between the emergence of markets and market actors, and privatization, corporate governance and restructuring. Its significance has to do with a view which unquestionably underlies many writings on transformation, namely the assumption that markets emerge, by and large, spontaneously once appropriate preconditions such as well-defined property rights or a market-oriented legal system are in place (for example, Åslund, 1995; EBRD, 1996). Yet if the emergence of markets necessitates the existence of certain formal and informal institutions (Hodgson, 1988; North, 1990) as well as economic actors which exhibit market-related skills and forms of behaviour, such an automatism can no longer be assumed to exist, since neither learning nor institution building are timeless events. Moreover issues pertaining to the knowledge of market participants about their economic environment (Swaan, 1997) and their mutual dependence in network-like structures now come to the fore (Brezinski and Fritsch, 1997). Similarly the question has to be addressed of whether, and how, pre-existing structures such as informal networks inhibit or support the development of new configurations. Thus an important question is whether the emergence of markets has to be understood as yet another instance of a process in which legacies of the past turn out to be both liabilities and assets for transformation (Grabher and Stark, 1997).

Against this background, the interrelationship of privatization and market creation can be conceptualized along various lines. Most obviously privatization together with liberalization contributes to the creation of new market actors: for example, when former state-owned enterprises, which formed an integral part of the state bureaucracy, are allowed to make investment, production and pricing decisions of their own, when citizens become shareholders of newly privatized enterprises, or when labour is no longer allocated through central agencies. Furthermore how market actors actually behave is jointly influenced by the institutional framework in which they are located, and by the incentives and constraints they face. Hence the system of corporate governance, which is both an important part of this institutional framework and a major source of incentives, is likely to shape market outcomes in substantial ways, as is the structure of economic relations in which market actors are embedded. Last but not least, it is precisely because of the relationship between the behaviour of market agents and the extent and the quality of restructuring that the welfare effects of the divestiture of state property depend on the wider reform context of privatization and become manifest only through the actual performance of markets.

The final part of the volume comprises chapters which try to address these issues explicitly. All three chapters take the notion of the network as the conceptual starting point for an analysis of the emergence of markets in Central and Eastern European countries. This is not surprising, given that the network approach has gained widespread acceptance in recent years as a useful conceptual tool for the analysis of economic structures such as markets or industrial networks in both sociology and economics (cf. Albach, 1993; Mayntz, 1993; Beije and Groenewegen, 1992).

In Chapter 13, Michael Keren compares the structure of inter-firm networks in centrally planned and market economies, arguing that socialist networks are much more stable than capitalist ones. He then examines the incentives that encourage enterprise managers in social-ist networks to venture into attempts at transformation and suggests that these incentives are not per se sufficient to induce transformation. Among other things, it may be the distance from the final user which matters here, for restructuring may be hampered if the cooperation of others, such as wholesalers, is necessary. At the same time, enterprises must be given clear signals that the old environment, with its unques-tioning life support by means of soft budget constraints, is no longer viable.

The chapter by Eckehard Rosenbaum analyses in more detail the specific ways in which the network approach has been used so far in economics and sociology and suggests that, in order to employ the concept in a fruitful manner, various types of networks have to be carefully distinguished. Against this background he then argues that a market has to be understood as a communicative network whose mode of operation is contingent upon the knowledge agents possess about the structure of this network. In view of the many obstacles network building has to face owing to indivisibilities, network exter-nalities and bounded rationality, Rosenbaum suggests that building markets is a far from easy task. At the same time, the development of markets does not necessarily start from scratch because informal net-works, which are the remains of central planning, and the knowledge agents possess about these networks, may in fact form the nucleus of markets of the future.

Klaus Meyer takes a somewhat different route. As with the preceding two chapters, the starting point of Chapter 15 is the insight that the textbook conceptualization of markets does not suffice to illuminate our understanding of real markets. This applies in particular to the automotive industry, which is characterized by the widespread exist-ence of stable exchange networks between car manufacturers and first-tier suppliers, and thus by structures which have to be located somewhere between, on the one hand, markets as traditionally under-stood and, on the other hand, hierarchies. Meyer traces the technolo-gical and economic reasons for the development of these networks and illustrates, with the help of the acquisition of Škoda by Volkswagen, how similar structures are beginning to emerge in the Czech Republic. He shows how foreign direct investment contributes to the integration of existing manufacturers of automobile parts into worldwide networks and thus helps to overcome barriers to trade whose origins lie more in the lack of social capital in the form of trust and reputation on the part of managers than in straightforward cost disadvantages.

## Conclusions

If there is such a thing as a single common message emerging from the contributions to this volume, it is what might be fashionably called 'the embeddedness of privatization'. That is, privatization is, and should be studied as, part of a broader process of economic restructuring and institutional change. We have argued above that such a broader perspective on privatization encompasses three dimensions: the political nature of privatization, the interrelationship of privatization, corporate governance and enterprise restructuring, and the emergence of markets and of market actors.

Almost 10 years into transformation, and with privatization close to completion or at least firmly under way, the choice between different privatization methods with all its political and economic connotations is now largely of historical interest. By contrast, enterprise restructuring, corporate governance and the emergence of markets are likely to remain on the agenda of both economic policy and research for some time to come. In this respect, the divestiture of state-owned assets is a crucial, arguably even the single most important, step. Nevertheless changes in ownership titles are but one part of the story, being closely interwoven as they are with the transformation of corporate governance, enterprise restructuring, network transformation and the emergence of markets.

Thus a major challenge to, and a promising venue for, future research on privatization is the analysis of the link between the transformation of corporate governance structures and the transformation of supplier, sales and communication networks. So far, these dimensions have largely been treated separately. However their complementarity is most visible in the case of enterprise restructuring. For enterprise performance is obviously shaped as much by the patterns of ownership and control as by the specific position of a firm within a network of demand and supply relationships. Indeed these features can be seen as two sides of the same coin in that the structures of corporate governance tend to leave their imprint on inter-enterprise networks, and vice versa. Just as it may take the long-term commitment signalled by a large owner to get suppliers and customers to engage in long-term relationships, so will ownership structures reflect the strength of network ties, in particular through the size of cross-ownership.

Clearly such analyses may come too late to have a bearing on privatization choices. However the analyses certainly help to make sense of the observable outcomes of privatization, and indicate how to support the needed post-privatization restructuring. At the same time, the analyses may help to address issues which have either been the subject of a lively debate even before the breakdown of communism but which, for lack of conclusive empirical evidence, have never been resolved, as regards, for example, the functioning and the relative merits of different systems of corporate governance, or they may help to address issues which have tacitly underlain much of economic analysis but were only brought to the fore by the unprecedented task of building a market economy from scratch, as with the complex bundle of formal and informal institutions and networks, on which markets are based. Thus, while the beginning of transformation was marked by a kind of knowledge transfer from West to East, its continuation may be characterized by the transfer of knowledge and experience from East to West.

# I

# The Political and Fiscal Dimension of Privatization

# 2
# Polish Mass Privatization: Success or Failure?

*Rainer Gesell*

## Introduction[1]

Mass privatization – like any privatization – is not an aim in itself, but serves various economic, fiscal and social–political objectives (Vickers and Yarrow, 1991). Mass privatization programmes (MPPs) are usually based on economic and political considerations. Fiscal objectives are only of minor importance since state-owned enterprises (SOEs) are given away. MPPs are in particular supposed to accelerate privatization by (a) omitting the valuation of SOEs, (b) circumventing lack of domestic capital, and (c) overcoming public resistance (Jermakowicz, 1996). MPPs, however, may result in dispersed share ownership, effectively leaving the corporate governance of mass privatized enterprises unchanged. To alleviate this problem, intermediaries are part of most MPPs.

In Poland, a MPP was implemented after a lengthy and controversial political debate in 1995. Compared to the well-known Czech and Russian MPPs, the Polish programme is not only a latecomer but also quite exceptional as it relies heavily on state involvement. This involvement is most obvious in the government-led creation of intermediaries. In the following, we analyse whether the Polish MPP accomplishes its political and economic objectives. First, its main features are presented. On that basis, the second and third sections discuss the record of the Polish MPP. The fourth section concludes the chapter.

## Objectives, design and characterization of Polish mass privatization

The Polish MPP was intended to ensure that Polish citizens participate in and profit from privatization by implementing 'economic enfranchisement'[2] through a free transfer of SOEs. The underlying political objectives are reducing public resistance towards privatization and creating a class of private owners who represent a pro-reform constituency. Simultaneously, the programme intends to introduce efficient ownership and control structures to mass privatized enterprises through the foundation of 15 National Investment Funds (NIFs). The basic features of the programme are the following:[3]

- **Voucher system.** Each adult Polish citizen was entitled to a 'share certificate' that can be exchanged for a package of shares consisting of one share from each NIF. Certificates are tradable and listed on the Warsaw Stock Exchange (WSE). They are restricted to investments in NIFs and cannot be used for investment in enterprises participating in mass privatization.
- **NIF scheme.** The NIFs are closed-end funds that are initially owned by the Treasury. Of their share capital 85 per cent is – from mid-1997 until the end of 1998 – transferred to certificate holders, with 15 per cent retained by the state for compensating the NIF management. Since the exchange of certificates started, the NIFs have been listed on the WSE. The NIFs have a supervisory board, a management board and a general assembly of shareholders. A peculiarity of the NIF construction is that the management of their assets can be delegated to 'management firms' (in most cases a consortium of Polish and foreign financial institutions).
- **Participating enterprises.** In total, 512 enterprises participate in the programme. Of their share capital 33 per cent is distributed to one NIF, 27 per cent goes to the remaining 14 NIFs, 25 per cent is retained by the Treasury and 15 per cent is transferred free to employees.

The Polish MPP is only one specific form out of various possible models of mass privatization. Generally, market-based and centrally regulated forms of mass privatization can be distinguished (Jermakowicz, 1996). The Polish programme is usually characterized as the prototype for a centrally regulated approach. This is true for the demand side of the scheme, the creation of intermediaries and the allocation mechanism of shares. With regard to the demand side, the range of certificate uses is restricted, as they cannot be used for direct investments into participating enterprises, but only for conversion into NIF shares. Financial intermediaries (the NIFs) did not evolve spontaneously. Rather they were set up, initially owned, and monitored by the government. Also members of the first supervisory boards and management firms were chosen by a government commission. The allocation mechanism was also restricted, as NIFs could only decide in which enterprises to have a majority holding, with the size of the stake being fixed.

The programme also includes some elements of a market-based approach with respect to the supply side and the voucher system: enterprises could, more or less, decide themselves whether to take part in the programme or not (decentralization of the privatization decision) and share certificates are freely tradable. In the next two sections, the implications of this particular design for the accomplishment of the programme's political and economic objectives are examined.

## Political objectives: overcoming public resistance and creation of a pro-reform constituency

### Evaluation criteria

Generally mass privatization can be expected to be a popular method of privatization, therefore it may be a way of getting privatization started. However popularity and political feasibility of a MPP are influenced by (a) the existence of similar popular alternative privatization methods (that may be supported by influential interest groups), (b) expected gains from participating in the programme, (c) the complexity of the programme and (d) inclusion of the public in the early stages of the programme. This issue refers to the programme's sequence, that is the succession of vouchers distribution ('demand'), establishment of intermediaries ('investment funds') and supply of enterprises.

The second political objective associated with MPPs is that it is a way to create a pro-reform constituency, helping to make reforms irreversible and serve the long-term political sustainability of privatization. This issue is of particular importance, as future governments may seek to derail privatization and use profits generated by privatized firms to subsidize loss-making SOEs. Using a median-voter model, Schmidt (1997) concludes that MPPs can commit governments to refrain from expropriating privatized firms. He identifies the following factors for reducing the threat of expropriation:

- Size of the programme: the more shares are distributed to the population and the larger the potential gains from participating in it, the lower the risk of expropriation.

- Range of participants: to reduce the risk of expropriation it is prefer-able to distribute shares equally to all citizens rather than to favour enterprise insiders.
- Continuity of shareholdings: people should be encouraged to retain shares and discouraged from selling them for cash.

To this list of factors we would like to add an additional requirement for creating a pro-reform constituency:

- Potential for early and rapid implementation. Given that the creation of a pro-reform constituency is needed most at the begin-ning of the second stage of transformation – after the period of 'extraordinary politics' is over and interest groups exert influence on political decisions – the programme should be able to be implemented fast.

### Assessing the Polish record

The Polish MPP only partly meets these criteria. This is due to the par-ticular starting point of Polish transformation, to naive expectations by the first Polish reform governments, and – most importantly – to its centrally regulated design.

The programme was not able to accelerate the Polish privatization process to any considerable extent: it neither encompassed most SOEs, nor was it quickly implemented. The enterprises covered by the pro-gramme account for only 6 per cent of SOEs existing at the start of transformation. Although the first proposals for mass privatization in Poland date back to 1988, the law covering the programme was adopted only in 1993. Its implementation started only during 1994 and lasted until the end of 1998.

The small size of the programme is mainly due to specific political constraints: as a result of socialist reforms during the 1980s, Polish enterprises gained a considerable degree of autonomy and (implicit) ownership rights were exerted by workers and management. Enterprise autonomy even increased in the first period of transformation. Thus the general Polish privatization approach reflects the strong position of enterprise insiders (Gesell and Jost, 1997): preferential employee and management buy-outs are the dominant form of privatization and only a few enterprises can be subjected to mass privatization without meeting strong resistance.

The delayed adoption of the programme and its slow implementation are partly due to the behaviour of the first Polish reform government, which relied on standard methods of privatization and intended to privatize SOEs by stock market listings. Mass privatization was only slowly adopted by the Polish government as a way to accelerate privatization (Btaszczyk and Dąbrowski, 1994; Winiecki, 1995). The main reason for the delays, however, is the centrally regulated design of the Polish MPP. To be sure, complex MPPs need more time to be implemented. More importantly, however, is that centrally regulated programmes are susceptible to delays as their implementation consists of a series of political decisions that give opponents of mass privatization opportunities for delaying or abandoning the programme. A rapid implementation of a centrally regulated MPP depends on a firm commitment of the government and a stable political environment, neither of which existed in Poland between 1990 and 1994.

Furthermore some features of the programme restrict its ability to win political support. The programme is rather complex, which makes it hard for ordinary citizens to understand its potential benefits. Additionally its sequencing brings in citizen participation late as enterprises to be mass privatized are selected and investment funds are founded *before* certificates are distributed. Contentious decisions – which are likely to delay the implementation of the programme – however, centre primarily on the inclusion of enterprises and the appointment of investment funds' members. Because citizens are last in line, they are not interested in pressing for faster implementation.

The programme also fails to meet most criteria for building up a pro-reform constituency. Its limited size and slow implementation wasted the chance of quickly building up a broad pro-reform constituency. On the other hand, citizens' participation was strong: 96 per cent of eligible Poles picked up share certificates. However most of them subsequently sold them: an opinion poll taken in December 1996 (CBOS, 1997) indicates that only 18 per cent of those interviewed intended to convert certificates into NIF shares. Given the considerable costs of conversion (investors have to open an account and pay for brokerage and the registration of certificates) the number of individual citizens holding NIF shares is likely to be even lower. Thus the creation of a continuous 'class of new owners' was spoilt by the inclusion of one of the few market-based features in the programme, the free tradability of certificates. However, by allowing for an early concentration of shareholdings (via concentration of certificates), the corporate governance of NIF may be improved. The introduction of certificates' tradability highlights the importance the programme's creators were assigning to enterprise restructuring.

An indicator for the – at least partial – dissatisfaction with the political results of the MPP is that during the 1997 election campaign the idea of endowing all Poles with part of the assets jointly created under Communism ('general propertization'), which was supposedly accomplished by the programme, has again been taken up by the Solidarność camp and new proposals for privatization are developed that link privatization with pensions reform.[4]

As the programme's failure to meet its political aims adequately is due its specific design that stresses the need to impose effective forms of corporate control on mass-privatized enterprises, its small size, delayed implementation and low popular support are put up with, fostering enterprise restructuring. But is the design really able to accomplish this task? This question is explored in the next section.

## Economic objectives: enterprise restructuring

The Polish MPP reflects some implicit assumptions on the relation between enterprise restructuring, privatization and corporate governance. In particular, its designers assume, that (a) deep restructuring depends on privatization, (b) ownership and control structures are determined by privatization, and (c) effective mechanisms of corporate governance are necessary for enterprise restructuring. This set of assumptions is discussed in the first subsection. On this basis, evaluation criteria are derived and applied to the Polish case.

### Restructuring, privatization and corporate governance

For macroeconomic stabilization measures to be followed by welfare enhancements, adjustments at the microeconomic level are necessary, which entails restructuring and liquidation of existing SOEs.[5] Restructuring encompasses several dimensions, including 'reactive' changes of enterprise behaviour (like labour shedding, wage reduction and plant closure), strategic aspects (such as export reorientation and changes of the product mix and of management structures) and 'deep' or 'active' restructuring, which involves new investments (Grosfeld and Roland, 1995; EBRD, 1995, pp. 128–38). In the following, the focus is on deep restructuring: given that the capital stock inherited from the socialist system has been economically devalued, as it was based on inappropriate assumptions about supply and demand conditions, new investments are required to induce general improvements of enterprise performance and secure their long-run economic survival.

Successful reconstruction of the state sector consists of (a) separating viable from non-viable enterprises and (b) subsequently liquidating non-viable and restructuring viable ones. Successful restructuring is dependent on the *ability* to restructure. This includes the potential to raise capital for new investments, sufficient economic competence to identify value-enhancing investments, and control of enterprises to ensure that resources are used in the way intended. The ability to restructure is a necessary but not a sufficient condition. Rather there must also be *incentives* to implement enterprise restructuring. Although the problem of the appropriate sequence of privatization and restructuring (whether SOEs should be first privatized and then restructured) is solved differently in Central and Eastern Europe, there are good reasons to assume that a government-led restructuring of SOEs is inappropriate.

Separating viable from non-viable enterprises requires precise knowledge on the current and future economic situation of SOEs. In order to gain such knowledge, governments would have to strictly control enterprises. However the well-known problems of planned economies highlight the fact that such control is impossible: removing the asymmetric distribution of information between state and enterprise management and tackling the problem of inappropriate incentives to disclose all relevant information would require administrative capacities that do not exist. Nor have state agents sufficient economic competence to correctly assess future prospects of SOEs. Even in the – hypothetical – situation of governments having all relevant information and economic competence to process it, the liquidation of non-viable SOEs is unlikely, as this would result in large-scale unemployment. As closures of SOEs are, contrary to those of private enterprises, not seen as an accidental event by the actors within enterprises, governments can be made responsible for them. Thus the state is *neither able nor willing* to mimic the screening function of capital markets. As far as restructuring measures of the state are concerned, the mentioned lack of administrative capacity and economic knowledge prevents such measures from resulting in SOEs behaving in a market-like manner. Additionally, given that enterprise managers will take into account that firm closures are unlikely, their behaviour is ex ante influenced by the expectation of soft budget constraints (Kornai, 1986).

Thus the state cannot sufficiently induce deep restructuring. What has to be examined is the mechanisms by which privatization causes behavioural changes to enterprises. To start with, hard budget constraints can be more easily maintained *vis-à-vis* private enterprises. This is a prerequisite for a functioning market economy as the coherence of an economic system requires that macroeconomic stabilization be supplemented by hard budget constraints at the microeconomic level (Brücker, 1997).

A second, equally important, aspect of privatization is that it implies a change in ownership and control structures that enterprises are facing.[6] But does it matter for restructuring how and to whom property rights of enterprises are transferred? Privatization only determines the *initial* distribution of property rights and, as the Coase theorem argues, such initial distributions may be irrelevant for economic efficiency as economic agents will voluntarily engage in market transactions that result in an efficient allocation of property rights. Thus efficient ownership and control structures of privatized enterprises would emerge irrespective of the method of privatization. Crucial for the applicability of the theorem are zero transactions costs. Some authors argue that this is the case with property rights assigned to privatized enterprises (see, for example, Vaubel, 1992). From such a point of view, privatization-determined ownership and control structures are quickly transferred and efficient forms of corporate governance would emerge irrespective of the privatization method.

However, although ownership and control structures evolve over time and their initial privatization-determined form may change, the assumption of zero transaction costs cannot be maintained. Most importantly, there are no developed capital markets at the start of transformation. This point is also accepted by proponents of the 'privatization method does not matter' approach. They argue that capital markets will quickly evolve after the retreat of the state from enterprises, but, this argument ignores interdependencies between markets and the governance of enterprises (Frydman and Rapaczynski, 1994): without effective coordination within the institutions that act on a market, neither are the prices generated adequate nor will economic agents within enterprises face the right incentives to respond to price signals in a social welfare-enhancing way. A model developed by Blanchard and Aghion (1996) presents additional arguments for the economic relevancy of the privatization method. These show that, after the transfers of SOEs to management and employees, the efficient realignment of shares is distorted as insiders will take into account the implications for their employment when deciding to sell shares to outside investors.

Thus the privatization-determined ownership and control structures are, at least in the short and medium term, relevant for enterprise performance: relying on a fast evolutionary development is no solution. But what are the best forms of corporate governance to induce enterprise restructuring? Generally enterprise behaviour is subject to incentives and controls imposed by the legal system, cultural expectations, markets and owners (Gray and Hanson, 1993). Legal and cultural constraints and incentives are exogenous to privatization.[7] Market-based incentives and constraints encompass competition on product, capital and labour markets. Most of these mechanisms are – at least at the beginning of transformation – underdeveloped in Central and Eastern Europe (ibid.). Additionally, as a result of the mentioned interdependencies between the functioning of markets and internal coordination and control in enterprises, most of them are unlikely to work properly without efficient owner control.

Shareholder control can be based on 'exit' and 'voice'. Exit implies passive behaviour of shareholders: they sell their shares if they are not satisfied with company performance. This causes a relative fall in share prices and, by making low company performance visible, render the company susceptible to takeovers. However, as capital markets are underdeveloped, exit is not an efficient option for corporate governance in Central and Eastern Europe. Thus active monitoring by shareholders ('voice') can be considered to be the most appropriate form of corporate governance during the early stages of transformation (ibid.). A prerequisite for effective active monitoring is a certain degree of ownership concentration, otherwise problems of coordination and collective action would arise.

The discussion indicates that successful privatization is more than a simple retreat of the state from enterprises. Rather effects on the ownership and control structure of privatized enterprises have to be taken into account. This leaves the state with the task of designing – via the devising of a privatization approach – effective forms of corporate governance. This, however, poses additional problems (cf. Frydman and Rapaczynski, 1994): (a) which political feasible solution is best suited to inducing enterprise restructuring; and (b) how can the risk of the state abusing its prominent role be avoided? Obviously the problem of a 'constructivist fallacy' in Hayek's (1967) sense is immanent when devising a privatization policy.

### Evaluation criteria

The following criteria are derived from the above discussion to evaluate a particular privatization approach with regard to enterprise restructuring:

(1) As governments cannot be expected to be willing and able to induce deep restructuring, *enterprises must be separated from the state* in order to depoliticize the restructuring process.

(2) *Reducing the potential for a 'constructivist fallacy'*: although state action is unavoidable where privatization is concerned, discretionary state interventions should be restricted and competition and market forces should be brought into the privatization process as soon as possible (Frydman and Rapaczynski, 1994). Additionally the realignment costs of property rights should be reduced, in order to set in motion as soon as possible an evolutionary process that, in the long run, is able to correct failures in the privatization-determined ownership structure.

These two criteria are applied below under the heading 'Restraining the role of the state'. The discussion earlier also stressed that privatization in Central and Eastern Europe is more than a retreat of the state from enterprises and that its impacts on ownership and control structures have to be considered. In particular, the following criteria have to be met:

(1) *New owners should accomplish basic requirements for restructuring*: they should have both abilities and incentives to implement restructuring. In the early stages of privatization, active control by owners is the most appropriate measure to accomplish this aim. For owners to be able to exert active control, a certain degree of ownership concentration is required.

Concentration of ownership is the economic rationale for integrating intermediaries into mass privatization: as other forms of endowing privatized enterprises with new owners – like the sale to strategic foreign investors – may be impossible for political reasons. Intermediaries concentrate dispersed share ownership and may be able to exert active shareholder monitoring. This, however, introduces the additional problem of 'controlling the controllers'.

(2) *Intermediaries*, in order to act in the interest of their owners, *must be free from state influence* and *governed themselves by effective incentive and control structures*. Although active owner control is most appropriate for the early stages of transformation, the contribution of a particular privatization approach to the development of alternative mechanisms of corporate governance is important in the long run. Thus:

(3) *The contribution to the development of capital markets* has to be included when evaluating a particular privatization approach.

## Assessing the Polish record

*Restraining the role of the state*

The state assumes a prominent role in a centrally regulated MPP. This is not necessarily a drawback, as long as (a) its role is restricted to the setting up of the programme, and, as this phase will consume some time (b) discretionary interventions by the state during that time are rendered difficult.

These two criteria are only partly met by the Polish MPPs. The state not only founded the NIFs and appointed their initial board members, but will continue to be a significant shareholder for years to come. Additionally there are a number of restrictions on private shareholders' voting rights for the first four years after the foundation of the NIFs (Ministry of Privatization, 1995). Although the Treasury stresses that it will perform a passive role as shareholder and leave the determination of NIFs' policy to the new private owners (Treasury, 1998, Ministry of Privatization, 1995), the credibility of this self-binding is reduced as (a) passive behaviour is not assured by an explicit provision in the Law on Mass Privatization and (b) the Treasury reserves the right to intervene in specific situations when the interests of small shareholders or those of the Treasury might be jeopardized (Treasury, 1998). Thus there is still room for active involvement of the state in the running of the NIFs.

The Polish approach uses market forces and competition only on a limited scale. Again this is in the nature of a centrally regulated MPP. However the visible hand of the state comes at some cost, as valuable information is not discovered by the competitive mechanism. For instance, the NIFs did not have to compete with each other over certificates. If they had had to, this would have generated information on the market appraisal of the NIFs' strategies at early stages of the programme. In its actual setting, this information only belatedly emerged after the NIFs listing on the WSE.

Thus the Polish MPP has only insufficiently restrained the role of the state, resulting in a high potential for a 'constructivist fallacy'. The next section discusses some of the impacts of this fallacy.

*Ownership and control structures*

*Basic requirements for restructuring* The Polish MPP endows mass-privatized enterprises with owners that are principally *able* to foster enterprise restructuring. The NIFs facilitate the access to new resources for mass-privatized enterprises as they are able to raise funds on the capital markets at lower cost than individual enterprises, owing to their diversified portfolio and the reputation effects of including foreign financial institutions in management firms. Additionally the management firms, via their relations with domestic and foreign banks, are able to improve the access to bank credits.

The ownership structure of mass privatized enterprises principally allows for active owner control and the implementation of restructuring measures: the leading NIF holds the largest block of shares and appoints the largest number of supervisory board members. Control by the leading NIF, however, is attenuated as it neither holds the majority of shares (only 33 per cent) nor is entitled to appoint the majority of board members (absolute majority minus one). Thus developments that are contrary to the intentions of the leading NIF are possible and can be observed.[8] Additionally the rather high number of majority holdings of each NIF (about 35), impose administrative and informational limits for the restructuring of all majority holdings. However attenuated control and administrative limits for active restructuring are not necessarily impediments to restructuring, as some major holdings can be sold to strategic investors (which subsequently restructure the enterprise themselves) and the NIF concentrates on a core of investments.

Although the Polish MPP allowed for the ability to restructure, there are shortcomings with regard to the incentives to do so. To start with, the Law on Mass Privatization does not include a provision that the NIFs' objective is enterprise restructuring. Rather it is said that 'The purpose of the funds is to increase the value of their assets, in particular by enhancing the value of shares of companies of which the funds are shareholders' (Art. 4). However restrictions on the scope of portfolio management, effectively imposing limits on the exertion of the exit mechanism, are an indication of the legislator's intention to stress the restructuring of mass privatized enterprises by its lead NIF.

The somewhat ambiguous legal provision, together with the construction of the NIFs, creates a complex incentive structure that is hard to establish on theoretical grounds. Formally it is the combination of a two-layer principal–agent relationship between 'owner of NIF' and NIF, and a three-layer relationship between NIF, management firm, and participating firms. To make things even more complicated, 'owners of NIF' change (so there may be some anticipatory behaviour) and the management firms are not monolithic actors, but consortia. The NIFs' behaviour can be interpreted as the result of a bargaining process between these various actors. The bargaining solution has multiple equilibria as the NIFs follow at least three distinctive strategies, one of which does not include restructuring.

NIF behaviour towards mass privatized enterprises varies considerably; at least two funds are following a more 'speculative' strategy (Kowalczyk, 1997) by mainly relying on exit and pursuing portfolio management. The remaining NIFs can be classified as 'venture capital funds' and 'industrial holdings'. We will refrain from a detailed evaluation of these various different strategies, but their existence is an indicator of a lack of clear-cut incentives in the programme to induce restructuring. The degree to which the restructuring behaviour of most NIFs is due to true economic incentives or to moral persuasion from the government is also hard to establish. Kowalczyk (1997: 22) assumes that, after the state withdraws from the NIFs, even more funds may show speculative behaviour.

*Ownership and corporate governance of NIFs*   The NIFs are not free from state influence and there are potentials for future discretionary interventions in the programme. The visible hand of the state resulted in a governance structure of the NIFs that is susceptible to open internal conflicts between supervisory boards and management firms. Members of supervisory boards are selected by the council of ministers, thus they are political, rather than economic, actors. Together with the relatively high compensation of NIF management, there is ample scope for hostile relations between supervisory boards and management firms. At the beginning of 1998, three NIFs terminated the contract with their management firm and one tried to do so. Whether these tendencies continue or evolve into regular, mostly conflict-free, forms of internal governance depends on the ownership structure that evolves after 'privatizing the privatization funds'; that is the listing of the NIFs on the WSE.

Moreover NIF management is constrained by active monitoring by shareholders and by capital market controls. The new ownership structure is determined by the exchange of share certificates and the subsequent trading of NIF shares. While 95 per cent of eligible Polish citizens picked up certificates, only a small fraction of them has or is going to change them into NIF shares and some pre-conversion concentration of share ownership has taken place.

As most certificates are no longer held by Polish citizens, it would be highly intriguing to know which institutions will emerge as major shareholders of NIFs. However, as the conversion process only finished at the end of 1998, there is only very preliminary evidence available and even NIF managers have no clear idea about the future owners of the NIFs.[9] The results of the first general meeting of NIF shareholders in 1997 (Rzeczpospolita, 1997) and disclosure requirements[10] can only be used as a crude indication: besides the Treasury which is still the dominant share-holder, two distinguished groups of 'large' investors can be identified: (a) members of the consortia running the management firms of the NIFs, and (b) some foreign and Polish financial institutions. Neither of these investors, however, has a stake that considerably exceeds 5 per cent[11] and in some NIFs there are no such 'major' investors.

The holdings of the consortia firms are most likely to be interpreted as signals to other financial institutions: by investing in their own NIF and committing some financial resources, they indicate that the NIF is thought to be a good investment opportunity. The intentions of the financial institutions are not known.[12] The NIFs themselves are in most cases interested in having another majority investor besides the Treasury. Fund managers stress that it is much easier to deal with the Treasury if a private (preferable renowned foreign) investor supports the position of the NIF management.

Although active monitoring by non-dispersed outside shareholders may be the most effective way of disciplining management and inducing restructuring, the listing of the NIFs on the stock exchange and the rela-tive advanced WSE render capital markets a potential control mecha-nism. Capital market control arises from disclosing relative performance and the threat of takeovers. As NIFs are closed-end funds, their relative performance can be measured by the development of the net value of assets per share and the associated premium and discount on share price. However, this measure is not entirely appropriate, given that book values only partly reflect the true economic value of assets. Also comparability is limited, as not all NIFs use identical accounting systems.

Resulting from differing performances, there may be takeovers of low performing funds. The potential of control by the market for corporate control is limited by the NIFs' size and the lack of domestic capital (Winiecki, 1995; Kowalczyk, 1997). However there is one incidence of a NIF takeover: a Czech investor bought a 10 per cent stake in NIF II and intends to run it itself. This indicates the existence of an emerging market for corporate control. However the design of the Polish MPP impedes the functioning of such a market:

- If the NIF to be taken over is managed by a management firm, the new owners have to first terminate the current management contract.

Although this can be done without giving cause, it has to compensate the management firm (Art. 24 of the Law on Mass Privatization).

- Where, the NIF to be taken over has no management firm, the law only outlines the procedure for NIFs exclusively owned by the Treasury. However the actual proceedings in the NIF II case involve the time-consuming process of public tender. Whether such proceedings will continue after the conversion of certificates is over is not clear yet. If they do, takeover processes will be delayed and made less attractive.

*Contribution to capital market development*   Apart from the impediments on the market for corporate control, the MPP unequivocally fostered the development of Polish capital markets by introducing a new financial instrument (the share certificates) and creating a new market, the market for NIF shares. Additionally listings of participating enterprises on the WSE will also increase market capitalization.

## Conclusion

The design of the Polish MPP reflects a compromise between political and economic objectives. The very nature of compromises is that neither aim is sufficiently accomplished. This is also true of the Polish MPP. Concerning political objectives, the high rate of participation is a success, but the MPP did not accelerate privatization, nor did it build up a broad reform-oriented constituency.

Delays in the programme are incurred because of its centralist design, which, however, has a series of features impeding the economic objective of the programme (enterprise restructuring): the state is not sufficiently constrained and there are no clear-cut incentives for restructuring. Additionally the peculiar construction of NIFs makes them susceptible to internal conflicts. How far these failures are resolved by the emerging ownership and control structure cannot be determined conclusively. However there are some indications of more effective forms of corporate governance: management firms are emerging as NIF shareholders and there are signs of an emerging market for corporate control.

## Notes

1. The author has profited from comments on an earlier draft of the chapter by Herbert Brücker and Tomasz Mickiewicz and other participants of the workshop. The usual disclaimer applies.
2. This issue is discussed in Poland under the heading of *'powszechne uwtaszczenie'*.

3. For a more detailed description see Thieme (1995).
4. See Gesell *et al.* (1998) for a discussion and assessment of these proposals.
5. The equally important issue of setting up new firms is not further discussed here.
6. Such a change can already be induced by credibly announcing a privatization programme: anticipating privatization, management may restructure in order to build up a reputation that enhances its chances on the managerial market. Such a change of incentives is dependent on the conditions that managers can see a relationship between their action and the resulting changes in enterprise profits, as well as that managers can expect to profit from their reputation. See Pinto and van Wijnbergen (1995) for case study evidence from Poland, and Brada (1996a) for a summary of the argument.
7. This is not entirely correct as, for instance, a privatization programme which causes a 'marketization' of society may also change the cultural expectations managers are facing.
8. One instance of such a development was the sale of a cement company: although the leading NIF intended to restructure it, it was forced by the other NIFs and the company's employees to sell it to a foreign investor.
9. Rumours indicate that about 50 per cent of certificates are now held by foreigners. Also the Catholic radio station 'Radio Maria' is supposed to have collected some certificates. However there are no exact numbers available.
10. In Poland, shareholdings exceeding 5 per cent have to be made public.
11. An exception is Expandia Polska SA which holds about 10 per cent of the shares of the second NIF. This is due to its takeover attempt, discussed below.
12. One could speculate that in some cases they will actively exert their ownership rights and try to take over the NIFs.

# 3
# On the Political Economy of Privatization in Eastern Germany

*Uwe Siegmund*

## Economics or political economy of privatization in Eastern Germany?[1]

Privatization in Eastern Germany has largely been deemed very special, efficient and unpolitical in the sense that the government and its privatization agent, the Treuhand, behaved in a welfare-maximizing manner (Brücker, 1997; Dyck, 1997; Fischer *et al.*, 1996; Freese, 1995). The government and/or Treuhand were right to choose privatization as the major aim to promote efficiency *and* to pursue other aims as well, to choose *negotiations* as the major privatization method and to choose a state organization somewhere between a bureau and a public firm (*Anstalt*) as the organizational form for the privatization agent. There were no other real and better alternatives available, given the conditions for the privatization in Eastern Germany. Efficiency aims dominated equity aims. If political conditions were taken into account in this economics of privatization approach they were explained ad hoc and exogenously given to the government and/or Treuhand. This seems to be an incomplete picture of eastern German privatization, because the Jasinski–Yarrow privatization paradox applied in Eastern Germany as it applied in other countries:

> Like public ownership itself, privatization is a policy of the state and is determined by political decision makers. The motives that drive privatization will be those of politicians and bureaucrats, which, as a consequence of the political agency problem, can not in general be identified with the public interest, social welfare or economic efficiency. This leads to the paradox (or dilemma) of privatization: the process of privatization is liable to be subject to the same kinds of

inefficiencies – deriving from the political and enterprise agency problems – as the SOEs that it seeks to eliminate. Put another way, government failure is both a motive for privatization and an obstacle to its efficient implementation. (Jasinski and Yarrow, 1996, p. 18)

There was a privatization policy in Eastern Germany that has to be described and analysed. Privatization is by its very nature a politico-economic process. A democratic government has to and will use mass privatization to gain and remain in power. On the one hand, democratic governments in transition countries were elected for privatizing. On the other hand, democratic governments privatized to be re-elected. Thus concepts of vote maximizing, budget maximizing and interest group pressure or capture have to be taken into account in analysing privatization in Eastern Germany. First attempts at this political economy of privatization approach were made by Czada (1996), Dickertmann and Gelbhaar (1994, 1997), Hau (1998) and Siegmund (1998, 1999).

This chapter will contribute to this approach by addressing three issues: the multiplicity of the Treuhand's aims resulting in an assignment problem; the choice of the privatization method, especially the puzzle of why auctions were not chosen by a seemingly welfare-maximizing government; and the political control of the Treuhand fostered by its organizational structure. At the end, conclusions will be drawn.

## The assignment problem of privatization

Mass privatization in transition countries was pursued with many objectives. This was also the case in Eastern Germany. Although the German privatization law clearly stated in the first sentence of Article 1, 'State property has to be privatized', it also declares the following objectives: to define the size and form of the property to be privatized; to restructure firms including their cross subsidizing; to liquidate non-viable firms; to give away property to cities, counties, new federal states and other state organizations (called 'communalization'); to deal with special property differently, for example, in agriculture; to reprivatize firms and assets; to save or create jobs; to foster small and medium-size enterprises; and to promote competition. Privatization proceeds should be used for restructuring firms, for reducing government debts and for distributing among Eastern German citizens.

Presented in a more systematic way, the Treuhand had to pursue three groups of aims (Figure 3.1). First, it had to pursue bureaucratic aims. Here the Treuhand had to act according to law and behave as a bureaucrat. For

*Figure* 3.1   Aims of the Treuhand

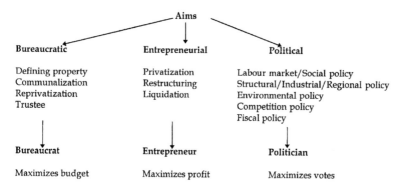

example, agricultural and forest land was only hesitatingly privatized before 1996 because it was reserved for reprivatization, which depended on a political bargain between the government, old owners and the courts. Second, the Treuhand had to pursue entrepreneurial aims. Here it had to act according to market signals and behave as an entrepreneur. For example, firms had to be liquidated, restructured or privatized according to their viability in the market. Moreover, as a kind of 'super entrepreneur', the Treuhand was supposed to take into account all the negative externalities associated with a transition shock and therefore to calculate the intertemporal welfare of East German citizens. The government or Treuhand never said what the externalities were and why they were negative. No attempt at a social welfare cost–benefit calculation was ever made either (U-Ausschuß, 1994). Do inefficient but subsidized firms that subtract value, that prevent workers from moving to new jobs and locations and that support wages far above productivity levels create positive or negative externalities? It seems more appropriate to consider the 'externalities' as political aims, which is the third group of aims the Treuhand had to pursue. Here it had to act according to the needs of the governments for re-election and behave as a politician. For example, the Treuhand created a third labour market by keeping employees in its firms and paying for job commitments.

What can be seen is the assignment problem involved in privatization. The Treuhand had not only vague objectives that were inconsistent and unranked (Schmidt, 1996), but also an overload of aims. This assignment produced confusion, lack of transparency, non-accountability and discretion in decision making by the Treuhand. Lawyers tried to bring in some ranking and classification but the interpretation of the privatization law was very wide, ranging from a duty to restructure first to a duty to privatize first (Bleckmann, 1992; Weimar, 1993). Thus the government and the privatization agent were free to choose from among the many aims and to charge each other with the responsibilities. It was possible that, without a change in the German privatization law, a change in government could have led to a completely different assignment of aims to the privatization agent.

The assignment of aims to the Treuhand was due to a political compromise in the reunification year, 1990. In the first half of the year an East German reformed communist and a weak interim coalition government favoured equality over efficiency aims, that is, the equal redistribution of property over its reallocation, and in the second half of the year a strong all-German conservative government favoured efficiency aims but deviated from this in spring 1991, when pressure from political opposition parties, trade unions and the new federal states increased (Kemmler, 1994). The assignment of aims was also due to over optimistic expectations about privatization proceeds based on too optimistic calculations of the East German capital stock and too much hope that there would be high West German and foreign direct investment in Eastern Germany. In the end, it was the privatization agent itself that declared privatization as its major aim to promote efficient firms. This was the virtue of the Treuhand managers and those politicians who put them in office.

What is privatization for? To give the best possible private entrepreneurs the control of assets – from the very beginning. Any other goal is a deviation and generates extra government interventions in the future business of private owners, interventions that are not compatible with normal business practices in a market economy. These extra government interventions will be corrected sooner or later by the market and have to be accepted by the government. Therefore the privatization agent should only be responsible for converting state property into private property (see BMWi, 1991).

The assignment problem in privatization can be compared to the assignment problem in macroeconomic policies: the central bank is responsible only for price stability, the trade unions and employers are responsible for (un)employment, and the fiscal policy is responsible for good growth conditions. If a government wants to regulate private property it can use independent regulatory bodies; if a government wants to redistribute income it can use taxes and transfers; if a government wants to promote competition it can open entry to the market. All of this is distinct from privatization – and therefore should be dealt with distinctly. For every single bureaucratic or political aim of the Treuhand there was already a parallel state agent in Eastern Germany that could have pursued the aim as well: just think of the Cartel Office and the Labour Office.

Of course, the assignment problem does not mean that privatization cannot be used for other aims, similar to money creation, that can also be used to create short-term employment. Moreover it is in the interest of the typical politician to use the privatization agent or the central bank to favour his constituency in order to be re-elected. The assignment problem of privatization focuses only on the fact that this leads to extra disturbances which make economic coordination by markets expensive, uncertain and vulnerable to political intervention. That is why the privatization agent should be as independent as the central bank, with a single and clearly specified objective. Other assignments are too costly. The assignment problem prevails even if the privatization agent is given a hard budget constraint in the sense of a fixed or declining budget. Decision making remains discretionary. The Treuhand had a soft budget constraint that exaggerated the assignment problem, but did not cause it.

This leads us to the large financial deficit of the Treuhand, and its explanation. I argue that the losses are mainly political costs. Thus Sinn and Sinn's (1992) arguments of a liquidity constraint of buyers, of a rising interest rate that reduces the attractiveness of the privatization investment, of falling attractiveness of firms for sale, and of refusing privatization to stop some West German firms from becoming monopolists are considered as secondary (similarly Brücker, 1998). Also considered secondary are the arguments that there were unproductive socialist firms, a demand shock and a supply wage shock. All of these arguments may explain a reduction in prices, but hardly explain negative prices for almost all firms. The liquidation value of firms would have been the lowest price minus some administrative costs incurred by the Treuhand.

The Treuhand said that it devoted the majority of its expenditures to restructuring, taking over old debts, and paying for environmental damage, and only a minority to 'true' privatization efforts (Table 3.1). Privatization revenues amounted to only one-fifth or DM76 billion out of DM332 billion for financing privatization; the rest was credited. The low proceeds reflect substantial price discounts for commitments by the investor to save about 1.5 million jobs and to invest about DM210 billion from 1991 to about 1996, which would have been about 20 per cent of the workforce and more than double the overall investment, respectively, in Eastern Germany in 1991. Lucke (1995) calculated that a job committed was subsidized by price reductions on average of about DM50 000 and a committed DM1 of investment by DM0.5. Thus the proceeds of privatization, *ceteris paribus*, would have

*Table* 3.1    Expenditures and revenues of the Treuhand[a]

|  | DM bn |
|---|---|
| Expenses for privatization, restructuring and liquidation[b] | 153 |
| Expenses for old debt relief | 99 |
| Expenses for cleaning up the environment | 43 |
| Other expenses | 37 |
| Total | 332 |
| Revenues | 76 |
| *Deficit* | *256* |

Notes:
[a] End 1994, including projected revenues and expenses of the Treuhand successors for 1995–8.
[b] In particular, investment subsidies, equity capital contributions, financing losses of firms, contributions to social plans, loans to firms, interest payments of the Treuhand.
Source:    Treuhand (1994b, p. 15).

been higher by about DM180 billion. Subtracting DM99 billion of old debts, the Treuhand would still have already made profits (332 – 99 < 180 + 76). The Treuhand's privatization proceeds would clearly have been positive without extra political aims. Part of the Treuhand's costs would have appeared in other state budgets. For example, parts of the Treuhand's price discounts would have appeared in the Labour Office's budget as wage subsidies or expenditures for the unemployed. Whether job and investment commitments during privatization are the least-cost policy instrument for preserving jobs and inducing investment depends on the opportunity costs of the Treuhand's price discounts.

Apart from economic calculation there was also a political cost calculation in which job and investment commitments served political interests. On the one hand, the conservative government did not want to be associated with indefinitely subsidizing East German firms and therefore presented privatization successes in the form of the number of privatized firms, especially to its West German electorate. On the other hand, in order to be re-elected it also needed the support of East German employees and therefore presented employment successes in the form of job and investment (that is, future employment) commitments to its East German electorate (Bundestag, 1994).

In summary, the East German privatization agent was not special as compared to other privatization agents in transition countries that privatized or restructured under political constraints that demanded a price. What was special was the size of the privatization loss: about

124 per cent of East German GDP in 1991. The Treuhand's budget constraint could be made politically soft because mainly West German taxpayers were paying and will continue to pay for the losses. Privatization agents in other transition countries had to have harder budget constraints, which was good for an allocatively efficient privatization, since this forced governments to sell, and even to auction off firms, for the highest price.

## Giveaways versus negotiations versus auctions

Many privatization methods have been used for mass privatization in the transition countries (EBRD, 1996). So it was in Eastern Germany (Table 3.2). Of these many methods, the Treuhand used direct sales as

*Table* 3.2   Privatisation methods of the Treuhand[a]

| Method | Applied to |
| --- | --- |
| *I Sale* | |
| *a Total privatization* | |
| Two-side bargaining | All types of assets[b] |
| | Liquidation cases |
| | MBO/MBI of small and medium-size firms |
| Multi-side bargaining | Direct offer to a few selected investors in process and complex industries (oil, chemistry, steel, paper) |
| | Direct offer to many selected investors in product and well-structured industries with small and medium-size enterprises (wood processing, furniture, textiles) |
| Public tendering | Small privatization (services) |
| | Real estate |
| *b Partial privatization* | |
| Shareholding | Few very large firms |
| Leasing | Agricultural and forestal land |
| Contracting out | Few small and medium-size firms (in so-called 'management KGs') |
| *II Giveaway* | |
| Reprivatization (restitution) | All types of assets |

*Notes:*
[a] Outside the Treuhand there was spontaneous privatization, reprivatization, privatization 'by law' in which courts decided the allcoation of property rights, and privatization by local governments.
[b] Often used in Treuhand subsidiaries, and until spring 1991.

its major privatization method, although the government and the Treuhand were free to choose their major privatization method from among three basic options: giveaways using vouchers, direct sales using negotiations and direct sales using auctions. What is not commonly known is that also in Eastern Germany, as in other transition countries, these three basic options were high on the agenda of policy makers at the beginning of the transition in 1990–1 (Figure 3.2). Thus the question arises as to why the Treuhand chose direct sales using multi-criteria, multi-side bargaining as its major privatization method, and rejected giveaways using vouchers and direct sales using auctions.

Giveaways to the East German population using vouchers were favoured by the civil rights movement that had brought about the peaceful political revolution and the party opposition to the reformed communist government in the first half of 1990 because they represented a third way between capitalism and communism (Fischer and Schröter, 1996). A combination of this method and sales to strategic investors was still being discussed as late as 1991 and was supported by a minority vote in the Council of Economic Advisors to the Ministry of Economics (MoE) (BMWi, 1991; Sinn and Sinn, 1992). Apart from efficiency considerations of corporate governance, three politicoeconomic arguments could be advanced to explain why giveaways using vouchers were not chosen as the basic privatization method in Eastern Germany. The German government(s) did not need extra political support to obtain the momentum needed for a market-oriented reform or for mass privatization. It (they) had had the political support to estab-

*Figure 3.2*   Options for privatization methods in Eastern Germany

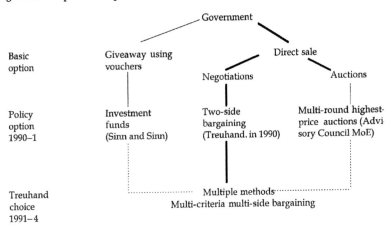

lish a Social Market Economy since the first free election in March and the first all-German elections in October 1990. Furthermore the all-German government had other political instruments with which to smooth the transition shock and buy votes, namely direct financial transfers to East German citizens. Moreover the underlying theoretical concept of voucher privatization was the concept of people's capitalism already developed in the 1950 and 1960s and used with the people's share privatization in Western Germany at that time. So the German government had unique experience in giveaways using vouchers that led it to believe that people's capitalism could not be created this way.

Instead of choosing voucher methods, the Treuhand chose direct sales by negotiations as its principal privatization method. Typically the Treuhand preselected and approached West German or international investors in the particular industry in which the East German firm was operating. Then it started to negotiate over multiple criteria with a small number of investors, often only one to three. Of course the Treuhand behaved in some of its sales activities as is done in normal business practice: for example, by checking the solvency of the investor or describing the object for sale. In making its sales decisions, however, it deviated from normal practice. It based the decision of whom to allocate the firm to on the 'soundness' of the business concept every investor was required to submit. Thus the Treuhand managers thought they knew better than the particular investor whether the business concept was appropriate to the firm in question. The Treuhand, therefore, must have had an idea of what it wanted to negotiate. It negotiated above all the number of jobs preserved or investment commitments and, only secondarily, other arrangements such as the sales price, risk sharing in cleaning up ecological damage, speculation clauses or dealing with restitutional claims (Schmidt, 1994).

But why were East German firms not simply auctioned off? Public auctions were favoured by many economic advisors to the government and parts of the business community in 1990 (Kemmler, 1994) and they were still favoured by the majority of the Council of Economic Advisors to the Ministry of Economics in 1991. And as spontaneous privatization in 1990/early 1991 had shown, many investors wanted to become the owners of East German firms as quickly as possible (Siegmund, 1998). Auctions have a lot of advantages compared to negotiations: for example, they increase competition among bidders, leave less discretion to privatizers, lower the cost of transacting, speed up the transfer of assets and lead to higher revenues. Of course auctions also have disadvantages.[2] But can we consider these disadvantages to really be the reason that auctions were not used for mass privatization in Eastern Germany, now that we know how the Treuhand actually did privatize? Brücker (1997, 1998) and others maintain that auctions could not have been used for a number of reasons.

First, it was technically and administratively too difficult to organize public auctions with multiple rounds of bidding by international investors. One has to keep in mind that the Treuhand had to sell about 14 000 medium-size and large firms, 35 000 small firms, parts of firms, real estate units or assets, and (later) about 1.4 million hectares of agricultural land. All of this was accomplished under a tough time constraint, although with a soft budget constraint. And then it chose time-consuming and complicated negotiating. It is no wonder that the Treuhand expanded its staff from 100 in 1990 to about 4000 in 1992, that the Treuhand managers were always under an extreme amount of stress, that investors became frustrated and that the public was suspicious of dirty deals. The Treuhand itself has shown that mass auctions were technically and administratively practicable (Treuhand, 1994a, vols 6, 8; TLG, 1996). Small privatization of shops, restaurants and other small services was accomplished using regional auctions with the help of local governments. It was carried out in less than one year by only a small Treuhand subsidiary organization, and there were not many complaints about the sales. Also real estate was successfully put out to public tender, a method which came close to public auctions.

Second, the Treuhand had to pursue many aims and, therefore, it had to use many decision criteria that could not be reduced to one criterion, that is, to the price, which in auctions is typically but not exclusively the major decision criterion. If the Treuhand could not reduce its many decision criteria, there was no chance of using auctions. But the Treuhand reduced its many criteria to three when making decisions. It based its decisions on the number of investment commitments, the number of job preservation commitments and the sale price. Since the Treuhand had been able to reduce the many criteria to three, reducing them to two decision criteria or even to one criterion should not have seemed an insurmountable problem. Furthermore the Treuhand responded internally to the problem of discretion in mass negotiations by standardizing them, issuing rules of behaviour and conduct, assigning clear responsibilities within its organization and closely monitoring and controlling its lower management. Thus negotiation design was, after all, not so very different from auction design.[3]

It was also argued that the Treuhand could rationally decide to whom to allocate a firm even when using many decision criteria by

just ranking them ordinally, that is, ranking the different business concepts. But ordinal ranking means nothing more than attaching shadow
prices to the many criteria chosen. In multi-criteria negotiations the
Treuhand managers conducted auctions 'in their heads' because there
was neither a single one-dimensional criterion nor reasonable rules for
shadow pricing between the criteria (U-Ausschuß, 1994). Also the
Treuhand managers were not bound by having to publicly announce
all of their decision criteria or explain any of their decisions. They
could pursue their own preferences, either to the advantage or dis-
advantage of the taxpayer.

Third, there were informational problems during East German transition, so that auctions did not deliver the best allocation of assets.
Unevenly distributed information among bidders, bidding failures
according to different information processing by bidders, and asymmetric bidders with different access to information and different abilities were major informational problems. Negotiations overcame these
problems by way of complex communication between auctioneer and
bidders, with the Treuhand utilizing information from one investor to
evaluate other investors, or to give other investors more information.
But because the Treuhand used multi-side bargaining, that is, bargaining with more than one bidder, or open bargaining, that is, bargaining
with potential bidders who might always enter negotiations, the same
informational problems in auctions applied to negotiations: information remained unevenly distributed, bargaining failures occurred
instead of bidding failures, and bidders remained asymmetric despite
negotiations. Furthermore multiple-round auctions could have communicated at least some of the supposed informational complexities to
bidders. Thus, at best, there is a neutral outcome, in that it would not
have mattered whether the Treuhand had used auctions or negotiations, once it moved away from bilateral negotiations. Treuhand
auctions would not necessarily have been worse than Treuhand
negotiations even in the presence of informational problems.

Finally, there was an 'aggregation problem', so that, the larger the
firm or the more technically related it was to other firms, the less able
it was to be auctioned off. Again this aggregation problem also applied
to Treuhand negotiations because providing better communication did
not solve problems with respect to the technical relatedness or size of
firms. It might have taken more time to provide more information, or
more effort to design an auction mechanism that covered some of the
peculiar characteristics, but it would not have been impossible to do
so. Natural monopolies, which are often technically related firms, have

been auctioned off in some transition countries, although not in Eastern Germany. Large firms could have been put up for auction simultaneously as a whole and in their smallest component parts, typically subsidiaries or factories. In the end a combination of parts could have been chosen that would have had the highest sales price for the Treuhand. And indeed, the Treuhand did use a similar approach for privatizing the East German travel agency Reisebüro. It first tendered the travel agent as a whole. Since this attracted only a few bidders, it broke the travel agency down into three parts (incoming travel, outgoing travel and travel shops) and simultaneously offered them for sale. It sold them immediately and successfully (*Die Wirtschaft*, 1993). It seems very likely that in Eastern Germany, as in other transition countries, the larger and more technically related firms (often natural monopolies) were not auctioned off because there was strong political opposition: fears of foreign ownership, of windfall profits earned by the new private owner, or of bankruptcy if no buyer could be found.

That auctions were not chosen was explained by the Treuhand as follows: 'Because the Treuhand often has to take into account many other criteria besides the price when privatizing firms, this method [public auctions] cannot be considered in the majority of cases' (Treuhand, 1991a, 4.4; see also Breuel, 1992). Because of the 'many other criteria,' namely, the many political aims, negotiations were chosen as the main privatization method in Eastern Germany. Opaque negotiations allowed complicated and changing political objectives to be pursued, be they job preservation commitments or hidden subsidies for declining industries. In general, it is no politicoeconomic surprise that there was *not one* transition country, including Eastern Germany, that chose direct sales using mass auctions of firms to private investors as the major privatization method.

Thus, with regard to privatization methods, Eastern Germany was no special case. It used a variety of privatization methods with direct sales incorporating a certain type of negotiation as the major method. The choice of privatization methods was politicoeconomically determined and not grounded in pure efficiency and welfare considerations. So was the choice of privatization methods in many other countries. The Treuhand pushed negotiations closer to auctions, a fact which may not be known internationally. Nevertheless the Treuhand should and could have auctioned off firms for the highest price because it was in a better position to do so than were similar institutions in any other transition country. Unfortunately the soft budget constraint eased the pressure to use auctions.

## A repoliticized privatization agent

The privatization agents in all transition countries were new political institutions. They were created from scratch, with novel privatization legislation, and deemed to be transitory institutions. The task of the privatization agents was to carry out the privatization policy of the government. They took different organizational forms, as a department of a ministry, a privatization ministry or an autonomous state organization, but none of them was independent of government intervention or interest group pressure, and all of them displayed bureaucratic behaviour. So it was with the Treuhand.

Initially the Treuhand was supposed to be under the auspices of Parliament and there were ideas of creating a Ministry for Eastern German Reconstruction, with the Treuhand at its heart. In the course of reunification in 1990, the Treuhand did not become a ministry (first step of depoliticization); rather it became subordinated to the government (second step) and therein to the minister of finance, who can be seen as the best representative of reformers and taxpayers during transition (Boycko *et al.*, 1995) (third step), and finally it became an autonomous state organization (fourth step). Real ownership rights were widely dispersed over different political and administrative hierarchical levels. Thus there was a whole set of principal–agent problems, with politicians on top fighting for survival in the politicobureaucratic market by maximizing votes, privatizers in the middle privatizing under political constraints, and firm managers at the bottom fighting for survival in the market by maximizing profits and seeking rents. (For details, see Siegmund, 1997a: Figure A1.)

Direct political control over the Treuhand by the government was guaranteed by various administrative rights, especially by appointing the highest decision-making body, the Administrative Board, and by establishing various financial rights, especially by approving the Treuhand's yearly budget and its refinancing on the capital market, and by having its expenditure behaviour closely observed by a credit committee. The largest, and therefore also politically most important, privatization cases were decided in the Administrative Board. These cases involved firms that had more than 1500 employees or DM150 million in returns or book value, or that needed more than DM100 million for restructuring. The structure of the Administrative Board mirrored the German tradition of corporatism: collective bargaining, codetermination, state patrimony and consensus (Table 3.3). From one perspective, the Treuhand was a codetermined firm with a

*Table* 3.3   Administrative board of the Treuhand[a]

| Interest group | Status | Number in 1991 | 1993 |
|---|---|---|---|
| (President) | Chief executive officer (CEO) of a large trade firm | 1 | 1 |
| (Vice president) | Self-employed accountant | 1 | 1 |
| Eastern German state governments | Premier of Saxony | 6 | 6 |
| | Premier of Mecklenburg–West Pomerania (1993, other minister) | | |
| | Premier of Saxony–Anhalt (1993, minister of economics) | | |
| | Premier of Brandenburg | | |
| | Minister of finance of Thuringia (1993, premier) | | |
| | Minister of finance of Berlin | | |
| Federal ministries | State secretary, Ministry of Finance | 2 | 2 |
| | State secretary, Ministry of Economics | | |
| Trade Unions | Head, German Trade Union | 4 | 4 |
| | Head, Trade Union of Public Workers | | |
| | Head, Trade Union of Chemical Workers | | |
| | Member of the board, Trade Union of Metal Workers | | |
| Employers | CEO of a large computer firm (1993, retired) | 9 | 6 |
| | CEO of a medium-size machine tool firm | | |
| | Self-employed consultant | | |
| | President of a large photo and chemical firm (foreigner) | | |
| | CEO of a medium-size firm (since 1993, vice-president) | | |
| | Member, executive board of a large trade firm (1993, retired) | | |
| | CEO of a large utilities firm | | |
| | CEO of a medium-size textile firm (1993, retired) | | |
| | CEO of a large electronics and consumer goods firm (1993, retired) | | |
| | Member, executive board of a medium-size machine tool firm (1993, new) | | |
| Others | Member (retired), board of directors of the Bundesbank | 1 | 1 |
| **Total** | | **24** | **21** |

*Note:*   [a]  The number of board members was reduced in 1993.
*Source:*   BMF (1991, p. 43), Treuhand (1991b, p. 23).

coalition of trade unions and East German state governments (labour) on the one side and of the government and employers (capital) on the other side in the board's decisions, in which the vote of the president had been decisive since 1993. From another perspective, the Treuhand was a labour-managed firm with the federal government being part of the labour-side. And the Treuhand was even a pure political firm if one thinks of employers as representing various interest groups and not capital. While this led to less political conflict than having a board of 'pure capitalists', it also hindered privatization and, especially, liquidation. Consensus was not difficult to reach because the taxpayer, as the third party, was not adequately represented in the board. The Treuhand was an off-budget organization, which was allowed to issue debt up to certain limits per year until 1994. These limits were approved by the Ministry of Finance's Treuhand Department and by a parliamentary subcommittee responsible for the Treuhand. Apart from these two direct property rights, the Treuhand was comparatively politically independent in its daily decisions, so that lawyers saw the Treuhand acting under mediating law (Übergangsrecht), which is in between public and private law (Weimar, 1993, p. V).

In the course of privatization the Treuhand became subject to more direct political control. This was due to the fact that the profitability of firms to be privatized declined and therefore many firms had to be liquidated – although there was already large-scale de-industrialization. The political importance per privatized or liquidated firm increased. In particular the so-called 'old industrial cores', agglomerations of firms in declining industries, had to be either liquidated or subsidized, in the hope that they would become new industrial cores (DIW *et al.*, 1996, Report 14). The industrial cores were subsidized by the Treuhand (and others) according to the political lobbying of the East German state governments. Brandenburg lobbied for the steel industry, Mecklenburg–West Pomerania for the shipbuilding industry, Saxony–Anhalt for the machine building and chemical industries, Saxony for the textile and machine building industries, and Thuringia for the microelectronics, optic, electronic and glass industries.

The Treuhand had come to terms with the East German state governments and the trade unions already in 1991 by signing a letter of intention, wherein subsidies for medium-term restructuring and slow liquidation were determined. Because of political pressure the Treuhand set up advisory boards and discussion forums on the municipal (Beiräte Niederlassungen) and state levels (Wirtschaftskabinette Länder/Treuhand). Furthermore the Treuhand was made the subject of an inquiry by Parliament in 1993–4. Although the inquiry's results were rather disappointing, it showed some organizational, legal and financial weaknesses in the Treuhand and, more important, made the managers on all levels think more about politics (U-Ausschuß, 1994).

The Treuhand was, for some time, less vulnerable to political control than similar institutions in many other transition countries. This can be attributed mainly to German policy-making tradition, with the Bundesbank being the best example. Nevertheless the Treuhand was not a private organization, but rather a state one, and adapted to political demands. It became more politicized in the course of privatization. Whether, on average, the Treuhand was more politicized than the Czech Ministry of Privatization, or less than the Hungarian privatization agencies, is difficult to prove. The Treuhand was less politically and differently, influenced, than privatization agents in other transition countries, though it was not an apolitical organization.

## Overcoming inefficient privatization policy

Democratic governments that engage in a policy of mass privatization must take into account politicoeconomic repercussions and conflicts, because efficiency does not coincide with equity. East German privatization was not special in this respect. The German government, like many other governments, used privatization policy itself as the major conflict resolution and redistribution institution; this policy was implemented by the Treuhand with its multiple aims, discretionary negotiations, semi-politicized organization and soft budget. Thus, overall, it is not clear whether efficiency or equity aims or, to put it theoretically, welfare or vote maximization, dominated the Treuhand's behaviour. In order to improve efficiency, and nevertheless promote equity and redistribution, these two aims, we have argued, should have been separated. If the German government and Treuhand had followed only efficiency aims, it would have privatized very likely according to the following shock approach recommendations.

(1) *Privatize only*. Do not assign any other goal to a privatization agent. Social policy should be pursued by means of taxes and transfers; competition policy should be implemented by an anti-monopoly office, and so on. Mixed goals blur responsibility and become expensive. If you have to or wish to assign another goal, give it a secondary priority. Use privatization for other goals only to achieve the political momentum (critical mass) for a market-oriented reform.

(2) ***Privatize using standard auctions***. Put a lot of effort into marketing the firms to create demand. Negotiations are time-consuming,
opaque, discretionary and expensive, and demand many controls.
If the privatization agent is (somehow) pressured to negotiate, he
can standardize negotiations and make them more auction-like.

(3) ***Privatize unpolitically but with rules***. Use a privatization agent
that is as politically autonomous as possible. Do not intervene. The
best rule to bind an independent privatization agent is to let him
auction the firm to the highest bidder. The second-best rules are
law, incentive contracts, monitoring and public control.

While this shock approach does not seem to many observers to be
politically plausible for Germany, let alone other countries, it would
nevertheless help to overcome the Jasinski–Yarrow paradox, which
states that inefficiencies in privatization policy are caused by governments that cause inefficiencies of state firms in the first place, for
example because of equity aims. Equity and redistribution, it has been
argued above, can be brought about by other policies than privatization policy. This would seem to have been especially appropriate in
Eastern Germany where those other policies were available and were
used anyway.

Voters, interest groups and governments have been learning from
the inefficiencies of state ownership. Why, then, should they not learn
from the inefficiencies in privatization policy, too – as they have been
learning from the inefficiencies of inflation and monetary policy all
over the world?

## Notes

1. I would like to thank the Egon Sohmen Foundation for financial support and
   Paul Kramer for improving my English.
2. For surveys of auction theory, see McAfee and McMillan (1987), Maskin
   (1992) and Schmidt and Schnitzer (1997).
3. This response of the privatization agent leads to a more fundamental problem
   in using privatization methods which has been called elsewhere the 'reversal
   of polarity problem' (Siegmund, 1997b). On the one hand, bargaining can be
   made more auction-like, as was the case in Eastern Germany. On the other
   hand, auctions can be made more bargain-like, as was the case in Russia, where
   auction design became the object of politicoeconomic bargaining.

# 4
# Fiscal Aspects of Privatization: the Paradox of Privatization Revenues

*Dirck Süß*

## Introduction: revenues from privatization: how important are they?[1]

Since the middle of the 1980s, privatization has become a popular economic policy all over the world. Besides increasing efficiency and decreasing political influence in the economy, the restoration of public finances has always been an important argument for putting privatization on the agenda. Apart from more indirect effects like hardening the enterprises' budget constraints and thus enabling politicians to cut subsidies, or higher tax proceeds due to more efficiency, the revenues from the sale of enterprises are generally seen as an important fiscal effect of privatization.

After the collapse of the socialist systems in Central and Eastern Europe towards the end of the 1980s most countries in that region jumped onto the privatization train. Privatization was seen as a key element of any successful transformation strategy. As in established market economies, privatization in countries in transition pursues a large and diverse number of objectives, but possible revenues usually play an important role (Süß, 1997). Many countries started the transition period with a heavy burden of high internal and external debt. In most cases the situation was worsened by a fiscal crisis that evolved in the course of the transition, caused by a drop in revenues and simultaneously increasing expenditures. Revenues from privatization were often seen as a welcome source of income during this period.

This chapter begins by examining the privatization process in Poland, the Czech Republic and Hungary from 1991 to 1996, with a focus on the revenues raised during this period. In the second section the results will be compared and the extent to which they were to be expected will be analysed. In the third section some factors determining privatization revenues will be presented. A fourth section concludes the chapter.

## Privatization in Poland, Hungary and the Czech Republic

Poland, the Czech Republic and Hungary all started the transition with large public sectors, but there were differences between these countries. In Poland and Hungary, far-reaching property rights reforms had already taken place in the time before the start of the transition period. Firms had become more autonomous and employees (Poland) and managers (Hungary) had secured rights of decision making and code-termination. Besides these reforms in state-owned enterprises (SOEs), in Poland the greater part of agriculture had remained private during the socialist era. In Hungary, private economic activity had become possible outside the state-owned sphere in some sectors, for example small shops and restaurants. In the Czech Republic, almost all enterprises were state-owned and coordinated through a system of strict central planning. These differences in the degree of liberalization and property rights reforms resulted in different shares of the private sector in the economy at the beginning of the actual transition process (see Table 4.1).

The countries also differed with respect to the overall economic environment and, of particular importance here, the situation of state budgets. Poland and Hungary were both suffering from severe macroeconomic imbalances: high inflation rates coincided with high internal and/or external debts. In Czechoslovakia, the inflation rate, budget deficit and external debt were low compared to the two other countries and international standards (Table 4.2).

The different starting positions concerning the distribution of property rights and the necessity to react to the economic situation resulted in the choice of different privatization strategies. Poland and Hungary both decided at first on a sales-oriented strategy, with a keen eye on possible privatization revenues to balance the budget and repay foreign

*Table* 4.1   Size of the public sector, % of GDP (1988)

| Czechoslovakia | Hungary | Poland |
|---|---|---|
| 99.3 | 92.9 | 81.2 |

*Source*:   Kornai (1992, p. 72).

*Table* 4.2   Macroeconomic situation at the start of transition (1989)

|  | Hungary | Poland | Czech Republic |
|---|---|---|---|
| Budget deficit (% of GDP) | –1.4 | –7.4 | –2.8 |
| External debt (US $bn) | 19.2 | 40.2 | 6.8 |
| (per capita, US $) | 1 846 | 1 058 | 660 |
| Inflation rate (annual average, %) | 17.0 | 251.1 | 2.3 |

*Source*:   EBRD (1995).

debt. In the Czech Republic, a more innovative privatization plan was drawn up: privatization was to be carried out with the help of a free-distribution voucher scheme.

In all three countries privatization can be divided into two large areas which usually proceed at different speeds and according to different rules: the small privatization, concerning smaller enterprises from the trade, crafts and service sector, and the large privatization, involving the big state enterprises which constitute the most substantial part of the socialist economies. In Poland, small-scale privatization was carried out by the municipalities. Most enterprises were auctioned, sold or leased to employees or managers for relatively low prices. Each municipality had its own privatization programme and was entitled to the revenues. Owing to the decentralized character of privatization, there are no figures for the revenues from the Polish small privatization (Earle *et al.*, 1994). Until the start of the mass privatization programme in December 1995, large-scale privatization in Poland was executed mainly in two ways: capital privatization (sale) and liquidation (in two variants). The sale of enterprises either as a whole to large core investors or of smaller parts to the public was planned to become the main method of privatization. Considerable proceeds were expected, but until the middle of 1995 only 142 out of over 8000 enterprises were sold. Privatization by liquidation has been the more important method. Under this programme enterprises are liquidated and assets sold individually. Often the new owners of assets are enterprise insiders. Revenues from the sale are used to pay enterprises' debts. Although privatization through liquidation became an important way to privatize, at the end of 1995 more than half of the Polish enterprises up for privatization were still state-owned (Dąbrowski, 1996). Revenues from privatization remained low in absolute terms and compared to the state budget deficit (see Table 4.3).

*Table* 4.3   Revenues from privatization in Poland

|  | 1991 | 1992 | 1993 | 1994 | 1995 | 1996 |
|---|---|---|---|---|---|---|
| Revenues (new Zloty mn) | 170.9 | 498.9 | 789.4 | 1 614.7 | 2 641.6 | 3 220.0 |
| % of GDP | 0.2 | 0.4 | 0.5 | 0.8 | 0.9 | 0.9 |
| Budget deficit (% of GDP) | 3.8 | 6.0 | 2.8 | 2.7 | 2.7 | 2.1 |

*Sources:*   Ministerstwo Skarbu Państwa (1996, 1997), BMWi (1997).

In December 1995, 512 enterprises entered the mass privatization programme and were turned over to 15 National Investment Funds (NIFs). Every Polish citizen could become a shareholder of these funds in exchange for vouchers which were sold for a nominal fee. The government kept 25 per cent of the shares, the sale of which could generate some revenue later. It has been a specific feature of the Polish case so far that employees were involved in the privatization process and enjoyed preferential treatment in many ways, thereby being able to safeguard the substantial control rights they had gained during earlier reforms (Mohlek, 1996).

In Hungary, the privatization programme was mainly based on direct enterprise sales. Raising revenues to pay back foreign debt was an important aim. After a phase of spontaneous privatization from 1988 to 1989, the State Property Agency (SPA) was founded to stop the process of uncontrolled transformation of public assets to semi-private joint ventures and to secure revenue for the state (Sárközy, 1996). Small-scale privatization was carried out mainly during the period 1991–2. The most frequently used method was an auction approach. Many smaller enterprises, such as petrol stations or hotels that belonged to chains of enterprises, were not part of the programme. The SPA planned to sell them en bloc. This decision, and the fact that many enterprises in the trade and service sector were already private following the liberalization of the 1980s in Hungary, meant that the small privatization programme was not as extensive as in the other countries (Lagemann *et al.*, 1994). In the process of large-scale privatization, several programmes were launched which also relied on sales either for cash or (partly) for so-called 'compensation vouchers' which were issued as part of the Hungarian restitution programme. Most commonly a case by case approach was applied. The privatization agency entered into lengthy negotiations with possible investors, thus keeping the process moving at a slow pace (Major, 1994).

*Table 4.4*  Revenues from privatization in Hungary

|                           | 1991  | 1992  | 1993   | 1994  | 1995   | 1996  |
|---------------------------|-------|-------|--------|-------|--------|-------|
| Revenues (HUF bn)         | 30.35 | 62.99 | 134.86 | 36.86 | 451.57 | 180.1 |
| % of GDP                  | 1.2   | 2.3   | 3.8    | 1.0   | 8.0    | 2.7   |
| Budget deficit (% of GDP) | 2.1   | 6.2   | 5.4    | 9.8   | 6.2    | 3.3   |

*Sources*:  ÁPV Rt. (1995), BMWi (1997), National Bank of Hungary (1996).

The establishment of a second privatization and holding agency and plans to introduce a new privatization law brought the process to a grinding halt at the end of 1994 (Mihályi, 1996a). After the new law was put into effect, privatization sped up again. Revenues from privatization were higher than in Poland in most years but, with the exception of 1995, they fell short of expectations (Table 4.4).

Because of the comfortable situation of the state budget, the Czech decision makers were not dependent on revenue and could afford to give away property instead of selling it. Quite early in the privatization process a restitution programme was introduced. Property confiscated under socialism was given back to former owners or their heirs. With respect to possible privatization revenues, such a restitution programme is relevant in two ways: firstly, giving away property means relinquishment of revenues in exchange for justice (Appel, 1995); secondly, a restitution programme can lead to uncertainties about ownership rights and scare off investors (Sinn and Sinn, 1992). Small privatization was conducted mainly through auctions open to all Czech citizens. Unlike the situation in Hungary, almost all small enterprises were included in the programme and, unlike the case of Poland, revenues had to be transferred to a central institution (Fund of National Property). More than 50 000 enterprises were privatized by the end of 1992, either by restitution (30 000) or by auctions (22 400) (Kotrba and Svejnar, 1994, pp. 152, 159).

What makes privatization in the Czech Republic unique with respect to speed, revenues, institutional setting and applied methods is the mass privatization programme for large enterprises. Under this programme more than 2300 large enterprises were privatized in two waves in under four years. Several institutions were involved in this procedure. The ministries of privatization and of finance were responsible for evaluating and choosing privatization projects. The Fund of National Property organized the actual privatization and were in charge of the proceeds (Kubin and Tůma, 1997).[2] The enterprises were assigned to the

*Table* 4.5   Revenues from privatization in the Czech Republic

|  | 1991 | 1992 | 1993 | 1994 | 1995 | 1996 |
|---|---|---|---|---|---|---|
| Revenues (Kr bn) | 18.5 | 38.4 | 25.9 | 30.6 | 25.9 | 24.5 |
| % of GDP | 2.6 | 4.9 | 2.8 | 2.9 | 2.1 | 1.7 |
| Budget deficit/surplus[a] (% of GDP) |  |  | +0.2 | +0.9 | +0.3 | −0.4 |

*Note:*   [a] In 1991 and 1992 the Czech Republic still formed a unit with the Slovak Republic.
*Sources:*   FNM ČR (various issues), BMWi (1997).

two waves of privatization and vouchers were sold for a small nominal fee to the general population. The management of the enterprises had to work out a plan for privatization within a short deadline. Possible methods of privatization were not only the transfer of shares in exchange for vouchers, but also the sale of shares to small investors, selling or auctioning the firm to a core investor or transferring the enterprise to a municipality or a public organization, for example social security insurance. Besides the obligatory preparation of a privatization plan by the management, anyone interested, whether of domestic or foreign origin, could propose a privatization plan to the Ministry of Privatization. Here the most suitable project was chosen and the enterprise was transferred to the Fund of National Property for privatization (Kotrba and Svejnar, 1994). Because free transfer for vouchers was not the only means of privatization, remarkable revenues from privatization could be obtained in the Czech Republic (see Table 4.5).

## The paradox of privatization revenues

How were the privatization revenues obtained affected by the different privatization strategies of the three countries? Comparing the results uncovers a surprise: revenues in Poland are significantly lower than in the other countries, in Hungary there are marked changes from year to

*Table* 4.6   Privatization revenues in % of GDP

|  | 1991 | 1992 | 1993 | 1994 | 1995 | 1996 | Average |
|---|---|---|---|---|---|---|---|
| Poland | 0.2 | 0.4 | 0.5 | 0.8 | 0.9 | 0.9 | 0.6 |
| Czech Republic | 2.6 | 4.9 | 2.8 | 2.9 | 2.1 | 1.7 | 2.8 |
| Hungary | 1.2 | 2.3 | 3.8 | 1.0 | 8.0 | 2.7 | 3.2 |

*Sources:*   See Tables 4.3 to 4.5.

year, while in the Czech Republic revenues developed more steadily and an average are only slightly lower than in Hungary.[3] There are several reasons why this result is indeed surprising and can be called the 'paradox of privatization revenues'.

- In the Czech Republic, the macroeconomic starting position, with low internal and external debt, was a lot better than in the other countries and privatization revenues were not really needed to stabilize the situation.
- The voucher method, which means giving away parts of enterprises and therefore the relinquishment of revenues was an important part of the Czech privatization.
- In the Czech Republic, a considerable amount of property was returned to former owners in the restitution programme. This also means no revenues for the state and can lead to a retreat of investors.
- In Poland and Hungary, revenues from privatization were seen as a welcome source of income to help balance the budget and pay back external debt. Therefore, besides arguments related to corporate governance issues, privatization via sales was chosen as the main method of privatization.

In short, the paradox is that the country which was least dependent on privatization revenues and where the chosen privatization methods were least likely to lead to considerable proceeds performed best with respect to direct income from privatization.

## Untangling the paradox

Prices are determined by supply and demand and the institutional setting in which these two come together. This basic insight of microeconomics sets the stage for a further inquiry into the determinants of the revenue paradox.

### Supply-side explanations

#### Different amounts of privatized property

A simple explanation for the differences in privatization proceeds would be that in the Czech Republic more property has been privatized so far. The more property sold, the higher revenues ought to be. The different amount of privatized property can be due to a larger public sector at the beginning of the transition period or faster privatization.

The public sector in the Czech Republic was larger than in the other two countries (Table 4.1), but private activities in Poland and Hungary almost exclusively took place in the agricultural, small trade and service sectors. Therefore the higher revenues from privatization due to different sizes of the public sector should mainly stem from small-scale privatization. In fact the revenues from small privatizations in the Czech Republic were considerably larger than in Hungary. They equalled 2.3 per cent and 1.8 per cent of Czech gross domestic product (GDP) in 1991 and 1992, respectively. In Hungary, only 0.2 per cent of GDP was earned during the same period in which small privatization was completed. (Unfortunately there are no figures for Poland.) But the differences in the size of the public sector fail to explain the high revenues from large privatization: enterprises included in these programmes dominated the economy and were wholly state-owned in all three countries.

Another possible explanation would be that, in the Czech Republic, privatization has progressed faster. Given the numbers of privatized enterprises, this explanation fits the problem. According to World Bank estimates, at the end of 1995 in the Czech Republic only 10 per cent of the enterprises were still state owned, compared to 22 per cent in Hungary and 54 per cent in Poland. But more important than the number of enterprises is the value of privatized property. Here the World Bank estimates that 40 per cent of the value of the former state sector was not yet privatized in Hungary as well as in the Czech Republic, while for Poland no estimates are available (World Bank, 1996a). Considering the fact that in Hungary most enterprises have been sold, while in the Czech Republic a large part has been given away, differences in the amount of completed privatizations cannot provide a satisfactory explanation for the paradox of revenues in a comparison of these two countries. For Poland, however, this explanation partly fits the problem: many of the valuable enterprises, namely the utilities, the privatization of which led to the boost in Hungary's revenues in 1995, are still state-owned.

### The problem of absorption

While the argument in the preceding part was that revenues are likely to be higher when more enterprises are privatized, it can also be argued that the opposite is true. Sinn and Sinn (1992) hold that the law of supply and demand also applies to the market for enterprises. A massive shift in the supply curve must lead to a drop in prices, for three reasons.

(1) **Portfolio effect**  The number of entrepreneurs willing to take high risks associated with a participation in former state enterprises is limited. The more enterprises sold, the more risk-averse investors have to be convinced to buy an enterprise. The more risk-averse investors are, the less likely they will pay high prices.

(2) **Microeconomic limitation of available credits**  To get credit from a bank in order to buy an enterprise a certain amount of equity is necessary. Since the total amount of equity in an economy is limited – especially in the transition economies – capital markets cannot supply willing investors with enough credits to buy enterprises for a reasonable price. The more enterprises are being privatized, the lower the average amount of money available for a single purchase will be.

(3) **Macroeconomic limitation of available credits (stock flow constraint)**  Existing stocks of enterprises cannot be sold in a short period of time because there are not enough liquid flows available. A rapid sale of stocks of property which were built up over a long period of time necessarily leads to low revenues.

These arguments seem to apply especially if privatization is carried out as fast as possible in a closed economy. In a more open economy, foreign direct investment and capital supply from abroad can contribute to solving the problem. Another possibility is to prolong the process and find a way to smooth the supply in a manner that makes it easier for the economy to absorb the enterprises into the private sector. Therefore better chances of foreign participation and a smoothing of the privatization process in time could be the key to the paradox of privatization revenues.

In many transition economies there is a fear of too massive foreign participation, leading to hindrance of FDI. In the countries considered here, the possibilities for foreigners to invest and participate in the privatization process were most unfavourable in Poland. For many forms of investment, for example some forms of joint ventures, participation in public enterprises or the purchase of land and real estate, special permission was needed. Unrestricted activities of foreigners are only allowed in enterprises that do not own or lease any real estate. Tax holidays for foreigners have only been granted on a discretionary basis (Borish and Noël 1996).

In Hungary, specific attempts have been made to get foreigners involved in privatization. They can become full owners of privatized enterprises, including all real estate. Foreign investment is protected by a variety of laws and considerable tax holidays have been granted. In the Czech Republic, foreigners were excluded from the small privatization, but in large privatization they had the same rights as Czech citizens. Registered foreign enterprises can buy real estate without any restrictions and investments are possible in any size or sector. Until 1993, there were some tax holidays (ibid.).

The conditions for foreign investment explain in part why Hungary and the Czech Republic have been able to earn higher income from privatization than Poland, but they do not explain why, in the first three years, revenues in the Czech Republic were higher than in Hungary. Taking the amount of foreign direct investment as an indicator of the openness of a country to foreigners also fails to confirm the hypothesis that the high revenues in the Czech Republic result from massive foreign participation. The cumulated foreign investments for the period from 1989 to 1996 show that Hungary's share was by far the largest, with 1288 US$ per capita, followed by Poland with 128 US$ and the Czech Republic with only 118 US$ per capita (EBRD 1997).

Besides enlarging the group of possible new owners, slowing down the privatization process and selling few enterprises at a time might also contribute to higher revenues. In Hungary and Poland, the privatization proceeded more slowly than was originally planned.[4] In Poland, the privatization was and still is the subject of continual political struggles which often lead to delays. In the course of these debates enterprises lost value and insiders were enabled to strengthen their position, which further slowed the privatization process (Rapacki, 1995). This slowdown due to political debates did not lead to higher revenues. In Hungary, the situation was similar. Privatization followed a more gradual approach from the very beginning. Single case decisions, in which the aim of gaining high revenues was often very important, dominated the process. But privatization was also often further slowed by political intervention. At times a number of large enterprises were not privatized at all but assigned to a state holding to stay under state ownership permanently. In other cases the state kept parts of the enterprises or golden shares to ensure future state influence. Later a new privatization law was worked out to speed up the process again, but uncertainties about the contents of the new law and the course of privatization in the future caused an almost total cessation of privatization in 1994. In Hungary, the delays of privatization caused by political interventions in the running of privatization programmes and the reorientation of the privatization policy did not lead to higher revenues either.

In the Czech Republic, it was an aim of the privatization programme to transfer large amounts of property as fast as possible. In a relatively short period more than 3000 enterprises were transferred to new owners by different methods. A large number of shares in enterprises were not immediately privatized but stayed with the Fund of National Property. Through this fund the state holds shares in more than 200 companies and remains the largest and most influential shareholder in the country. Since the completion of the second wave of privatization, sales have become the most important method of privatization and the Fund of National Property keeps selling shares for cash, still earning remarkable revenues (Mejstřik, 1994; Borish and Noël, 1996; OECD, 1996).

Thus a slowdown of privatization can lead to higher revenues from privatization if it reflects a prudent sequencing and is conducted by market-compatible instruments but is unlikely to yield higher income if it results from political interference.

### Demand side explanations

Differences in the revenues from privatization might be a result not only of differences on the supply side but also of differences on the demand side. Prices potential investors are willing to pay depend on how the enterprises are evaluated. While evaluating enterprises is a difficult task even in economic systems that are not going through a period of transition, evaluating enterprises properly under transformation conditions is almost impossible (Ulrich, 1995). The value of an enterprise is calculated by the discounted flow of future earnings. Under transformation conditions all determinants of future earnings such as prices, wages, governmental regulations or income of the population and resulting ability to buy the products of an enterprise are rapidly changing in unknown directions. Analysing the influence of these factors on the evaluation of enterprises is beyond the scope of the present chapter. Therefore we focus on some indicators which should affect any rational investor's decision: growth, inflation, unit labour costs and labour productivity (see Table 4.7).

The conditions for investment determined by these four factors have developed quite differently in the countries analysed here. Surprisingly they were most advantageous in Poland. It was the first country to return to the path of growth. Increasing growth rates have a positive influence on investors' expectations about future development of aggregate demand. The steady decline of the inflation rate contributes to a further stabilization of expectations, while declining unit labour costs and rising labour productivity are indicators for growing competitiveness.

*Table* 4.7    Growth, inflation, unit labour costs and labour productivity in Poland, Czech Republic and Hungary, 1991–5

|  | 1991 | 1992 | 1993 | 1994 | 1995 |
|---|---|---|---|---|---|
| **Growth rate**[a] (annual change of GDP in %) | | | | | |
| Poland | –7.0 | 2.6 | 3.8 | 5.2 | 7.0 |
| Czech Republic | –14.2 | –6.4 | –0.9 | 2.6 | 4.8 |
| Hungary | –11.9 | –3.0 | –0.8 | 2.9 | 2.0 |
| **Inflation rate**[a] (annual change of consumer goods prices) | | | | | |
| Poland | 70.3 | 43.0 | 35.3 | 32.2 | 27.8 |
| Czech Republic | 56.7 | 11.1 | 20.8 | 10.0 | 9.1 |
| Hungary | 35.0 | 23.0 | 22.5 | 18.7 | 28.2 |
| **Unit labour costs**[b] **in US$** (annual change in %) | | | | | |
| Poland | 66.5 | –8.7 | –8.8 | –7.3 | 15.1 |
| Czech Republic | –14.8 | 32.8 | 25.8 | 13.2 | 6.9 |
| Hungary | 29.4 | 7.6 | –9.6 | –1.0 | –8.7 |
| **Labour productivity**[b] (annual change in %) | | | | | |
| Poland | –11.9 | 17.1 | 14.5 | 19.2 | 9.6 |
| Czech Republic | –16.6 | –7.6 | –3.5 | 4.0 | 20.5 |
| Hungary | –17.9 | 10.7 | 18.5 | 7.3 | 11.2 |

*Sources:*    [a] BMWi (1997), [b] EBRD (1996).

The comparatively better results in terms of privatization revenues in Hungary and the Czech Republic cannot be explained by the indicators considered here. The two countries merely performed better in lowering the inflation rate. Growth rates were negative until 1993. The good privatization results of the Czech Republic in particular cannot be explained by better conditions for investment influenced by labour productivity or unit labour costs either: steadily growing labour costs and declining productivity are not factors likely to attract investors and increase the value of enterprises. The similar trend in the development of labour productivity and labour costs in Hungary and Poland is also insufficient to explain the gap in revenues between these two countries. Consequently, from the analysis of these macroeconomic figures, no further insight into the paradox of revenues is gained. On the contrary: in the country in which the considered indicators developed best, the lowest revenues were earned and vice versa.

Expected pay-off from a particular investment is determined not only by economic data but also by the risk associated with it. Political risk has a substantial influence on investment decisions. In the Czech Republic, several factors served to reduce the political risk associated with the reform of property rights: the introduction of a restitution programme was a clear commitment to the guarantee of property rights; only one government was in charge of the whole privatization programme, which was introduced and executed at a high speed; deadlines within the programme were usually met; distributing property to a large part of the population in the mass privatization programme was an additional instrument to prevent future governments from reversing privatization. All these features of the Czech privatization programme reduced the political risk for investment, which contributed to higher revenues.

Hungary had a longer tradition of reforms than the other countries. It had been more open and market-oriented for quite a while and the main course of privatization and liberalization was never questioned. The high foreign direct investments that flowed into the country are a proof of the good reputation Hungary enjoyed among investors. The low revenues in 1994 should not be associated with higher political risks in that period but with confusion stemming from a reorientation of privatization policy during that time.

Again in Poland the situation was different. Especially during the early transition period there was a lot of political unrest. The government and, with it, the favoured privatization policy changed several times. Privatization increasingly became a subject of political debates and conflicts, a process most likely to scare off possible investors and to lower their willingness to pay. Another factor with negative effect on the value of an enterprise is the dilution of property rights by influential employees and unions. In Poland, the influence of this group has been traditionally strong, contributing to the low privatization revenues.

From this it follows that political stability and the general direction of privatization policy and economic reforms in transition countries have a stronger influence on possible privatization revenues than 'hard' economic facts.

## The institutional design

In a world with positive transaction costs and incomplete knowledge, institutional and organizational factors have a substantial influence on prices. Therefore the specific institutional conditions of privatization in the three countries have to be considered when revenues are compared.

Revenues will be high if an enterprise is sold to the investor who is willing to pay the most and if at the same time there is a mechanism forcing the buyer to reveal his true preferences. Theoretically it can be shown that a competitive approach is able to solve both problems. Competition among buyers is a good mechanism to reveal important information spread among many individuals (Hayek 1937, 1978). Two forms of information are particularly important to evaluate enterprises:

(1) Knowledge about the enterprise and its microeconomic surroundings such as the quality of the capital stock, internal organization of production, specific skills of employees, possibilities for restructuring the enterprise, or important sources of raw materials. Insiders like managers and employees are most likely to have this kind of knowledge.

(2) Expert knowledge which is not necessarily tied to the enterprise: modern management skills, knowledge about global markets and competition in specific branches or access to external sources of capital. Insiders are not likely to have this kind of knowledge, but it is probably available to outsiders such as internationally experienced managers or foreign investors.

During the transition period not only do potential investors have limited knowledge about the enterprises, but also the ministries and agencies in charge of privatization do not really know what the enterprises they are trying to sell might be worth. Therefore they should be interested in making use of the decentralized knowledge as far as possible. Since this information is spread among many individuals it should be an aim of the privatization agencies to involve as many potential buyers as possible in the privatization process.

Competition will force investors to try to make use of the knowledge available to them as good as possible to estimate the value of an enterprise. Since there is always the danger that a competitor is willing to pay a higher price every bidder will reveal his true preferences, making it possible for the seller to maximize revenues.

By using competition as a mechanism of discovery, two problems are solved at once: a large amount of information is collected and processed, so the best use of an enterprise can be found and the potential buyers are forced to reveal their preferences. Ideally this mechanism has to be supported by a high degree of transparency. Transparency of the process will prevent corruption and preferential treatment so that no one can acquire any property rights without paying the appropriate price. From these theoretical considerations the hypothesis can be derived that revenues will be high if the institutional design of the privatization process ensures competition and transparency and prevents preferential treatment. The mass privatization programme in the Czech Republic included the following features:

- Anyone interested in an enterprise had the chance to prepare a privatization project. While insiders had to prepare a project, thereby revealing relevant knowledge, outsiders, including foreigners could prepare a proposition if they were interested. In this way a lot of insider and outsider knowledge was revealed and could be used in coming to a decision.
- The privatization ministries chose among several projects the one that was most suitable. This provided an incentive for everyone interested in an enterprise to reveal their knowledge and preferences in order to come up with the most appropriate proposition.
- A division of powers and rights among several levels, such as the management of the firm, which had to prepare a project, the Ministry of Privatization, which made the decision and the Fund of National Property which was in charge of the actual privatization of assets and the collection of revenues created a system of checks and balances that led to a high degree of transparency and prevented preferential treatment.

Although in Hungary it was always pointed out that competition plays a vital role in the privatization, the process can be better characterized as a bargaining approach. In many cases the SPA engaged directly in lengthy negotiations with single investors. Such an approach can lead to lower revenues, for several reasons:

- important outsider information about the value of an enterprise can be lost if only selected investors are invited to make an offer;
- during the time-consuming bargaining process the enterprises lose value, and the buyer will pay lower prices the longer the procedure lasts (Major, 1994);
- case-by-case bargaining includes the possibility of strategic behaviour. If an investor knows that the SPA is willing to sell, it is always an option for him to try to renegotiate certain terms of a contract, including the price (Schmidt and Schnitzer, 1997).

Besides these disadvantages of a case-by-case privatization, the role of the management of Hungarian firms should be mentioned. Without the consent of the management hardly any firm could be privatized. This does not necessarily mean lower revenues, because an enterprise will be worth more to an investor if he knows that incumbent managers are willing to cooperate and their specific knowledge can be used as a resource in the future. On the other hand, it will not be the management's first aim to maximize sales revenues for the state. It is more likely that managers will be interested in increase in capital, new investments, job guarantees, or other side arrangements in contracts that will have a negative influence on the price.

In Poland, competition has played a very limited role in the privatization process so far. Employees have been preferentially treated in all forms of privatization. In many cases they have had the right to initiate the commercialization and privatization by themselves. After privatization has started employees enjoy special rights to become shareholders in the new enterprise or to buy the assets in the event of liquidation. If such preferential treatment is granted to the employees per se, they have no incentive to reveal their true preferences or any insider knowledge they might have about what the enterprise is worth. Therefore the state cannot expect to earn high revenues. At the same time, outside investors will be careful about involvement in former state enterprises if they face strong employee councils, because employees are likely to be interested in safe jobs and high wages, rather than profit maximization – a factor which is most likely to lower the willingness to pay of potential investors.

## Conclusion

The comparison of the different approaches to privatization in Poland, the Czech Republic and Hungary led to the surprising finding that a mass privatization programme involving substantial free transfer of assets does not necessarily mean lower total revenues. If free transfers are combined with the sale of enterprises to core investors or the sale of shares via the stock exchange, as was the case in the Czech Republic, considerable revenues can be earned. Important factors influencing the level of income from privatization are political and economic stability and the institutional design of the privatization programme. A stable environment contributes to a higher evaluation of enterprises due to lower risk associated with the investment. An institutional design providing competition and transparency attracts investors, raises the amount of information to evaluate enterprises, and prevents corruption and preferential treatment of insiders.

## Notes

1. I would like to thank Frank Bönker, László Csaba, Péter Mihályi, Hans-Jürgen Wagener and the other participants of the conference for useful comments on this chapter. Financial support from the Deutsche Forschungsgemeinschaft (DFG) is gratefully acknowledged.
2. There was one Ministry of Privatization in the Czech Republic and one in the Slovak Republic. On the national level, the Ministry of Finance acted as Ministry of Privatization. Following this scheme, three Funds of National Property were created.
3. For similar results, see Antczak (1996).
4. In Poland, it was planned to finish privatization within five to seven years; in Hungary, the original aim was to privatize 50 per cent of state assets within three years.

# II

# Privatization, Corporate Governance and Economic Restructuring

# 5

# Changing Models of Corporate Governance in OECD Countries

*Pieter W. Moerland*

## Introduction

Corporate governance has to do with the way in which business firms are run; that is, how these are managed and controlled. As the term suggests, it concerns the governance of corporations: more specifically, firms whose publicly traded shares of equity capital are listed on a stock exchange. Those firms are characterized by a separation of ownership and management, which poses the well-known agency problem between management and outside capital suppliers, such as external shareholders. In their survey article on corporate governance, Shleifer and Vishny (1997, p. 337) commence by posing the following three questions: 'How do the suppliers of finance get managers to return some of the profits to them? How do they make sure that managers do not steal the capital they supply or invest it in bad projects? How do suppliers of finance control managers?'

Most advanced market economies have solved those problems reasonably well by creating a panoply of disciplining mechanisms which keep managers alert and force them to return profits to the providers of finance. Nevertheless, in practice, there is a rich variation across OECD countries in their typical systems of corporate governance. The main economic blocs in the world show marked differences with respect to the role and position of states (compare MITI in Japan and the French government), industrial labour relations (lifelong employment in Japanese firms, collective bargaining in Europe, the conflict model in Anglo-Saxon countries), financial systems and institutions (universal banks in Germany and city banks in Japan) and so on. Corporate systems in different areas of the capitalist world differ with respect to their historical origins, their structures of ownership and control, and their conduct and performance. In particular, differences in the mechanisms of capital mobilization and the roles of domestic banking systems can be observed. In the United States, 99 per cent of the top 400 companies are publicly quoted on a stock exchange, as opposed to only 54 per cent on average in the European Union (EU) countries. In Germany and Japan, large banks play a vital role in financing and monitoring the corporate sectors, while in France, Italy and Spain, tight family and state ownership are rather common features. These and other institutional differences seem to influence economic behaviour, including the manner in which corporate restructuring takes place. Whereas in the Anglo-Saxon world hostile takeovers were commonplace during the 'roaring eighties', such manoeuvres were virtually unknown in most countries of continental Europe and in Japan. In the latter, other disciplinary mechanisms are prevalent, primarily through the involvement of banks and financial holding companies in corporate decision making and restructuring. These salient differences raise a number of questions concerning the effects of varying institutional settings on managerial behaviour and corporate control. Until recently questions of this type seldom arose.

Since the collapse of virtually all economic systems that were based on central planning in formerly communist countries, such as in Eastern Europe, the Soviet Union and China, academic and political attention has shifted in the direction of market-based economies. Formerly state-owned enterprises are being privatized and stock exchanges are emerging in a process of transition towards an economic system that is based on the market mechanism for efficient allocation of scarce resources. Also, in those transition economies, important questions are being asked with respect to optimal corporate governance, such as: Who should be the new owners of business firms? Should ownership be concentrated or dispersed? Which property rights should be allotted? Of course, the emerging market economies are attempting to learn from the corporate governance experience of the more advanced economies.

This chapter confines itself to only one part of the various advanced economic systems: their corporate business sectors (corporate enterprises that are listed on a stock exchange). We present a comparative analysis of corporate governance structures in several important OECD countries. The first section presents a brief explanation of the separation of ownership and management in a listed corporation, and some indication is given on the geographic presence of listed corporations.

Ownership and control structures are at the heart of the corporate governance issue. The second section is devoted to three important characteristics of ownership structures: the identity of shareholders, the distribution of ownership and the property rights allotted to shares of equity. The third section deals with different control structures and disciplinary mechanisms to mitigate the agency problem of managers *vis-à-vis* external shareholders. In the fourth section, two general classes of corporate governance systems are distinguished and elucidated: the market-oriented system and the network-oriented system. The OECD countries can be roughly divided up according to this classification of corporate governance systems, with the Anglo-Saxon countries being market-oriented and continental European countries and Japan being network-oriented.

The final section compares the merits and drawbacks of both classes of corporate governance systems. Furthermore recent developments in several important OECD countries are described: models of corporate governance are changing for a number of reasons.

## Rationale for presence of listed corporations

The question of why firms come into existence was left unanswered in traditional neoclassical economic theory. That problem – just what makes a firm come into being – was first addressed by Coase (1937), who viewed the firm as an alternative to the market. The actual choice of one of those two coordinating mechanisms is determined by their relative efficiency in terms of information costs. Thus the market and the firm are, in Coase's view, to be considered as substitute devices for organizing economic activities. The birth, transition and death of the firm are no longer to be seen as exogenous events (as in traditional economic theory), but rather as the outcome of an endogenous process of economic optimization. In the classical firm, the entrepreneur combines the functions of ownership and management in his own person. But what is the economic rationale for the organization of the open corporate firm with publicly traded shares of equity? In other words, what forces cause the separation of ownership and management to be an efficient organizational form? The traditional economic explanation for the open corporation emphasizes scale economies, specialization of managerial capabilities and shareholder diversification. One can imagine that the desire for a transition from a privately held firm (with a single owner–manager) into a publicly held firm (with some separation of finance and management) arises if the restrictions of the former organizational form become (too) severe.

At least three possible restrictions can be distinguished with respect to the classical firm. First, the owner–manager's personal wealth may be insufficient to finance all profitable investment projects, thus creating opportunity losses from underinvestment. Second, by investing his personal wealth entirely in his own firm, the owner–manager lacks the opportunity of risk diversification through investing his money in the market portfolio. As a consequence, he runs the unique risk of his own firm, having not only systematic risk but also unpriced, firm-specific risk. In addition to this, he also invests his human capital in the same firm, so that he absorbs specific risk on his financial as well as his human capital. Third, alienation of divisible residual claims (property rights) is not possible without losing the status of full owner, which implies that the entrepreneur's personal wealth lacks liquidity. All three drawbacks call for economic sacrifices, which can be translated into opportunity losses: of profitable investments forgone, of risk diversification forgone and of wealth liquidity forgone.

Thus the motives for a stock market flotation, which transforms the firm into a publicly held corporation, is a desire to push back the opportunity losses of under investment, risk specialization and illiquidity. However, whatever the motives may be, the publicly held, open corporation suffers from agency problems due to the separation of ownership and management. All this implies that a kind of trade-off exists between suppressing the opportunity losses of the classical firm and creating agency costs by attracting capital from outside.

The breakthrough of listed corporations took place during the second half of the nineteenth century. The Industrial Revolution caused a mobilization of large amounts of money for investment in factories, mines, infrastructure and so on. Especially in the United Kingdom, the listed corporation prospered, giving rise to the development of the stock exchange. Nowadays the relative presence of listed corporations is not equally distributed across the OECD countries, according to relevant indicators such as the GDP.

Stock exchanges in the main Anglo-Saxon countries such as the United Kingdom and the United States are rather well developed. Comparatively large numbers of firms are publicly listed. As already mentioned, in the United States, 99 per cent of the top 400 companies are listed on a stock exchange, while in the United Kingdom almost 80 per cent of the largest 700 companies have a listing (Franks and Mayer, 1997a). The United Kingdom occupies a special position within the EU.

Some 40 per cent of all listed companies in the European countries are UK companies. The number of listings on the London Stock

Exchange (LSE) exceeds even the number of listings on the New York Stock Exchange (NYSE) and on the Tokyo Stock Exchange (TSE). The number of listings within the countries of the European Union exceeds those of the NYSE and the TSE by a wide margin, while total EU market capitalization lags behind. This indicates a lower mean market value per company in the EU in comparison with companies listed on the NYSE and the TSE. The presence and relative significance of listed corporations is larger in the Anglo-Saxon part of the world than elsewhere.

## Ownership structures

Corporate ownership structures can be characterized by the distribution and composition of shareholders. The distribution may vary from a single shareholder to a multitude of shareholders. In between are majority holders, large blockholders, blocking minorities, constellations of core shareholders and all kinds of relative concentrations. The degree of concentration or dispersion will generally be thought to have relevance for a firm's agency and control structure. The same holds true for shareholders' identity: insider versus outsider, active versus passive, corporate raiders. Shareholders are residual claimants whose property rights may be restricted in one way or another. Below we pay attention to three distinct characteristics of corporate ownership structures: the identity of shareholders, the distribution of ownership and property rights.

### Identity of shareholders

The identities of shareholders vary across countries and also over time. In the United Kingdom, nearly 60 per cent of domestic market capitalization was held by institutional investors in 1993; this relatively high percentage had grown from 19 per cent in 1963. Thus, over three decades, a dramatic increase in institutional shareholdings had taken place in the United Kingdom, mainly via pension funds. The share of private household holdings declined over that time interval from 56 per cent to 19 per cent. In Japan, institutional shareholdings are also important, but there, unlike the United Kingdom, banks are dominant parties. After 1987, Japanese banks were legally restricted to holding equity stakes up to 5 per cent of a firm's stock (prior to 1987, up to 10 per cent). Typically some five or six banks form a consortium of financiers of Japanese *keiretsu* (industrial groups), one of them acting as the main bank (city bank) and the others as satellites.

Outside the United Kingdom and the United States, other companies are an important category of shareholders. In Germany, more than 40 per cent of a firm's shares are in the hands of another non-financial firm. This percentage has remained rather stable over time; it amounted to 44 per cent in 1960. Also in France, Italy and Japan, intercorporate shareholdings and industrial grouping form salient characteristics of share ownership. In the United States, private households are still the most important category of shareholders but the percentage is gradually declining in favour of indirect holdings through all kinds of funds.

### Distribution of share ownership

The degrees of dispersion or concentration of shareholdings also show marked differences across countries. Generally speaking, firm size and concentration of shares are inversely related. But, given a certain firm size, there are nevertheless large differences in average concentration ratios across OECD countries.

In the United States, the largest five shareholders hold, on average, a quarter of the outstanding shares of a firm, that is the concentration ratio $C_5 = 25$ per cent. Very large corporations have smaller $C_5$ values: for example, General Motors 6 per cent, Exxon, IBM and General Electric all 5 per cent. Compare the $C_5$ values for Japanese corporations, such as Toyota: 22 per cent, Matsushita: 20 per cent and Nissan: 25 per cent (Roe, 1993). The average concentration ratios are relatively high in Germany, where the holdings of the largest five shareholders average over 40 per cent (Prowse, 1995). Also the pattern of single largest shareholders shows an interesting differential across countries. The figures pertain to samples of the largest 170 companies in those countries. Recently only in 16 per cent of the largest 170 UK companies did a single shareholder own over 25 per cent of the shares, as opposed to the case of Germany, where in nearly 85 per cent of the largest firms there was such a major shareholder, and of France, where the figure was almost 80 per cent (Franks and Mayer, 1997a).

Also, in other continental European countries, a relatively high degree of concentration is apparent. The $C_5$ ratio of all Dutch non-financial firms amounts to 49 per cent. In Italy, concentration is extremely high, with $C_5$ amounting to no less than 87 per cent. From these figures it becomes clear that concentration of share ownership is (much) greater in corporations based outside the United States and the United Kingdom, where ownership is widely dispersed among a large number of individuals and institutions. In continental Europe and Japan, families, financial institutions and other corporations hold considerable stakes of equity.

## Property rights

Common shares of equity are residual claims which give the holders, in principle, cash flow rights and control rights with respect to the firm. Cash flow rights represent rights on dividends and liquidation surpluses. Control rights give shareholders some say in the firm, mainly by using voting rights in the annual meeting of shareholders.

Those property rights are, again in principle, proportional rights, which, for example, are encapsulated in the maxim: 'one share – one vote'. However, in practice, control rights in particular are very often restricted in one way or another. In the United States, Sweden and other countries, a number of corporations issue dual class shares, one class with and another class without (or with reduced) voting rights. In the Netherlands, Germany and Switzerland, voting rights of common shares are, in many cases, restricted for reasons of establishing defensive mechanisms against hostile takeover attempts. In continental European countries, the phenomenon of intercorporate holding pyramids is rather popular. All these mechanisms serve to violate the maxim of 'one share – one vote' by breaking the proportional correspondence between cash flow rights and control rights.

In addition, free-riding in the case of share ownership widely dispersed over a multitude of small individual shareholders effectively means a separation of cash flow rights from control rights. However the control rights might then be mobilized by a bidder who obtains a critical proportion of the rights and, as a consequence, does not suffer from the free-rider problem. Generally speaking, insiders of a corporation (management, families, founders) may have specific incentives to separate the cash flow rights from the control rights of common shares. They try to retain control over the firm, while attracting additional financial capital from outside. This enables them to expand business activities without losing private benefits from control.

From this short review of characteristics, it becomes clear that there are salient international differences with respect to identity, distribution and property rights of corporate share ownership. Those aspects are interrelated to some extent. This will be elaborated further in the next section, on control structures.

## Control structures

Control mechanisms serve to deal with the agency conflicts between managers and outside capital suppliers, such as shareholders. These mechanisms can be subdivided in a number of ways.

(1) They may either encourage the manager to align with the interest of outside shareholders (for example, a compensation scheme) or discourage the manager from deviating from it (for example, a market for corporate control).
(2) There are direct disciplinary mechanisms (for example, a supervisory board) and indirect ones (for example, stock market pricing).
(3) A third distinction concerns the type of residual rights that are involved: the cash flow rights or the voting rights of shares.

Being a residual claimant may pertain to the ownership of residual cash flow rights or to the ownership of residual control rights, or both. The classical entrepreneur is the sole residual claimant of the private firm, owning both types of residual rights simultaneously. In principle, a common share of stock in an open corporation combines cash flow and voting rights in a proportionate way: the rule of 'one share – one vote'. Control devices relate to either cash flow rights or voting rights, or both. Now we are able to classify several well-known disciplinary mechanisms in terms of the type of rights involved.

(1) Managerial remuneration schemes may contribute to the alignment of interests by linking compensation to stock prices, for example through payment in stock options or shares of stock. These plans create incentives that are based on the cash flow rights of shares.
(2) A supervisory board may exercise direct monitoring and disciplinary activities with respect to managerial behaviour. When the shareholders are represented in the board, they can vote for candidates who may be expected to watch over their interests. If necessary, corrective measures can be taken, such as replacement of poor management.
(3) The stock market has disciplinary power (as the stock price reflects shareholders' dissatisfaction) when stockholders decide to sell their shares because of poor management. This puts pressure on the stock price and increases the firm's cost of capital. In fact those shareholders sell their financial claims (cash flow rights), irrespective of the

presence of voting rights. The stock market thus offers a cash flow right-based control mechanism.

(4) The market for corporate control engenders disciplinary power through the transfer of voting rights. In the case of a proxy contest, the focus is on voting rights per se, while in the case of a hostile takeover, voting rights transfer is accompanied by cash flow rights. Under majority voting rules, a majority shareholder (holding a majority of voting rights) can fire the manager, if this is deemed necessary.

In addition, there are the disciplinary forces stemming from the managerial labour market and, of course, from the output markets.

In fact alternative control mechanisms are available and may replace each other or complement each other. The optimization of a firm's control structure implies finding a balance between encouraging the manager to comply with shareholders' interests and discouraging him from pursuing solely his own. Disciplinary forces can mitigate the agency conflict between management and outside shareholders. Thus there is a 'panoply of internal and external monitoring devices' (Fama, 1980, p. 295) which impose, alternatively or complementarily to each other, the limits to managerial discretion.

Disciplinary mechanisms differ significantly, however, across countries and also across time. Why does the use of the external market for corporate control appear almost exclusively in Anglo-Saxon countries? Are alternative disciplinary devices equally effective in monitoring managerial behaviour? Below follows a brief discussion of the various disciplinary mechanisms that are at work in different OECD countries. In that respect, the advanced market economies are subdivided into two classes: market-oriented corporate systems and network-oriented corporate systems.

## Market-oriented and network-oriented corporate systems

The structure of corporate ownership – identity, concentration, property rights – is clearly interrelated with the structure of control. Large shareholders have incentives to monitor managers directly, while atomistic shareholders abstain from direct monitoring because of free-riding. Then indirect monitoring via the stock market or the market for corporate control is likely to occur.

Some shareholders have a multifarious relationship with corporations, for example universal banks in Germany and suppliers or customers in

Japanese *keiretsu*. Those relationships make the agency problems more complex and also give rise to new agency problems, for example with shareholders who restrict their relation with the corporation to only share ownership. In the literature on corporate governance, a classification of countries is often made into two categories, such as market-based systems versus bank-based systems or outsider systems versus insider systems. This chapter distinguishes between market-oriented systems and network-oriented systems.

Market-oriented corporate systems are characterized by well-developed financial markets, large-scale presence of open corporations with widely dispersed share ownership, and active markets for corporate control. Network-oriented corporate systems are characterized by closely held corporations, group membership of corporations, and substantive involvement of universal banks in financing and controlling corporate firms. Exponents of the market-oriented systems are the Anglo-Saxon countries, such as the United States and the United Kingdom. The network-oriented system is prevalent in many countries of continental Europe and in Japan. Of course, the distinction between market-oriented systems and network-oriented systems is a matter of degree.

Capital mobilization via stock markets is rather important in the Anglo-Saxon countries. Many corporations in the Anglo-Saxon countries are widely held by a multitude of small investors. Especially in the United Kingdom, institutional investors hold blocks of shares in many companies. By the Glass–Steagall Act of 1933, commercial banks in the United States have been prevented from holding corporate equity on their own account. Shareholders and debtholders are largely separated, with large companies relying more heavily on diffusively held bond financing.

In most countries of continental Europe and in Japan, corporate financial capital has been mobilized to a substantial degree by banks, insurance companies, families and national states. In the group of Germanic countries (including Germany, Switzerland and Austria), industrial expansion in the late nineteenth century was facilitated largely by the emergence of the so-called 'universal banks' (*Universalbanken*). Nowadays the banking sector still plays a prominent role in financing and controlling corporate enterprises. The large German banks (such as Deutsche Bank, Commerzbank and Dresdner Bank) act as suppliers not only of bank loans but also of equity capital. They possess blocks of shares on their own account, which provides them with substantial voting power in many corporations. In addition, through their trustee holdings, they can exercise the voting rights of a considerable number of shares that are deposited with them by their clients (*Depotstimmrecht*). Moreover the banks are generally represented on supervisory boards by directors (sometimes serving chairmen) of corporations with which they have a primary financial relationship. The blocks of shares held by the banks are mostly considered as a form of long-term equity holdings.

In the Latin countries of the European Union (including Italy, Spain, France and Belgium), the ownership structure of corporations can basic-ally be characterized by family control, financial holding companies and cross-shareholdings, and state ownership. In Italy, powerful fami-lies (such as the Agnellis) and multinational (industrial) groups have control over nearly all of the listed companies. Widely held public companies can be counted on the fingers of one hand. The stock exchanges are comparatively underdeveloped, so that ownership and control structures are rather closed. In Spain, cross-holdings and bank holdings are common phenomena. Furthermore state intervention in corporate affairs cannot be neglected. In France, rivalling financial holdings, bank equity holding (*banques d'affaires*) and state ownership have long been predominant forms of capital supply. In 1981, however, the entire French banking system was nationalized, making the state an important shareholder in many major corporations. In the last few years, the French government has reversed a number of these nationalizations, leaving financial holding structures and bank equity holdings (particularly by Banque de Suez and Banque Paribas) as the most important forms of equity ownership. In Belgium, holding com-panies and family ownership prevail. The Société Générale de Belgique (founded in 1822) controls no fewer than 25 of the top 115 Belgian concerns, which comprise approximately half of the industrial sector in that country.

Industrial structures in Japan are characterized by the presence of sizeable industrial groups, *keiretsu*, such as Mitsubishi, Mitsui, Sumitomo and Dai-ichi Kangyo. Some of these groups originated from previously powerful *zaibatsu* (family-controlled holding companies), which were outlawed after the Second World War, but still exist on a restructured basis. Other *keiretsu* were established in the 1950s by large banks. Most groups are both diversified and vertically integrated. Within each group, a close relationship exists between its manufactur-ing members and a limited number of financial institutions, both banks ('city banks') and insurance companies. Usually those financial institutions provide the non-financial firms of the group with debt as well as equity capital. Furthermore bank employees are frequently appointed in managerial positions of other group firms, while bank officers, in many cases, are members of the group firms' board of directors. Thus industrial groups are centred around major financial institutions, and there is a general understanding that these commitments are for the long term.

Another distinct feature is reciprocal shareholding among member firms with close trading ties. In many cases, these cross-holdings are accompanied by interlocking directorships. Since these relationships have a mutual character, policy making by individual firms may not only, or primarily, reflect their individual interest, but will be embedded in the interests of the group as a whole. Assessing the ownership and control structures in both types of corporate systems leads to the following conclusions (Moerland, 1995).

(1) The ownership structures in network-oriented systems are more concentrated than in market-oriented systems; in network-oriented systems there are more intimate relations with shareholders than in market-oriented systems.
(2) The external market for corporate control plays an important role in market-oriented systems, but not in network-oriented systems.
(3) A monitoring board has greater disciplinary power in network-oriented systems than it does in market-oriented systems.
(4) The relative importance of the managerial labour market shows a mixed picture; the external functioning of the managerial labour market and performance-linked compensation schemes are rather important in market-oriented systems, while internal managerial mobility is characteristic of network-oriented systems.
(5) The stock market's disciplinary power tends to be greater in market-oriented systems than it is in network-oriented systems.

## Evaluation of changing models

Which system of corporate governance works best? In the long run, only institutional settings with favourable cost–benefit conditions are likely to endure. Obviously, up to now, market-oriented as well as network-oriented systems have survived, side by side. Does this imply that the alternative ownership and control structures are to be considered as equivalent corporate governance devices?

Of course, the answer to this question is an empirical matter. Unfortunately there is no clear empirical evidence on the relationship between corporate performance and corporate control. Therefore we shall try to delineate several theoretical arguments with respect to the costs and benefits of alternative governance structures and disciplinary devices.

The merits and drawbacks of one system seem to be, to some extent, the reverse of those of the other system. For example, the advantages of direct control by large shareholders and separate supervisory boards in network-oriented systems are presumably compensated by more liquid and efficient financial markets in market-oriented systems. Clearly there is a trade-off between control and liquidity. Market liquidity tends to improve the pricing process in financial markets, to lower the cost of capital (Amihud and Mendelson, 1986) and to tighten the disciplinary forces of stock exchanges.

Direct control in network-oriented systems is commonly based on relatively stable, intimate, long-term relationships between capital suppliers and the firm. Those capital suppliers will be better informed, as quasi-insiders, about managerial behaviour and performance than anonymous capital suppliers in market-oriented systems. Also the problem of free-riding will be less severe than in an environment with widely spread share ownership. This makes the need for external corrective measures through the market for corporate control less pressing, since the main owners may be in a position to take disciplinary measures directly if this is deemed necessary.

However monitoring by large shareholders may be detrimental to small shareholders, since they may profit from private benefits at the expense of the latter. Large shareholders often have multifarious relationships with a firm (compare the German universal banks) which raises new agency problems between them and the other shareholders. Furthermore large shareholders bear excessive firm-specific risk, which could otherwise be borne at lower cost by well-diversified small shareholders.

Because of the complexity of costs and benefits of corporate governance aspects it is difficult to indicate which system is 'superior'. Moreover the systems are developing over time. Over the last few years, even a process of mutual convergence seems to be occurring.

The dominant role of banks in Japan and Germany is likely to diminish as a consequence of several developments. Regulatory changes in Japan have initiated a liberalization of financial markets, which has stimulated the development of bond and commercial paper markets, to the detriment of bank loans. During the last few years, the reputations of a number of leading Japanese banks have been damaged by financial scandals and by massive losses on their outstanding loans. In Germany, a political discussion is unfolding on the pros and cons of banking power in the business sector and industrial policy. In particular the numerous supervisory board positions occupied by bank executives are criticized in politics and business circles.

Contrary to these tendencies in network-oriented systems, the role of banks and other financial institutions seems to become more pronounced in market-oriented systems. In the United States, a long period of banking restrictions is likely to come gradually and partially to an end, opening up opportunities for banks to intensify their relations with business firms. Other financial intermediaries, such as mutual funds, insurance companies and pension funds, are becoming important shareholders of American industry.

A shift is going on towards institutional intermediation in channelling capital flows from individual households to corporations via investment funds, pension funds and insurance companies. These professional institutions hold internationally diversified portfolios, the performance of which is periodically evaluated against international yardsticks, such as the Morgan Stanley Capital International Index. Both this international standardization of investment policies and performance measurement urge large internationally operating corporations to orient themselves towards universal financial objectives and parameters. In this respect, a more explicit orientation towards stock price behaviour by corporate managers in network-oriented systems can already be observed in comparison with, say, 10 or 15 years ago.

Globalization of competition has taken place in an increasing number of industries: motor cars, electronics, chemicals, financial services and so on. Those output markets are perhaps the most severe disciplinary mechanisms of all. Corporate firms in different parts of the world will have to adjust their governance structures when these appear to be less efficient than elsewhere. Also an increasing interaction exists between different governance systems as a consequence of international mergers and acquisitions, foreign investments, intercontinental joint ventures and so on. Furthermore large (multinational) corporations have their shares listed simultaneously on the important stock exchanges in the world, such as New York, Tokyo, London, Frankfurt and Paris. Since the world is developing in the direction of a 'global village', an increasing degree of reciprocal influence and osmosis will exist between the various corporate systems, implying a tendency to convergence.

# 6
# Corporate Governance: a Systemic Approach with an Application to Eastern Europe

*Ralph Heinrich*

## Introduction[1]

There has been a long-standing debate on corporate governance in mature market economies.[2] Recently issues of corporate governance have also come to the fore in the transition economies of Eastern Europe and the former Soviet Union. Improving corporate governance has been singled out as one of two priorities in the recent memorandum of understanding between the International Monetary Fund (IMF) and the Russian government. Deficiencies of corporate governance have also been blamed for the recent balance-of-payments crisis in the Czech Republic, where disappointing growth in labour productivity despite relatively high investment rates, together with excessive wage increases and the lack of attractiveness of the Prague stock market for foreign investors, led to an overvaluation of the exchange rate and an unsustainable current account deficit.

However the debate on corporate governance has been largely inconclusive. In what follows we will argue that there are complementarity and possibly substitutability relationships between certain governance instruments. These relationships have profound implications for understanding how individual corporate governance instruments work, how they interact within a corporate governance system, and for informing the debate about reforming them.

The first section below surveys the existing literature, while the second section offers an interpretation of efficient corporate governance as a system of complementary elements. An important result of the theory is that policies aimed at changing only a subset of relevant parameters and instruments may be ineffective or even counterproductive because they fail to solve systemic inconsistencies and may even add to them. Inter alia, this can explain why systems might differ quite widely in performance even though they may look quite similar along some lines of governance. The third section offers an application to corporate governance problems in the Czech Republic. The conceptual framework of the second section is used to identify where economic policy created inconsistencies or failed to remove them, and suggests reforms that would be consistent with the governance instruments already in place. A fourth section concludes the chapter.

## Corporate governance: the debate

The need to govern agency relationships in firms arises from the separation of ownership and control. This separation is motivated by a discrepancy in the firm between promising investment projects and internally generated investible funds. If the problem of corporate governance is not solved satisfactorily, outside finance will remain limited. Hence the efficient allocation of capital crucially depends on efficient corporate governance. Moreover it has recently been argued that there is a positive causal relationship between the degree of financial development and economic growth in emerging markets.[3] This implies that, by improving financial systems, and hence corporate governance, countries can grow faster.

The problem of corporate governance is solved in any given firm by using a menu of governance instruments. A non-exhaustive list includes incentive pay (Kole, 1997), monitoring and intervention by boards of directors (Baysinger and Hoskisson, 1990), monitoring and intervention by shareholders (Zeckhauser and Pound, 1990), the market for corporate control with the attendant takeover threat (Grossman and Hart, 1980), debt and the attendant bankruptcy threat (Jensen, 1986), monitoring by debtors (Hoshi *et al.*, 1990), monitoring by regulators and financial market analysts (Holmström and Tirole, 1993), the market for managers (Fama, 1980) and product market competition (Nickell, 1996).

Typically one governance instrument is singled out and it is shown how its existence in the real world can be rationalized as a solution to agency problems between management and the owners of capital. Empirical investigations have sought to establish links between the performance of firms and the presence of certain governance instruments.[4]

The literature is mostly silent about the presence or absence of governance instruments other than the ones under study.[5] Given that in reality all firms are using a menu of instruments, two interpretations can be given to this omission. Either it is held that the efficacy of the governance instruments under study is neither enhanced nor impaired by any other instruments the firm might be using, or the argument could be that all firms always choose the set of governance instruments not studied such that it is optimal given the use which is made of the instruments under investigation.

Neither of these two interpretations is satisfactory. The latter begs the question why the instruments under study might not be chosen optimally if all others are, or, if they are always chosen optimally, why one should attribute differences in performance to differences in the use of particular governance instruments. Moreover, there is empirical evidence of non-trivial unresolved agency problems (for example, Blanchard *et al.*, 1994). The former interpretation flies in the face of some obvious interdependencies between governance instruments. One example would be incentive pay and a liquid stock market. The former is used to motivate managers, the latter is used by investors to exit if they are unhappy. These two instruments are complementary for four reasons. First, for incentive pay to induce managers to maximize long-term firm value, a liquid stock market is needed. If the stock market is illiquid, owners can manipulate share prices, and incentive pay tied to the share price will not work. By the same token, tying pay to accounting measures rather than the stock price will not provide incentives to maximize long-term firm value. Second, a liquid stock market is obviously needed for exit to work. Third, having managerial pay tied to the share price will strengthen the efficacy of the threat of exit in that it will induce managers to care about keeping shareholders satisfied. Fourth, the more liquid the market in a firm's stock, the more dispersed its ownership structure tends to be. Incentives for 'hands-on' monitoring will then tend to be weak owing to free rider problems, and hence incentive pay to control managers is more valuable than in firms with more 'hands-on' monitoring.

By focusing on instruments in isolation, the literature is unable to explain satisfactorily the existence and use of such a variety of different combinations of instruments as is observed in reality. The empirical results of this literature can be highly misleading. Suppose two governance instruments are substitutes in improving performance. Then a firm not using one instrument may be using its substitute and may still perform well. Conversely, suppose two instruments are complements. Then two firms might differ in performance despite making the exact same use of a given instrument, simply because one of them has failed to use the complementary instrument. A regression of performance on one instrument without controlling for the use of the other might in both cases wrongly find no significant relationship. By way of example, a frequent finding in the empirical literature is that management remuneration in the United States appears to be less sensitive to firm performance than the theoretical models would predict. One explanation for this finding may be that there are other governance instruments complementary to or substituting for performance pay.

As a second example, the finding that top management remuneration is significantly higher in the United States than in some European countries, a difference that is largely due to large returns earned on stock options, is often taken as evidence of a failure of corporate governance in the United States in the sense of managers setting their own pay and being too generous at the expense of shareholders. However it might rather be evidence of the larger role incentive pay has to play in a consistent and efficient system with little 'hands-on' owner monitoring as compared to a system with strong 'hands-on' monitoring. In the former system, owners bear agency costs in the form of sharing capital gains with management, while in the latter system owners bear agency costs in the form of expending resources on direct monitoring and of not being able to diversify away risk. Nothing is implied by this argument on which solution is more efficient.

Finally, there is increasing evidence of the generic systems of corporate governance, namely the US and Japanese systems, appearing to lead to remarkably similar outcomes despite using very different instruments. For instance, Hall and Weinstein (1996) find no evidence that US firms behave more myopically under distress than Japanese firms, even than *keiretsu* firms. This supports the notion that little may be gained by studying individual governance instruments in isolation, and that what matters is understanding how individual instruments work together in a consistent system of corporate governance.

At the policy level, the debate has boiled down at its most basic to the question of whether countries in which securities markets are perceived as playing a dominant role in governance need to give a larger role to financial intermediaries or whether, conversely, countries in which intermediaries are perceived as playing a dominant role should move to expand the role of securities markets (Allen and Gale, 1995). While there have been advocates for both alternatives, the debate has suffered from the same defects as the theoretical literature: a failure to consider the interplay of governance instruments.

This failure is all the more deplorable at the policy level because the interdependency of governance instruments raises important issues concerning the proper assessment of the causes of inefficiencies in corporate governance, the possibly adverse consequences of piecemeal reforms in one part of the system for overall performance, and the need for and possibility of coordinated reforms in all or many instruments simultaneously.[6]

Recently recognition of the interdependencies between governance instruments and the systemic nature of corporate governance has been rising. There are some papers which explicitly address the multiplicity of governance instruments and the characteristic variation of systems of corporate governance across countries (for example, Berglöf, 1997,

*Table* 6.1   Stylized characteristics of alternative models of corporate governance

| 'Market-based' system | 'Bank-centred' system |
| --- | --- |
| A.  Instruments chosen at the firm level | |
| 1.  Dispersed stock ownership, primarily by households and institutional investors | Concentrated stock ownership or proxy control by banks |
| 2.  Little cross-shareholding between firms and little bank ownership of firms, active market for corporate control | Substantial cross-ownership between firms, substantial direct and indirect bank ownership, no significant market for control |
| 3.  Little bank involvement in firms' operations | Substantial direct involvement of banks in firm operations (monitoring, decision making, restructuring) |
| 4.  High-powered management incentives (through pay-performance link at the firm and through market for managers) | Low-powered management incentives |
| 5.  High ratio of bonds to loans in firm liabilities | Low ratio of bonds to loans in firm liabilities |
| B.  Instruments chosen at the policy level | |
| 1.  Far-reaching disclosure and accounting requirements in stock market, substantial minority shareholder protection, barriers to large shareholder activity | Limited disclosure and accounting requirements, limited minority shareholder protection, few barriers to large shareholder activity |
| 2.  Rules favourable to or at least not actively hostile to corporate bond market | May have legal obstacles limiting the size of the corporate bond market |
| 3.  Bankruptcy legislation tends to emphasize protection from creditors | Bankruptcy legislation tends to emphazise protection of creditor claims |

Shleifer and Vishny, 1997). However these papers do not really explain why there are many instruments and remain rudimentary at best in their explanation of interplay.[7]

Finally there are some useful recent papers which (a) distinguish between instruments the use of which the firm can optimize and instruments which are exogenously given to the firm; this is useful because it allows us to give structure to the argument that governance mechanisms are chosen optimally by firms; and (b) argue that the choice of governance mechanisms is responsive to changes in the firm's environment and give empirical examples (Kole and Lehn, 1997; Agrawal and Knoeber, 1996). However this literature has yet to develop a formal model of corporate governance as a system and it has not succeeded in the final analysis in explaining why firms use combinations at all and why they use the combinations they are using.

At the risk of oversimplification, Table 6.1 gives a highly stylized summary of the features which distinguish the two generic types of governance systems identified in the literature.[8] The following paragraphs provide a suggestive story of possible complementarities between governance instruments along the above dimensions.

## Complementarities in corporate governance

In what follows, we will be using the term 'complementarity' in the sense of Edgeworth and Pareto; that is, two governance instruments are complements if and only if using more of one of them raises the return to using more of the other one.[9]

### On complementarities between bankruptcy procedures and the concentration of ownership and debt[10]

The US bankruptcy code, particularly Chapter 11, emphasizes the protection of firms as going concerns. This is achieved by an automatic stay on creditors, including bonds and secured loans, and by keeping management in control of the reorganization process. The idea is to prevent some creditors from prematurely liquidating the firm at the expense of other creditors, shareholders or other stake holders, or to prevent creditors from endlessly haggling without reaching an agreement. By contrast, the German and Japanese bankruptcy codes emphasize control by debtors, in that the incumbent management is removed from control, and secured debt claims are not stayed. This procedure can be expected to result in quicker solutions with lower administrative costs, but it might also result in premature liquidations or stalemate. So we may define the US bankruptcy code as 'low' on creditor protection and the German and Japanese codes as 'high' on this dimension, with no value judgements implied. The extent to which premature liquidation or a stalemate in negotiations over reorganization pose a significant problem depends crucially on the degree of concentration of the ownership of both debt and equity of the firm. In Japan, and also in Germany, most corporate debt is in the form not of bonds but of bank loans. Moreover most firms have relatively close, long-term relationships with a few major creditors. Generally, ownership concentration is lower in the United States than in Germany and Japan.

Complementarity between bankruptcy codes and ownership concentration then means that, under a bankruptcy code 'high' on creditor protection, the benefit from raising ownership concentration is higher than under a bankruptcy code 'low' on creditor protection. By the same token, the benefit of raising creditor protection in bankruptcy is higher under concentrated than under dispersed ownership.

Why would this kind of complementarity obtain? Close long-term relationships between creditors and borrowers imply that creditors tend to be rather well informed about the financial situation and the prospects of the firm. For this reason, renegotiations of claims in bankruptcy among a few long-term creditors are less likely to fail and to lead to premature and inefficient liquidation than in situations with a large number of dispersed, uninformed creditors. A similar argument holds for equity owners. In Germany and Japan, significant portions of equity are held by other firms with business ties, and which therefore tend to be well-informed about the economic situation of the firm. Free-rider problems are likely to be less pertinent, and negotiations are more likely to lead to efficient outcomes if smaller numbers with larger individual stakes are involved. So if the bankruptcy code is 'high' on creditor protection, the benefit from moving from a dispersed to a concentrated ownership structure is higher than if the bankruptcy code is 'low' on creditor protection.

The drawback of the strong position of management in Chapter 11 is of course that it may enable management to force secured creditors into concessions and prevent even efficient liquidations. This is why a system with a comparatively weak position for creditors tends to support risk diversification on the part of creditors through dispersed ownership: that is, the benefit of moving from concentrated to more dispersed ownership is higher if the bankruptcy code is 'low' on creditor protection.

Moreover, when the ownership of the firm's debt and equity is highly dispersed, a US-type Chapter 11 bankruptcy provision may have the advantage of making it harder for secured creditors to force a liquidation of the firm, even though its overall value would be higher as a going concern. That is, with dispersed ownership, the benefit from moving from high to low creditor protection (read: from low to high protection of the firm as a going concern) is higher than with concentrated ownership.

As a result, there may be complementarity and a good fit between a bankruptcy system which emphasizes creditor control and institutional arrangements favouring concentrated ownership of equity and debt, and a good fit between bankruptcy codes which favour managerial control and institutions favouring dispersed ownership of debt and equity.

## On complementarities between ownership concentration of debt and equity

The separation of ownership of equity and control of the firm is one source of agency problems. One instrument available to mitigate it is debt. By raising the leverage of the firm, fixed payment obligations are raised, and hence the risk of bankruptcy is increased for a given distribution of stochastic earnings flows. Hence management is prevented from diverting all of the firm's free cash flow to inefficient uses. Moreover, to the extent that bankruptcy may result in management losing control and the associated rents, higher leverage may improve incentives for management to exert effort in order to lower the risk of bankruptcy by improving the distribution of earnings flows. However leverage creates its own set of agency problems. Creditors contract for a fixed payment and hence do not share in the 'upside' of any risky investment projects the firm may undertake. Therefore creditors have an inherent preference for excessively low-risk projects. By contrast, equity owners fully share in the 'upside' of risky projects but are limited in their 'downside' liability to the size of their equity stakes. Therefore they have a preference for excessively high-risk projects.

Creditors can mitigate these problems by holding small stakes in the debt of many firms and thus diversifying their risks. This will be all the more valuable the more diversified the ownership of equity, because the more diversified equity owners' portfolios, the more they will want to see the firm undertake risky projects, and hence the more intense will be the potential conflict of interest between creditors and equity holders. So dispersed ownership of debt and equity are complementary to each other. By implication, institutional arrangements which favour liquid, transparent stock markets with strong minority shareholder protection are complementary to arrangements which support liquid bond markets.

Conversely, another way to mitigate the conflict of interest between creditors and equity holders is for equity holders to hold large, concentrated stakes and thereby to intentionally forgo some of the advantages of portfolio diversification. This will reduce their willingness to make the firm undertake excessively risky projects. And, again, the gain from reducing the conflict of interests will be all the larger if creditors are unwilling or unable to diversify and hence have a strong preference for low-risk projects. So moving from dispersed to concentrated ownership of equity will have higher benefits if debt is concentrated than if it is dispersed.

But, of course, equity holders will find it easier to enforce their preferences on the investment decisions of the firm if they hold large stakes than if their ownership is diffuse. On the one hand, this is as it should be, given their larger exposure to risk. On the other hand it also strengthens equity holders' ability to impose their preferences on those of creditors. In this case, therefore, it may be useful in the interest of minimizing the agency costs of conflicts of interest between creditors and owners for creditors to have a countervailing influence on the operations of the firm. So the dominant position of German banks in exercising proxy votes and their strong representation on company boards can be understood as an insurance device preventing major shareholders from exposing the firm to excessive risk. Similarly Japanese banks may want to maintain influential positions relative to firms for these reasons. From a policy point of view, then, the more concentrated equity ownership, the more sense it makes to allow creditors to exercise a modicum of control as well, be it via proxy voting, representation on boards or direct ownership stakes.

Taken together, these arguments provide a broad rationale explaining why we tend to observe characteristic combinations of institutions of corporate governance along the dimensions of stock market and bond market regulation, bankruptcy procedures, concentration of ownership and bank control. If these arguments are valid, they have important implications for the design of economic policies in transition economies.

## Corporate governance in the Czech Republic

The deficiencies of the policy-oriented literature on corporate governance in mature market economies are mirrored by the debate on privatization and corporate governance in transition economies. There is a broad consensus that establishing sound corporate governance should be one of the most, if not *the* most, important goal of privatization (Gray, 1996). There is also an awareness that privatization by itself will not be sufficient for sound governance but has to be accompanied by suitable policies in other fields (Brada, 1996b) and that the choice of privatization programmes can in turn have considerable influence, positively or negatively, over the emergence of sound corporate governance (Frydman *et al.*, 1996).

However the literature has remained inconclusive on balance.[11] It is in danger of falling into traps similar to those mentioned above, namely to attribute differences in performance to differences in only some aspects of the governance system and to advocate certain policies without due consideration for the relevant interdependencies between many policies which influence the efficiency of a corporate governance system.

For instance, the Czech Republic's mass privatization policy was seen as a model for other transition economies until recently (Borish and Noël, 1997). However recent balance of payments problems, which were rooted at least in part in poor productivity growth despite high savings and investment rates, suggest that there may be serious governance problems in Czech enterprises (Buch and Heinrich, 1997). Some observers view these as a result of the Czech privatization strategy, but if it is true that, to be effective, a menu of governance instruments must work together, then the failure may rest, not in the privatization strategy, but in a failure to implement other reforms complementary to this particular privatization strategy.

This section looks at the use and interplay of governance mechanisms and at recent attempts at improving the workings of the governance system in the Czech Republic. The main existing deficiencies consist of an opaque and illiquid stock market, potential conflicts of interest besetting the relationships between banks and firms, the continued potential influence of the state in the banking sector and an ineffectual bankruptcy enforcement. It will be argued that the current Czech system consists of an incoherent combination of instruments.

The mass privatization programme begun in 1991 had created 1635 publicly held stock companies by 1995. As a result, stock market capitalization in the Czech Republic stands at 33 per cent of GDP and is much higher than in other transition economies. It is also higher than in some countries with 'bank-centred' systems of corporate governance, such as Germany. Also similar to 'market-based' systems, the bulk of shares in these firms is owned by individuals and institutional investors. This is a direct consequence of the privatization policy, under which firms were auctioned for vouchers previously distributed to citizens for a nominal fee. Rather than participating in the auctions themselves, most citizens invested their vouchers in investment privatization funds which then invested in firms on behalf of citizens.

In the first privatization round, investment funds acquired 66.2 per cent of the total book value available, and 75 per cent of the privatized firms were characterized by concentrated ownership of investment funds of at least 30 per cent (Matesová and Seda, 1994). Ownership structures are thus not as fragmented as originally expected. However the law places tight limits on the exposure of funds to individual enterprises and hence also on their ability to exert control. In this, too, the Czech Republic resembles 'market-based' systems. Although over 300 investment companies were originally founded, only about 50 of them play a significant role in the corporate governance of firms through their board membership in privatized firms.

Thus the ownership structure created in the Czech Republic would be complementary to a market-based system of corporate control. As such, it would require transparent and efficient stock markets. The reason is that individual investors cannot be relied upon to monitor firms. Likewise institutional investors in mature market economies usually do not participate actively in the monitoring of firm managements, but merely act as specialized portfolio investors on behalf of their shareholders. The additional agency relationship between individual investors and funds is usually also governed by the exit option afforded by a liquid stock market.

However the Czech stock market has been notorious for its poor regulation and its lack of transparency and liquidity. Minority shareholder protection has been minimal. In fact the vast bulk of trading is carried out outside the official exchanges at undisclosed prices (Pistor and Spicer, 1996). Thus economic policy has failed to create an important governance instrument complementary to the ownership structure created by mass privatization.[12] Agency problems between funds and individual investors are largely unresolved. Given the absence of an effective voice at shareholder meetings, the main mechanism to influence fund managers should have been exit. And, indeed, hefty discounts on the funds' share prices of up to 80 per cent on the market value of the underlying portfolios as well as a considerable dispersion in the secondary market prices of different funds indicate that many investors have tried to take that avenue.[13] But the persistence of large discounts suggests that funds have been largely indifferent to the message sent by deserting shareholders.

The problems with the corporate governance of the investment privatization funds have prompted legislation to encourage the emergence of unit trust funds. Roughly half the funds established for the second privatization wave have been founded as unit trusts rather than joint stock companies (Egerer, 1995). They are required to redeem their shares on demand at the market price of the underlying portfolio. Setting up funds as unit trusts rather than joint stock companies has been motivated, on the one hand, by the high costs of convening shareholder meetings but, on the other hand, also by the disappointment of investors with the high discounts at which the shares of the original joint-stock investment funds have been trading. The bulk of the new funds has been set up as open-end funds, which means they can attract additional outside capital. This can be expected to provide stronger incentives to fund managers to generate profits for shareholders in order to attract more capital and to maximize proceeds from management fees. Thus the move to encourage the emergence of unit trust funds tends to strengthen the role of the stock market in providing corporate control via movements in share prices.

However, in contrast to the generic 'market-based' governance system, banks have also been in a position to play a significant role in corporate governance in the Czech Republic. This potential role comes through the fund management companies which are mostly owned by major banks. To what extent banks use their power to improve the performance of Czech enterprises and thus to contribute to the success of the privatization process cannot yet be evaluated definitively. One concern is that the dual role of Czech banks as lenders to firms and as owners of the fund managers owning the same firms can give rise to conflicts of interest. In mature market economies, the bankruptcy code is a major vehicle to govern such conflicts of interest by clearly delineating the rights and duties of shareholders in the event of distress, by providing expedient means to change either the ownership structure or the financial structure of troubled companies should conflicts between creditors and shareholders become too great, and by eliminating nonviable firms from the market.

But the Czech bankruptcy code and courts are so ineffectual that it is hard for banks to enforce their claims against debtors. It is only since April 1993 that creditors have been legally allowed to take bankruptcy cases to court (Brom and Orenstein, 1994). The bankruptcy law has been amended twice in order to simplify the process and to make it more difficult for debtors to shield themselves from creditor claims. Creditors enjoy seniority over other claims. On paper, the Czech bankruptcy law does not look inherently flawed, and yet the number of bankruptcies has remained small. Up to mid-1996, there had been fewer than 500 bankruptcy cases opened, none of which involved a major enterprise, and none of which had been completed. The major obstacles to the effectiveness of bankruptcy legislation appear to be excessively cumbersome procedures and inadequate resources devoted to the court system, leading to substantial backlogs in unprocessed filings and pending cases (Zemanovicová and Zitnanská, 1996). In addition, some creditors are protected by government guarantees.

Because of the inefficiency of bankruptcy procedures, banks may feel that the only way to secure servicing of their loans is to use their influence over firms via fund management companies. As a result, fund managers may be more concerned with protecting the loan business of banks than with protecting the interests of shareholders (Matesova and Seda, 1994).

Moreover the lack of effectual bankruptcy procedures, together with tax disincentives to write off non-performing assets, has burdened the banks with a rather large amount of non-performing loans. The need to recapitalize out of profits may induce banks to treat the firms they indirectly control as captive customers and to saddle them with overly expensive new loans. Another serious concern about the prominent role banks can assume in Czech corporate governance is that the major banks have remained largely state-owned and that the state may use its ownership stake to prod the banks into supporting its industrial policy objectives. Thus, while the spontaneous emergence of investment funds controlled by banks has created a potentially important role for banks in the Czech corporate governance system, policy makers have again failed to provide complementary instruments of governance, namely sound bankruptcy enforcement and a sound ownership structure for the banks themselves.

Many observers have criticized the Czech approach on the grounds that a 'market-based' system of corporate governance was inappropriate for transition economies. The above analysis suggests that (a) the problem in the Czech Republic may not have been the attempt to implement a market-based system, but the failure to do so coherently, and (b) the same problem can beset governance in a 'bank-based' system.

## Conclusion

The debate about corporate governance, both in mature market economies, and in transition economies has suffered from a failure to give due consideration to interdependencies between different instruments of corporate governance. As a result, the debate has remained inconclusive and offers little advice for policy makers. The approach offered in this chapter suggests that, to the extent that instruments of corporate governance are complementary, they are usefully studied as systems. This has a number of strong implications. First, studying individual governance instruments in isolation may yield misleading conclusions. Second, there will be at best a limited number of efficient systems, and they will differ along many dimensions. Third, failure to establish some complementary elements may dramatically reduce the overall performance of the system. Fourth, establishing an internally coherent system may be more important than the choice between alternative generic systems. Further research is needed into the details of interrelationships between instruments of corporate governance, on the likely impact of the current global integration of capital and product markets on systems of corporate governance, and on the appropriate responses of national regulatory authorities.

### Notes

1. I thank Frank Bickenbach, Claudia Buch and Herbert Brücker for helpful discussions on an earlier draft. All remaining errors are of course my own. Financial support from the Volkswagen Foundation is gratefully acknowledged.
2. See, for instance, Chew (ed.) (1997) and OECD (1998).
3. See, for instance, Levine (1997).
4. See, for instance, Zeckhauser and Pound (1990).
5. Recently some authors have formally studied more than one governance instrument. In particular, some have studied capital structure, that is the interplay between pecuniary incentives and bankruptcy threats as a way to provide corporate governance (for example, Aoki, 1994).
6. Similar issues in the conduct and assessment of policy have recently been highlighted for the case of sequencing the transition (Gates *et al.*, 1996; Friedman and Johnson, 1996).
7. For example, Shleifer and Vishny (1997) argue that one system as a whole better protects minority investors and hence has its comparative advantage in bringing these investors to the market at the cost of restricting 'hands-on' governance by large investors, while the other system has its comparative advantage in securing influence for large investors at the cost of being less welcoming to small investors and hence failing to tap all sources of capital.

8. See, for example, Mayer (1998), Berglöf (1997), Kaplan (1997), Shleifer and Vishny (1997).
9. The formal theory of systems of complementary elements has been developed by Topkis (1978) and Milgrom and Roberts (1990).
10. For a comparative view on the economics of bankruptcy in the United States, Germany, France, Japan and the United Kingdom, see White (1996) and Eisenberg and Takashira (1996).
11. Frydman, Phelps, Rapaczynski and Shleifer (1993) advocate banks as the main agents of corporate control. Fries (1995) emphasizes the need for, and possible ways to encourage, markets for corporate control. Udell and Wachtel (1995) advocate markets for the governance of large firms and banks for small firms.
12. One way to overcome this problem is an endogenous evolution of the ownership structure towards more concentrated ownership by firms or banks. This is indeed happening to some extent. However given the inefficiency of the stock market, such a redistribution of ownership rights entails large transaction costs which could have been avoided by an economic policy recognizing interdependencies between governance instruments in the first place.
13. In mid-1994, for instance, the discount on shares of the top 10 investment privatization funds ranged from 28 per cent to 78 per cent (Egerer, 1995).

# 7
# Empirical Analysis of Corporate Governance in Transition

*Wendy Carlin*

## Introduction

The practical problem of trying to understand the transition has focused attention on the nature of the firm in a capitalist economy and on the role of corporate governance in catch-up growth and for economic performance more generally. The limited capacity of economic theory to provide an explanation for the different patterns of ownership and control of companies across mature market economies is matched by the relatively small volume of empirical research investigating the relationship between the structure of ownership and control and performance.

It is possible that, in time, the experience of transition economies will provide vital information for the development of a coherent theory of ownership and control. A common marketization shock has been imposed on existing enterprises in more than two dozen countries. A great variety of privatization methods have been adopted within and across countries, creating the basis for the analysis of the performance of firms with different ownership structures at a point in time as well as that of firms as they move from one ownership category to another over time.

The aim of this chapter is to take stock of the state of research that analyses enterprise sector restructuring, the emergence of post-privatization structures of ownership and control and their implications for performance. The first section below sets the scene by presenting a selective survey of recent literature from outside transition studies addressing the issue of corporate governance and its role in economic performance. The second section turns to the transition economies and presents a simple two-stage framework into which the bulk of the theoretical and empirical work on enterprise sector reform in transition can be fitted. In stage one, the marketization shock occurs and its implications for enterprise restructuring are examined; in stage two, privatization occurs and the implications for performance of the post-privatization ownership structure are investigated. The third section takes up the issue of empirical testing by reviewing the evidence on post-privatization performance. Attention is given to what can be learnt about the process of privatization as well as about its effects through the proper statistical treatment of the problem of selection implicit in comparing results from different types of privatization. The final section draws the results from the Western and transition literatures together.

## Setting the scene: corporate governance in market economies

Table 7.1 presents a summary of some recent approaches to the study of corporate governance in market economies. The majority of the discussion of corporate governance in transition economies, with its emphasis on the problems of managerial entrenchment and the paucity of external finance for investment, has been conducted along the lines of Shleifer and Vishny. Their definition of corporate governance is a narrow one. They see it purely in the context of the problem of the supply of external finance to firms. An agency model is used where the firm is a private body defined by a set of principal–agent relationships. Different systems of ownership are represented by different dominant principal–agent problems: a system characterized by dispersed ownership is one in which the owner–manager relationship presents the central corporate governance problem; in a system characterized by concentrated ownership, the key problem is that between the large shareholder and minority investors. In each case, external finance will only be provided by, respectively, outside or minority investors if the manager or the large shareholder can undertake not to exploit their private benefits of control. These private benefits range from outright theft to empire building to staying on the job when they are incompetent (Shleifer and Vishny, 1997).

Shleifer and Vishny propose that a functional system of corporate governance will be one in which there is ownership concentration to enforce profit-seeking behaviour: this will be straightforward in a system with a large shareholder but will occur through the mechanism of the hostile takeover in a system with no controlling shareholder. The other requirement for efficiency is that the legal rights of suppliers

*Table 7.1*   Cross-country studies of corporate governance

| Starting point | Key concepts | Claims |
| --- | --- | --- |
| 1.  Shleifer and Vishny Definition of corporate governance as the external finance problem. The quality of corporate governance should provide an explanation for firms having access to external finance in some countries but not others. | Agency problems (exploitation of the private benefits of control): owner versus manager; large shareholders versus small shareholders. | Access to external finance requires (1) concentrated ownership either through a controlling stake or through the takeover mechanism; and (2) legal protection of the suppliers of external finance. |
| 2.  La Porta *et al.* Differences in legal protection of investors and differences in finance and ownership across countries. | Legal traditions of civil law and common law, rights of investors and enforcement of rights: do these favour investors or managers? | Historical origin of the legal system determines the level of investor protection. Higher legal protection (associated with common law rather than civil law systems) implies less need for ownership concentration which increases access to external finance and reduces capital costs. |
| 3.  Mayer Stylized fact of similar patterns of investment finance (overwhelming reliance on retentions to finance investment) but different patterns of ownership and control across advanced market economies. | Ownership from within the corporate sector (concentrated holdings) allows committed owners to overcome the problem of externalities in control and sustains implicit contracts between stakeholders. Ownership outside the corporate sector fosters external evaluation of the use of assets and facilitates changes in use. | Patterns of ownership and control do not primarily affect sources of finance or methods of disciplining poor managers. They may influence the kinds of activities (as indicated, for example, by industry specialization) economies are able to succeed in. |

of external finance be protected. The authors suggest that the demands on the legal system are less in the case of concentrated ownership through a large shareholder. Indeed they suggest that for most countries the demands on the legal system of the dispersed ownership model are too heavy to be attainable. Hence, in practical terms, only the large shareholder model is likely to be available for most countries and reform efforts should concentrate on improving legal protection for suppliers of debt and equity.

The study by La Porta *et al.* (1998) proposes a bolder hypothesis and one that has been less prominent in transition debates. The authors suggest that a key determinant of access to external finance in a country is its legal code. Legal codes divide into common law (United Kingdom, United States, ex-Commonwealth countries) and civil law types. Three variants of civil code are the German (German-speaking and several East Asian countries), Scandinavian and French. They classify 49 countries according to legal code and gather detailed information on investor protection, enforcement and ownership concentration. The data suggest that an explanation for the rather low ownership concentration in common law countries is the greater degree of investor protection. The authors hypothesize that this increases the access of firms to external finance.

At the other extreme are the French civil law countries with weakest investor protection and high ownership concentration. Interestingly the authors find that, while poor countries systematically have weaker law *enforcement*, there is no correlation between per capita GDP of a country and the legal system of investor right protection. Hence, as exemplified by France and Italy, it is possible to get rich in spite of having an unfavourable legal code – the authors mention in passing that part of Poland was influenced by the French legal code in the nineteenth century while Hungary and Czechoslovakia adopted the German civil code in the early twentieth century.

Mayer's papers in this field[1] have sought to provide empirical information about two issues central to the agency approach to corporate governance: the patterns of investment finance in advanced market economies and the mechanisms through which managers are disciplined in poorly performing companies. Empirical results from flow-of-funds analyses using aggregate data indicate that, across the advanced countries, there is considerable similarity in the patterns of investment financing and, perhaps even more striking, a very tiny use of new equity as a source of finance even in the United States and the United Kingdom (for example, Corbett and Jenkinson, 1997). In a comparison of investment finance in Germany, Japan, the United Kingdom and the United States from 1970 to 1994, Corbett and Jenkinson show that, while Japan can still be characterized as 'bank-financed' (although the share of investment financed by bank loans halved between the early 1970s and the early 1990s), contrary to stereotypes, bank finance has not played an important role in Germany over that period. Germany, the United Kingdom and the United States are all mainly internally financed, with market sources of finance playing a small (often negative) and declining role.

Turning to management discipline, in studies of poorly performing companies in the United Kingdom and in Germany, it is shown that there is a relationship between poor performance and management turnover. But in neither country was higher ownership concentration associated with higher management turnover in the presence of poor performance. Although there was an active market in blocks of shares in both countries, they did not appear to perform a disciplinary function: they were not related to management turnover. These results cast doubt on the idea that concentrated ownership or changes in ownership are the mechanisms through which corporate governance, in the sense of imposing ex post monitoring on management, is exercised.

These results are in line with Kaplan's findings (1994a, 1994b) that the disciplining of managers in terms of salary cuts and dismissal as performance of a company falls below a given threshold is quite similar in companies in the United States, Germany and Japan. The major differences in ownership and control structures across these countries do not seem to produce differences in this aspect of the exercise of corporate governance.

Mayer emphasizes that ownership concentration, takeovers and changes in share stakes may have a rather different role than that of ex post monitoring. Assuming that effective ex post monitoring is in place, the difference between a financial system with concentrated ownership by non-financial companies, another where banks play a major ownership role and a third where ownership of large companies is much more dispersed and hostile takeovers occur may be that each is able to sustain a different set of activities. For example, a committed owner may be necessary to induce investment in the relationship by complementary factors such as workers, suppliers or customers, as well as managers. Whereas Shleifer and Vishny emphasize the ability of large shareholders to exploit their position and expropriate other stakeholders, Mayer highlights the role of the commitment to the continuation of an activity that is represented by a large shareholder.

Although much remains unresolved, one way of viewing this debate is the following. There is a trade-off which different *successful* financial systems resolve in different ways. The trade-off is between, on the one hand, encouraging commitment of the manager (in an entrepreneurial capacity) and of complementary factors to often irreversible investments in human capital, and the dangers of large shareholders exploiting the private benefits of control. On the other hand, a financial system which minimizes the possibility of large shareholder exploitation of other parties is unable to take full advantage of long-term relationships and risks opportunistic behaviour by managers, but can benefit from the ability to switch asset use quickly.[2] However, to be successful at all, a financial system must first establish some threshold level of ex post monitoring of management.

What can we conclude for the analysis of transition from this bird's-eye view of the debate about the role of corporate governance in the market economies? Our understanding of the way institutional arrangements interact with economic performance is still limited and, until recently, most research has focused on corporate governance arrangements within 'successful' advanced economies or on comparisons between such economies. But there are a number of directions for empirical work in the transition economies that may help to resolve these questions in the longer run.

As noted in the introduction, interest in the role of ownership in transition means that we will certainly have a better description of the structure of ownership at the outset of the market economy period in these economies and of changes in ownership than has been the case anywhere else in the world. In countries beginning with a total absence of mechanisms for ex post monitoring of managerial performance by corporate governance institutions, the opportunity for learning about the characteristics of the threshold level of corporate governance is enormous. Especially in the case of poorly performing companies, analysis is needed of managerial turnover and sales of share stakes (also supervisory board composition and changes where there are two-tier boards).

## A two-stage approach to the transition literature on restructuring and corporate governance

### Stage one: marketization shock and reactive restructuring

A simple two-stage framework has emerged in the analysis of enterprise reform in transition. The first stage follows the change of regime from the planned economy to a market economy. The 'marketization shock' entailed the introduction of market forces in goods, services and factor markets. Price liberalization and macroeconomic stabilization to enable market signals to function formed part of the marketization package. War, the collapse of trading relationships without the proximity of alternative markets and the weakness of government help to account for the cross-country variation in the length of time between the marketization shock and the recovery of aggregate output (Åslund *et al.*, 1996).

The concept of the soft-budget constraint has proved a remarkably powerful tool in the analysis of enterprise behaviour subsequent to the marketization shock. Budget softness is measured by the weakness of the link between an enterprise's financial performance and its command over current and capital resources. In the planned economy, there was no clear link from financial performance to managerial compensation or tenure. Exit of the enterprise through closure was not a route through which the manager could lose control. Equally the planner could not promise to reward managerial effort because the absence of an outside option for the manager (no managerial labour market, no private sector) meant that any incentive structure would lack credibility. The planner could not undertake not to toughen the manager's target once good performance had been demonstrated (Roland and Sekkat, 1996). The marketization shock reinstated the connection between financial performance and access to resources, introduced the possibility of exit of firms and allowed for the creation of new private sector activities.

Irrespective of ownership changes, the marketization shock produced a wave of restructuring activity by the managers of state-owned enterprises. The tightening of the budget constraint by the withdrawal of ex post state subsidies had the effect of inducing managers to exert the effort to cut costs by shedding labour and to seek markets for output where the cost of the perceived threat of closure outweighed the effort required and the riskiness of restructuring. Case study evidence revealed enormous heterogeneity between enterprises in their responses, but there appeared to be systematic components of the variation explicable in terms of the basic theory of restructuring in response to a hardening of the enterprise budget constraint (Carlin *et al.*, 1995).[3]

Interesting new insights into the stage one restructuring process have been provided by studies of former Soviet Union (FSU) countries. Barter transactions as a response to the collapse of output and input planning have persisted much longer after the beginning of the reforms in some of these countries, suggesting much deeper disruption to supply chains as a consequence of the collapse of previous trading arrangements than was the case in Central and Eastern Europe. The Baltics represent an interesting intermediate case indicating that both geographical proximity to Western European markets and a shorter period of communist rule may have made the recreation of a market economy easier.

Two recent studies of Moldova and Georgia (Djankov, 1997; Djankov and Kreacic, 1998) emphasize the persistence of the phase of disorientation and disorganization (for example, Blanchard, 1997, ch. 2) as managers of SOEs (or former SOEs) display passive behavioural responses of the kind documented by Carlin *et al.* (1995). In the face of virtual total absence of sales, younger workers have left enterprises, yet the managers have continued to hold on to capital equipment and other assets, expecting orders to appear that would restore full capacity utilization without the need for them to take any action. In the Moldovan study, specific attention was paid to the possible role that training programmes for managers could play in inducing improved performance. A manager having attended a training programme was the biggest determinant of the extent to which the enterprise was engaged in market as opposed to barter transactions (Djankov, 1997). The type of training appeared to make no difference to its effectiveness, which suggests that the training may have performed the function of introducing managers in this economy to some very basic notions of how a market economy operates.

Outside observers were often surprised by the speed with which reactive restructuring took hold in the leading transition economies. The speed of trade reorientation by the Central and East European countries was also frequently referred to as remarkable. This new evidence from the FSU highlights the possibility that the rapid reaction of enterprise managers in Central Europe may have been influenced by the diffusion of information about market economies through trade and FDI contacts and the return of émigrés. The evidence from the countries studied most heavily in Eastern Europe suggested that an understanding of the changes in incentives associated with the marketization shock provided a good explanatory model for the observed pattern of behavioural responses by incumbent managers of SOEs. The late reformers may provide new information about the role of managerial human capital and learning in the reform process.[4]

## Stage two: privatization and deep restructuring

In the early transition literature, it was often claimed that privatization was probably necessary but not sufficient to elicit deep restructuring. The term 'deep restructuring' was used to refer to a second set of actions that enterprise managers would need to take, over and above those needed to break even, in order to produce an efficient growth and profit-oriented firm. The claim was based on the idea that, once enterprises were operating under tight budget constraints, privatization could result in ownership structures that placed no constraints on managerial behaviour (in addition to those produced by competitive pressure, which would affect state-owned as well as privatized enterprises). Hence managers could continue to enjoy the private benefits of control of firms in the form of incumbency.

Nevertheless privatization was seen as an essential part of the process of depoliticizing enterprises: reducing dependence on state orders, on ex post government subsidies and on protection by the state from closure. In short, privatization was a way of locking in the marketization shock and promoting reactive restructuring, but would not automatically produce static and dynamic efficiency. Deep restructuring was normally assumed to require profit orientation as an objective of the owners that could be imposed on managers, the requisite human capital to identify profitable opportunities and the means to implement (that is, to finance) the associated investment.

A hierarchy of ownership structures ordered by their compatibility with deep restructuring has gained widespread currency in the literature. Outside ownership was typically viewed as preferable to inside ownership subject to the proviso that the outside ownership structure produced effective control over management. To this end the concentration of voting shares in the hands of an outside owner was viewed as the feasible structure. Because of the underdevelopment of the capital market, reliance on surveillance of performance by takeover raiders using verifiable public information on companies was not seen as a feasible structure of control in the presence of dispersed outside ownership.

Foreign owners were usually ranked first as profit-oriented owners with the requisite human and financial capital to push through deep restructuring. Less clear was the ranking between different types of domestic outside owners. Domestic strategic investors, banks and investment funds with controlling stakes were credited with different combinations of profit orientation, human and financial capital resources and agency problems.

In firms without an outside controlling owner, managerial owner-ship was identified as providing superior profit orientation to that asso-ciated with worker ownership. Worker ownership could entrench the veto by workers over forms of restructuring that would threaten their jobs: this would depend on workers' perception of opportunities for employment or for income support outside the enterprise. On the other hand, initial worker ownership could provide a route to deep restructuring via the ousting of an entrenched incompetent manager if there was a market for shares.

## Evidence on restructuring, privatization and corporate governance in transition

The empirical investigation of ownership and performance using firm-level data sets has gathered pace in the last two years. The attempt to test for a causal connection from ownership structure to performance focuses attention on the question of the way in which enterprises acquired their private owners. There are two interesting questions: first, did the characteristics of enterprises and their managers differ system-atically across methods of privatization within and between countries and, second, how has post-privatization ownership affected firm per-formance? Unfortunately there has been less attention given to the first question than to the second. We do not have a clear picture of how systematic the connection was between privatization methods and enterprise characteristics. For example, the typical assumption in the literature is that foreign ownership of former state-owned enter-prises best facilitates the process of deep restructuring. But, unless we know the characteristics of these enterprises, the conditions relating to post-privatization employment adjustment or investment attached to the sale, and how they were selected for foreign ownership, it is not possible to test this assumption.

There are two issues at stake in the analysis of selection effects. On the one hand, we are interested in finding out whether there was a difference in the observable characteristics of the enterprises which ended up receiv-ing a different privatization 'treatment'. If the observable characteristics were different then we can assume that participants in the process could have known about them. However, a second issue arises if there were dif-ferentiating characteristics which were not observable in pre-privatization performance. The most obvious is the quality of management. From the literature on pre-privatization restructuring, it is clear that the design of the privatization process could create incentives for managers to reveal or to conceal their quality prior to privatization. If some methods of privatization created an incentive for managers to reveal their quality while others led to concealment, the use of observable characteristics such as pre-privatization performance would not capture this dimension of selection bias.

An understanding of whether privatization per se, or particular methods of privatization, selected enterprises by quality is important not only for the correct interpretation of the results of privatization but also for the broader evaluation of approaches to privatization across countries. Detailed trade information for manufacturing indicates that transition countries have varied considerably in their ability to move up product quality ladders, with Hungary, the Czech Republic and Slovenia upgrading their exports much faster than Poland or Russia (Carlin and Landesmann, 1997). An obvious question is whether privatization programmes have played any role in this. The dominant privatization method has been different in Hungary, the Czech Republic and Slovenia, suggesting that country characteristics such as size and openness of the economy may dominate any privatization effect. But this simple interpretation neglects the possible role of privatization methods, since systematic selection of enterprises by quality could have occurred through different primary methods.

### Did methods of privatization select enterprises by quality?

In the general discussion of privatization, a particular method has sometimes been associated with the 'best' or 'higher quality' state-owned enterprises. In some cases, privatization design has sought deliberately to associate enterprise quality with a specific method of disposal. East Germany provides probably the clearest example of this intention. All core business activities of enterprises were evaluated for their potential viability and bids from outside investors sought by the privatization agency. Enterprises viewed as potentially viable but for which there was no outside investor interest could be disposed of through management buy-outs (MBOs); non-viable enterprises were slated for rapid closure. By prioritizing direct sales, the Hungarian and Estonian privatization programmes followed a policy similar to that in East Germany. Both countries pursued more decisive closure/bankruptcy programmes than was typical elsewhere.

In Poland, typical descriptions of the privatization programme indicate that, apart from the small number of large firms picked out for public offer in the early showcase privatizations, the best enterprises were acquired by managers through MBOs. Accounts of Russian privatization stress that the priority was speed and that the lack of information available to outside investors, the weakness of the legal framework for the protection of their rights and the control by insiders over the selection of the method of privatization were likely to result in dominant stakes in the best firms being acquired by insiders.

There are now a number of studies that provide information on selection and make explicit their attempt to deal with the selection problem in the analysis of post-privatization performance. The studies considered here provide information on medium-sized firms in Poland, Hungary and the Czech Republic (Frydman *et al.*, 1997), on large Polish firms (Grosfeld and Nivet, 1997), on the sample of Czech firms included in the large privatization programme (Marcincin and van Wijnbergen, 1997) and on a representative sample of Russian firms (Earle and Estrin, 1997).

Contrary to the frequent claims in the literature, Grosfeld and Nivet failed to confirm that privatized large Polish firms in their sample were stronger performers prior to privatization than were those that were commercialized or remained in state ownership. Frydman *et al.* also failed to find any systematic difference in the observable pre-privatization performance and characteristics in their sample of medium-sized firms between those that remained in state ownership and those that were subsequently privatized. However they did find that firms that were privatized to insiders, that is, to managers and workers, were superior in their pre-privatization performance to those privatized by other methods. Earle and Estrin's results confirm the 'stylized fact' that the voucher privatization in Russia was biased against outsiders taking controlling stakes in the best firms.

One study that investigates this issue in depth refers to the Czech privatization process. A misleading impression has sometimes been given of the Czech privatization process when the role of other bidders prior to the disposal of shares through the voucher auctions is neglected. About one half of property in the 'large privatization' pro-gramme (amounting to about one-quarter of all property privatized) went through the voucher process rather than, for example, through direct sales and, of those firms, the voucher stake for the median company was 80–90 per cent but only about 50 per cent when firms are weighted by the size of their assets (Marcincin and van Wijnbergen, 1997).

The model used in this article centres on the simple idea that enter-prises can be privatized through a method that produces dispersed ownership or through one that produces concentrated ownership. The latter is assumed to be superior in terms of generating rapid restructuring. However the government, with its eye on electoral support, is constrained in its choice of method by the need for speed so as to enhance the credibility of the programme and by the fact that the number of investors available in a short period is limited. Restructuring potential depends on both observable and unobservable characteristics and the government is assumed to choose the privatization method for each enterprise based on observable restructuring potential, increasing the probability that the better enterprises would be privatized via the second method.

By using a two-stage estimation process to separately identify the selection effect, Marcincin and van Wijnbergen found support for the hypothesis that the firms sold wholly through vouchers were of lower quality than those for which vouchers comprised only a part of the disposal. This is an important finding in its own right; showing that a privatization process with a tight deadline was able to sort enterprises by quality. It also raises interesting questions about the role of managerial consent to outside ownership and casts doubt on the claim that voucher privatization in the Czech Republic to outsiders was only possible because managers expected that dispersed ownership would result and that they would retain control. An interesting possibility is that the better firms prior to privatization were those with better managers who at the privatization stage were willing to exchange control for access to finance that could be facilitated through an outside strategic investor.

The feature of the Czech voucher process of combining speed with selecting 'better' ownership structures for 'better' enterprises may prove to be important in understanding the consequences of voucher privatization in a comparative setting, alongside the more widely discussed cross-country differences in ownership of voucherized firms. As noted above, the opposite selection of 'worse' ownership structures for 'better' firms was confirmed by Earle and Estrin as the outcome of Russian voucher privatization.

## Does privatization matter for performance? Does ownership structure matter for post-privatization performance?

Recent work has shown the benefits of using different approaches to uncovering the impact of privatization. Frydman *et al.* (1997) argue, for example, that valuable information may be gleaned by separating the cost reduction and revenue-increasing components of profitability. They suggest that reactive restructuring would be captured by cost-cutting, but signs of deep or strategic restructuring would be reflected in revenue increases. Accounting profitability may be a poor discriminator because of the possibilities for the manipulation of recorded costs in order to minimize tax liabilities and the possibility that manipulation may be systematically related to profit orientation and managerial ability. The authors' hypothesis is that all firms will display reactive restructuring in the face of the marketization shock, but that privatized ones will be marked by superior revenue growth performance in the post-privatization period as compared with firms that remain in state ownership.

Some caution is needed in interpreting the results because of the remaining methodological problems and the very small sample sizes once ownership is divided into seven categories (for example, there are 10 or fewer firms in four of the categories). Although country dummies are included, the fact that some forms of ownership occur only in one country means that there will be a confounding of the country and the ownership effect (for example, all firms owned by a privatization fund are Czech and all worker-owned firms are Hungarian). Subject to these serious caveats, the performance of the medium-sized firms in the Frydman *et al.* sample appears to differ according to their new ownership structure. Concerns about selection bias are lessened by the finding, noted above, that there was no difference in observable pre-privatization performance between privatized firms and SOEs. The superior pre-privatization performance of insider-owned as compared with outsider-owned firms allays the concern that managers seeking to secure ownership on favourable terms had an incentive to conceal capabilities prior to privatization.

Taking Frydman *et al.*'s preferred performance variable, revenue growth, privatized firms outperformed SOEs. Differentiating privatized firms by the dominant owner, the best performers were firms owned by privatization funds, by foreigners and by managers. Strikingly, partially privatized firms with the state as the largest shareholder showed a similar revenue growth performance to this group. However further investigation revealed that firms in this group performed in line with those owned by their second largest owner, suggesting a passive role of the state in partially privatized firms. Weaker performance indistinguishable from that of SOEs was shown by the small sample of firms with a domestic non-financial institution owner and by worker-owned firms.

These results appear to provide some support for the prediction that employee ownership in transition would slow down the restructuring process. Such firms display less cost cutting and labour shedding than do

SOEs, and show no better growth of revenue. Manager-owned firms seem to be just as entrepreneurial as fund or foreign-owned ones but shed less labour than do SOEs, thus failing to register a superior productivity performance. The achievement of manager-owned firms is also diminished somewhat by the finding that the performance of insider-owned firms was better than that of other firms before privatization.

For the much larger sample of Czech firms, Marcincin and van Wijnbergen showed that, after correcting for the selection bias, the observed post-privatization performance of fully voucherized firms was weaker, confirming the hypothesis that outside ownership matters for performance.

The most detailed study of Russian privatization using enterprise-level data is provided by Earle and Estrin (1997) in an exhaustive examination of the characteristics of a representative sample of about 300 'old' enterprises immediately after the completion of voucher privatization in mid-1994. Using their results, the structure of initial ownership following the privatization programme in Russia can be summarized as in Table 7.2. Following mass privatization, the role of the state remained considerable: considering all 'old firms', the proportion of employment in firms in which the state remained a dominant owner (with a stake of at least 40 per cent) was 38 per cent. Just looking at firms that were at least partially privatized, one-fifth of employment was in firms with the state as the dominant owner after privatization. Of those with a dominant private owner, over 70 per cent were in insider-dominated firms and three-quarters of those were in worker- rather than manager-dominated firms.

Table 7.2 shows that the ownership outcomes differed according to the method of privatization used. Insider ownership was far more prevalent with leasing privatization (lease buy-outs by workers that occurred before the main privatization programme) and with the selection of Option 2 privatization (through which employees secured 51 per cent of shares at 1.7 times the book value of the firm). These two methods accounted for 70 per cent of the firms privatized. The dominance of insider ownership is clear but was not uniform across privatization methods.

While fewer than one in 10 firms had a dominant outside owner, one in four had an outside blockholder with a stake of at least 25 per cent. More detailed analysis provided support for anecdotal reports that banks and 'other firms' were often not true outsiders: their presence as outsiders was most common where insiders were dominant in the firm. By contrast, investment funds appeared to gravitate towards

*Table 7.2*  Post-privatization ownership and privatization methods in Russia

| Dominant owner | Post-privatization structure (by dominant owner) | | Ownership | Methods of privatization | | |
| | All old firms | At least partially privatized | At least partially privatized | Leasing | Option 1 | Option 2 |
| | *% of firms (weighted by employment)* | | *% of firms (unweighted)* | | | |
| State | 38 | 20 | 8 | 1 | 21 | 4 |
| Private | 62 | 80 | 92 | 98 | 78 | 96 |
| Insider | 45 | 59 | 77 | 95 | 51 | 81 |
| Worker | 35 | 44 | 51 | 71 | 34 | 49 |
| Manager | 6 | 8 | 15 | 21 | 8 | 15 |
| Other | 4 | 5 | 10 | 0 | 9 | 15 |
| Outsider | 9 | 12 | 9 | 3 | 12 | 11 |
| Other | 7 | 9 | 6 | – | 14 | 5 |
| No. of firms | 327 | 241 | 238 | 66 | 65 | 104 |

*Note:*  The firms privatized according to Option 3 (an MBO based on a performance contract) are omitted because there were only three cases in the sample and it was of negligible importance in the privatization programme.
*Source:*  Earle and Estrin (1997) Tables 4, 5, 14.

firms where insiders did not have a majority (for example, in Option 1 companies through which insiders received 25 per cent of shares free and could purchase up to 15 per cent more at nominal prices). For a given insider stake, the preference of investment funds was revealed to be for blocks in companies that were not dominated by manager–owners.

To get around the problem of the endogeneity due to the possible selection bias in privatization, Earle and Estrin proposed the use of the method of privatization as an instrument exploiting the correlation between privatization method and ownership structure in an instrumental variables approach to estimating the relationship between ownership structure and performance. They used a multidimensional restructuring index (capturing mainly reactive restructuring) and labour productivity as their performance variables. They found that privatization was associated with a very small but significant positive effect on performance. Managers as owners produced a larger impact. While outside ownership appeared to have no significant effect on performance in the ordinary least squares (OLS) regressions, it did in the instrumental variables (IV) specifications, providing support for the idea that weaker firms were available to outside owners. Evaluation of these results is difficult because of the fact that the survey was conducted immediately after the privatization process.

In a very different approach, Grosfeld and Nivet examined the behaviour of a sample of large Polish firms over a lengthy period that includes pre-reform data. Their sample selection criteria dictated a quite specific sample, namely firms that were present continuously from 1988 to 1994. By comparing the average performance of sample firms, which accounted for between one-quarter and one-third of manufacturing output over the sample period, with the industrial sector of the economy as a whole, it is clear that these represented the block of large firms that have been slow to privatize (only 16 per cent privatized by 1994) and where the recovery of output has been delayed (no output growth by 1994, compared with the rise in aggregate industrial output from 1992).

The focus of the paper is on wage-setting behaviour and on investment. An examination of wage setting provides a useful method of gathering information as to the objectives of the firm and helping to identify the dominant decision-making parties. By using a wage equation that includes firm-specific and industry variables it is possible to examine the extent to which extent changes in wage reflect rent sharing as compared to the conditions external to the firm such as the industry wage or the regional unemployment rate. This provides an indication of how the balance of power is distributed between different agents in the firm. The greater is the power of workers, the weaker the influence of external conditions on the wage that is paid and the larger the extent to which workers would be expected to capture the gains from productivity increases. An entrepreneurial firm seeking to maximize profits in order to maximize the availability of internal funds to finance investment or to distribute profits so as to improve its access to market funds would be expected to display less rent sharing with wages tied more closely to the industry wage or unemployment.

Because of the sample used, Grosfeld and Nivet have rather few privatized firms (24 of the 173 firms in 1994) and they focus on the distinction between SOEs, commercialized/corporatized former SOEs and privatized firms. Most of the latter were privatized to strategic investors or by public offer. There is no overlap between the Polish firms in this sample and the much smaller ones investigated by Frydman *et al.* Their results support the hypothesis that commercialization represented a breaking down of the power of workers in SOEs: they found that insiders captured the bulk of the productivity gains in SOEs but that the link from firm-specific productivity to the wage was much weaker in commercialized enterprises. In the privatized firms, there was no positive effect of firm-specific productivity gains on wages – indeed the data suggested that, far from firm-specific productivity gains being shared with employees, there was a negative impact, pointing towards the vigorous attempt of managers to widen profit margins.

Investment has been regarded as a defining characteristic of deep restructuring, hence there is interest in the question of whether the amount of investment (for example, investment as a percentage of value-added) differs systematically between state-owned and privatized firms and between firms of different ownership types. Secondly, the analysis of investment behaviour can, in a similar way to that of wage-setting behaviour, throw light on managerial motivation and profit-orientation. Grosfeld and Nivet estimated an investment equation including accelerator and cash-flow terms along with ownership dummies. They found that only the ownership dummies were significant. Thus it appears that differences in ownership dominated the standard determinants of investment. In particular, the predicted ranking that privatized firms would invest most (almost twice the sample mean) followed by commercialized ones, which in turn would invest more than SOEs was confirmed. This is consistent with the differences in wage behaviour: the absence of rent sharing with employees in the privatized firms indicated strong profit orientation; the investment equation confirms that this was reflected in higher investment.

In a second analysis, an investment function was estimated for each ownership group separately. For each group, lagged profits were a significant determinant of investment, but sensitivity to the profits variable was much greater for the privatized firms. Only for the SOEs was the output growth term significant. An interpretation favoured by the authors is that, by comparison with privatized firms, investment in SOEs was influenced by the short-term evolution of sales. The strong role of the cash-flow variable for privatized firms could reflect financing constraints or it could be a proxy for expectations, perhaps indicating that current profitability is seen as a better indicator of prospective profitability than is recent growth of output.

Grosfeld and Nivet's results for very large Polish firms demonstrate a clear difference in behaviour between those still in state ownership and those that had been privatized (see Table 7.3 for a summary). Commercialization emerged as an effective strategy for wresting control from employees. The investment behaviour of commercialized firms was more similar to that of privatized firms than to SOEs. The dimension on which privatized firms stood out most clearly from the rest was output growth. Growth performance was not only stronger but the growth of output of privatized firms was much less influenced by sectoral output growth than was the case for other types. This is fully consistent with the more 'entrepreneurial' behaviour of privatized firms observed by Frydman *et al.* About half of the privatized firms had a strategic outside owner and the other half were sold through public offer. The finding of deep restructuring behaviour in this group highlights the need to find

*Table* 7.3   Investment in large Polish firms, 1992–4

| | State-owned | | |
| --- | --- | --- | --- |
| | *SOEs* | *Commercialized* | *Privatized* |
| No. of firms (1994) | 85 | 61 | 27 |
| *I/Y* (%) | 4.8 | 6.0 | 11.2 |
| Coefficient on accelerator term | 0.026 | Not significant | Not significant |
| Coefficient on profits term | 0.146 | 0.289 | 1.025 |

*Note:*
Coefficients are significant at 5 per cent or at 1 per cent. Not significant means not significant at 10 per cent.
Average number of employees 2613. *I/Y* = share of investment in value-added.
*Source:*   Grosfeld and Nivet (1997) p. 4, Tables 6, A2.

out more about the ownership and control structure of these privatized firms.

The emerging picture of a clear effect of privatization on deep restructuring, with outsider owned firms showing superior performance and worker-owned firms failing to outperform SOEs, is not fully confirmed by a detailed study of the investment behaviour of Czech firms. Lizal and Svejnar (1998) examined investment in a large sample of Czech firms over the period 1992 to 1995. Their descriptive data did show that foreign-owned firms had the highest investment shares and cooperatives the lowest, but private limited liability companies and those owned by private individuals had fairly low investment levels throughout the period – certainly not clearly higher than for SOEs. Both private and state joint stock companies had higher (and fairly similar) investment levels.

Unlike the studies of Frydman *et al.* and Grosfeld and Nivet, the Czech data set includes new start-up firms, although the cut-off point of more than 25 employees (and more than 100 employees in the final year sample) excludes the small new firms. Any new firms included in the data will tend to be in the lower-size classes and in the legal forms of limited liability and individually owned. As noted above, these firms have shown relatively low investment levels and the behavioural equations suggest that investment in the large category of limited liability was hampered by financial constraints. Apart from these smaller private firms and cooperatives, the Czech data suggest that financial constraints as proxied by a cash flow term did not play an important role in determining investment levels. Instead it was the accelerator term that seemed more often to be important. Taking joint stock companies, while the accelerator term was significant for state and foreign-owned ones, investment in those privately owned was not systematically related to either the growth of sales or past profits. As an illustration of the results, Table 7.4 shows the results for the investment equation for 1995 for state-owned, private and foreign-owned firms.

Tables 7.5 and 7.6 summarize the results from these five studies, showing, first, the results for selection, privatization and ownership effects and, second, those for evidence of differences in behaviour indicative of profit orientation and deep restructuring. These studies suggest that firms partly privatized in which the state has a substantial shareholding perform better than SOEs. There is some indication that the state may be passive, since firms tend to behave like those owned by the second largest owner. The need for further investigation of

Table 7.4 Investment in Czech firms, 1995

| | State-owned | | | Private (domestic) | | | Foreign-owned | |
| | SOE | Joint stock | Limited | Joint stock | Limited | Indiv. | Joint stock | Limited |
|---|---|---|---|---|---|---|---|---|
| No. of firms | 125 | 725 | 25 | 218 | 648 | 36 | 48 | 111 |
| Mean employment | 327 | 823 | 845 | 486 | 242 | 198 | 912 | 358 |
| I/Y (%) | 7.2 | 19.6 | 21.1 | 17.7 | 8.6 | 5.9 | 16.8 | 24.2 |
| Long-run coeff. on accel. term | 0.012 | 0.073 | N/A | 0.040 | 0.090 | Not sign. | 0.237 | Not sign. |
| Long-run coeff. on profits term | Not sign. | Not sign. | N/A | Not sign. | 0.056 | Not sign. | Not sign. | Not sign. |

Note: Number of firms is approximated by number of observations divided by four. Fewer observations were available for the regressions.
Coefficients are significant at 5 per cent or at 1 per cent. Not significant means not significant at 10 per cent.
Source: Lizal and Svejnar (1998) Tables 6, A2, A7.

Table 7.5  Summary of results: selection, privatization and ownership

| | Poland, Hungary, Czech Republic (Frydman et al.) | Czech Republic (Marcincin and van Wijnbergen) | Poland (Grosfeld and Nivet) | Russia (Earle and Estrin) |
|---|---|---|---|---|
| Sample description | Medium-sized firms: 1990–92 E = 360 | 'Large privatization' sample, 1991–5 | Large firms only: 1988–94 E = 2613 | Representative sample, mid-1994 |
| Number of firms | 178 | 560 | 173 | 327 |
| **1. Selection** | | | | |
| Were better firms privatized? | No | N/A | No | N/A |
| Of privatized firms, was pre-priv. performance better for insider than outsider? | Yes | N/A | N/A | Yes |
| Were other selection effects found? | | Yes: pre-priv, fully voucherized worse than partly voucherized | | |
| **2. Privatization effect** | | | | |
| Did privatized firms perform better than SOEs? | Yes | N/A | Yes | Yes (small effect) |
| **3. Ownership effect** | | | | |
| Better owners | than SOE: privatization fund; foreign co.; managers; part-privatized | some strong outside ownership | N/A | than SOE: manager; outsider (incl. banks and invest. funds) |
| Worse owners | no better than SOE: worker; domestic non-financial co. | fully voucherized | N/A | than SOE: dispersed outsiders |

*Table 7.6*    Summary of results: behaviour of firms

|  | Poland<br>(Grosfeld and Nivet) | Czech Republic<br>(Lizal and Svejnar) |
|---|---|---|
| Sample description | Large firms only:<br>E = 2613, 1988–94 | Population of med. and large firms, 1992–5 |
| Number of firms | 173 | >2000 |
| **1. Investment behaviour**<br>Do privatized firms invest more than SOEs? | Yes | Yes if foreign owned; but investment is low for some types of private |
| Is investment behaviour different for private compared with SOEs? | Yes | No clear pattern |
| **2. Wage-setting behaviour**<br>Do privatized firms display more profit-oriented wage setting? | Yes | N/A |

partial privatization, including that of Czech firms, is indicated. All studies point towards worker-owned firms as performing weakly and often indistinguishably from SOEs. The interesting issue of whether worker ownership facilitates the transfer to outside owners is not addressed directly in any of these studies, but the tendency for worker ownership to go together with outsider block holdings in Russian firms points in this direction.

Some signs of entrepreneurial behaviour by managers as owners were identified. The samples contain little information about foreign-owned firms and, although there is some indication that banks as owners have proved less effective than other financial institutions, the evidence is thin.

## Corporate governance in transition economies: unanswered questions

As this survey of recent work investigating ownership, enterprise behaviour and performance in transition economies has made clear, systematic econometric study is at an early stage. Many more studies with different samples and from different countries will need to accumulate before we can feel confident that the results so far are reliable. It is striking that each study presented here has taken a different approach to dealing with the selection bias/endogeneity problem – even with these data sets, replication using different methods is called for. The brief mention of recent studies focusing on reactive restructuring in FSU countries highlighted the possibility that the late and more slow-moving reformers may provide new information on the consequences of the marketization shock and the role of human capital and learning in the adjustment to the market economy.

Most of the analysis of corporate governance and enterprise sector reform to date in transition has sought to identify the impact of changes in property rights or differences in ownership structures on the behaviour of individual firms. Less attention has been paid to developing an understanding of how well the corporate governance system in the economy as a whole has developed. This is not surprising in the light of the discussion in the second section of this chapter, which reported that there is no clear consensus regarding the threshold characteristics of an effective system of corporate governance. While some authors suggest that, in market economies with effective systems of corporate governance, the different structures of ownership and control provide a different mix of governance via ownership concentration and legal protection of investors, others point to the apparent similarity of financing patterns and triggers for disciplining managers. They hypothesize that differences in ownership and control structures across countries are linked less to ex post monitoring of managers and more to identifying the kinds of activities each financial system best supports. We need, for example, to understand what it is that produces the disciplining of managers at similar levels of performance in such disparate ownership and control systems as Japan, Germany and the United States.

In transition economies, the careful monitoring of institutional developments in the legal code and its enforcement (including bankruptcy), the role of external finance in investment, the nature of bank finance and of bank–firm relationships and the concentration of ownership in the economy as a whole should be pursued alongside the analysis of individual enterprise behaviour. We need to begin to utilize the information from firm-level studies in conjunction with country-level characteristics, to assemble the bigger picture of the systems of corporate governance that are evolving. The systematic study of the large group of transition economies may eventually throw light on puzzles such as the relative success of Italy in postwar catch-up growth in spite of its very poor financial system (poor legal code, lack of financial institutions to impose ex post monitoring, lack of mechanisms to shift resources to different uses) and the relative failure of the United Kingdom in catch-up growth despite its apparently more efficient financial system.

## Notes

1. Relevant papers include: Mayer (1990), Franks and Mayer (1997b), Franks *et al.* (1997).
2. This is consistent with the arguments presented by, for example, Porter (1990) and Soskice (1994) that there may be an institutional basis for a country's competitive advantage.
3. For a survey of evidence on restructuring up to 1996, see Carlin and Landesmann (1997).
4. An earlier study of Russian shops pointed in this direction (Barberis *et al.*, 1996).

# 8
# Privatization and Corporate Governance in Transition Countries: Beyond the Principal–Agent Model

*Wladimir Andreff*

## Introduction

Privatization appears to be a success story in transition countries when assessed with quantitative criteria. This is not the whole story, however. Privatization has met various difficulties and is still plagued by two basic unresolved issues, corporate governance and residual state property in privatized enterprises, both indicating a partial qualitative failure. Therefore one cannot avoid looking at some theoretical implications of the observed results of privatization as regards management coalitions, the blurred dividing line between shareholders and stakeholders, financial–industrial groups, interlocking directorates, the violation of shareholders' rights and the corrupt redistribution of capital and property rights. Could it be that the standard approach to privatization, in particular the principal–agent model, has been too simplistic or even inaccurate for transition countries? Both empirical evidence and limitations of the mainstream approach to privatization suggest a renewed analysis at the dawn of the second stage of privatization now starting in transition countries.

## The quantitative success story of privatization

The share of private production in GDP is now significant in most transition countries (Table 8.1). It was over 50 per cent in eight Central and Eastern European countries and in Russia by the end of 1995. In some countries, such as Hungary, the Czech Republic and Slovakia, it reached 80 per cent in 1997. However the share of the private sector in GDP grows as the result of three cumulative factors: the transfer of public assets to private ownership, the increase in the number of new private start-ups net of bankruptcies, and the higher growth rate of production in the private sector compared to the growth of the still existing state sector. Taking privatization in this macroeconomic sense is relevant to assessing whether privatization is likely to have boosted macroeconomic efficiency and growth in transition countries. We have undertaken a rough econometric test by regressing the index of GDP growth (*IG*) on the share of the private sector (*SPS*), for a sample of 25 transition countries with Table 8.1 data. Whereas there are several factors explaining economic growth, private ownership must facilitate or even boost it if privatization triggers economic efficiency. Thus the regression coefficient of *SPS* must be positive if it is to confirm that privatization paves the way to economic efficiency and growth, even though the observed results must be taken with a pinch of salt owing to the very rough statistical data for *SPS*.

At the beginning of privatization, in 1990, the coefficient of *SPS* was not positive and was not significant at 5 per cent; the adjusted correlation coefficient being very small. The share of the private sector, while small, did not explain GDP growth at all. In 1995, the coefficient of *SPS* was positive, and 41.7 per cent of the variance of the economic growth index was explained by the linear regression with significant coefficients ($p < 5$ per cent). The hypothesis of a positive relationship between economic growth and privatization cannot be rejected. In addition, we have calculated the rank correlation between *IG* and *SPS*. In 1990, we found $r_s = -0.44$ which confirms the absence of a relation between economic growth and private ownership. In 1995, the coefficient of rank correlation is $r_s = 0.65$ and means a significant relationship at 5 per cent between the two variables. Thus we can associate the increase of the private sector and the recovery of economic growth, although Central and Eastern European countries and Newly Independent States (NIS) are still different in this respect.

*Table 8.1* Share of private sector (SPS) as a determinant of GDP growth

| | 1990 | | 1995 | |
| --- | --- | --- | --- | --- |
| | SPS | Constant | SPS | Constant |
| Coefficient | –23.395 | 97.952 | 30.114 | 86.477 |
| t–student | 1.396 | 47.024 | 4.264 | 27.724 |

Number of observations = 25     n = 25
$R^2 = 0.078$     $R^2 = 0.441$
Adjusted $R^2 = 0.038$     Adjusted $R^2 = 0.417$

*Source*:  UNECE (1996); World Bank (1996a).

Progress in small privatization has been both swift and comprehensive. The outcome of large privatization is less bright. Out of the total number of big state enterprises which had been privatized by mid-1995, according to OECD (1995) estimates, trade sales of state assets and enterprises account for 6204 cases, 13 per cent of large privatization. The privileged method was management–employee buy-outs (MEBO: 43 per cent of all cases), followed by mass privatization (23.5 per cent) and other methods (13 per cent), basically municipalization and restitution.

At a microeconomic level, the first basic performance criterion to be assessed is the effect of privatization on enterprise profitability, otherwise one could not understand why privatization was so urgently needed to get enterprises' balance sheets out of the red. Based on a large sample of industrial enterprises in seven Central and Eastern European countries, a recent assessment (R. Anderson *et al.*, 1997) shows that the Czech Republic and Hungary – where privatization has advanced most – had the highest percentage of profitable firms in 1995, and Romania and Bulgaria the lowest. Between 1992 and 1995, the profitability of firms had improved in almost all countries. In the whole sample, labour productivity growth averaged 7.2 per cent in privatized firms and –0.3 per cent in state-owned firms. However, had the sample been extended to Russian and NIS firms, this optimistic evaluation would have been dampened: recent data show that reported profits were steadily declining in nominal terms in most Russian enterprises (Gavrilenkov, 1998). All the quoted results for Central and Eastern European countries must be qualified somewhat. In 1992, these countries (except Poland) were still deep in the economic slump while, in 1995, economic recovery reached a peak (except in Hungary). Enterprise profitability must have dwindled in Central and Eastern European countries with lower rates of economic growth in 1996–7. Another limitation of the above-mentioned study is that it defines as privatized any firm that has more than 33 per cent of its shares transferred to private owners. This is debatable on the grounds of both corporate control theory (Andreff, 1996a) and the present pattern of share ownership in transition countries. Several privatized enterprises in the sample might well be still under state control, so that observed differences in performance between genuinely privatized and state-controlled firms partly disappear.

Privatization was expected to reduce the so-called 'underground economy' that was blossoming in former centrally planned economies. Such a belief rests on liberal economic thought, urging that excessive administrative rules and regulations were the causes of illegal economic activities. If we wish to find a sign, if there is any, of the quantitative failure of privatization in transition countries, the following evidence is important: on average, the share of the informal economy has increased together with privatization in most transition countries, although the opposite had been expected (EBRD, 1997). Our guess is that something went wrong with some qualitative dimensions of privatization, even though the second stage of privatization, started in 1995–6, was more concerned with unresolved qualitative issues.

## Corporate governance and residual state property: qualitative limitations

The major problem with non standard (that is, non-trade) methods of privatization is the resulting large-scale insider ownership. According to the principal–agent model, insiders would prove ineffective owners, lacking the incentives to restructure privatized enterprises. Actually the great bulk of the privatization literature assumes that, as residual claimants of the firm's net income, shareholders stand last in line for the distribution of gains or losses and, thus, have the appropriate incentives to make accurate discretionary strategic decisions (Easterbrook and Fischel, 1991). In particular, the capacity to monitor managers – and through them other employees – is crucial for share-holders. It is effective if their property rights are not improved by managerial rent seeking (larger offices, retraining sessions on Caribbean seashores) and by managers maximizing take-home gains (higher wages, bonuses). When shareowners are able to monitor and discipline managers, profits are higher than otherwise. Such an assumption underlies numerous assessments of the quality of corporate governance on the basis of firms' profitability. Before raising some doubts (in the next section) against this view, which reduces corporate governance to a monitoring relationship between owners and managers (more generally between outsiders and insiders) we will accept it for a first survey of the qualitative limitations of privatization in transition countries. For the standard model, the more scattered the distribution of corporate capital, the higher the shareholders' information cost for monitoring managers. Thus emerges the principal–agent problem in which the principal possesses less information than the agent (moral hazard) and must design a suitable procedure for inciting managers (agents) to act according to the principal's interests (maximizing profit and asset value). Quite logically, Shleifer and Vishny (1997) argue for block shareholdings, no matter who the blockholders are. It is a great pity that post-communist reformers in transition countries, obsessed by the speed of privatization and despite warnings supporting long-term privatization of profitable enterprises (Andreff, 1994a), selected and implemented those (non-trade) privatization methods which do not guarantee the emergence of hard-core shareholders. The objection against these warnings, that privatization would have taken decades (Schaffer *et al.*, 1998), does not really hold if we have to spend decades on improving ineffective corporate governance structures.

With the principal–agent model in mind, one can range all corporate governance structures along a scale: at the extreme (worst) end there are state-owned enterprises (SOEs); then come privatized firms with insider control (by managers or workers, or both) and finally private and privatized enterprises with a variety of types of outsider control by banks, institutional investors (investment funds, insurance companies, pension funds), domestic private shareholders and foreign investors. There is usually no corporate governance problem in a small firm. For large firms, asset trade privatization is supposed to provide strong corporate governance with either a single majority owner or a 'hard core' of monitoring shareholders. The latter could have only a minority share in the company, but this share must be higher than that of any other coordinated group of shareowners. Such effective owners should restructure the newly privatized firm and adjust it to new market conditions. Nevertheless a qualification of what restructuring means is needed.

Grosfeld and Roland (1995) have distinguished between defensive and strategic restructuring. Defensive restructuring means taking measures that seek to reduce costs and scale down enterprise activity by cutting obsolete production lines, shedding labour or getting rid of non productive assets. Such measures may be part of both deep restructuring and survival-oriented behaviour of managers and workers in privatized firms. Strategic restructuring is based on a thoughtful business strategy developed in response to the need for a profound redeployment of assets and implies the introduction of new products, new processes, new technologies and thus new investment projects. Strategic restructuring requires effective corporate governance by residual claimants. Therefore profitability and productivity are supposed to reflect, through the scope and depth of restructuring, the quality of corporate governance. It follows that a frequently tested hypothesis is whether, as a result of restructuring, privatized firms perform better than SOEs, and outsider-controlled firms outperform insider-controlled firms in terms of profitability and productivity.

Unfortunately, since 1995, we have witnessed a multiplication of studies with non-converging results.[1] As expected by the model, various studies have shown that privatized firms outperform SOEs or improve their performance after privatization. Nevertheless, in many studies, the result is subject to a selection bias: was it privatization which fostered enterprise performance or was it better performance that led enterprises to be selected for privatization? Moreover widespread strategic restructuring had not been observed in transition countries up to 1996 (Carlin and Aghion, 1996). Surveying empirical studies to date leaves us with some robust findings. Foreign owners of former SOEs engage in strategic restructuring by bringing in expertise and capital. On average, private firms are more profitable than SOEs and, in line with the discussed model, this difference reflects more defensive restructuring in SOEs. For privatized firms, the picture is rather blurred, but more studies find insider-controlled firms engaged in survival-oriented adjustment. The most recent mainstream survey (Frydman *et al.*, 1997) shows that, in terms of revenue growth and employment reduction, firms owned by outsiders enjoy an advantage over SOEs, firms in which investment funds are the largest owners perform rather well, firms owned by domestic non-financial companies exhibit a weaker performance, while insider-owned firms shed labour at significantly lower rates than either SOEs[2] or private companies and do even worse on costs and revenues. Employee-owned firms not only behave like SOEs in terms of their revenue performance, but also perform worse than SOEs in terms of labour shedding. This quite orthodox conclusion is a strong case against the effectiveness of privatization programmes that put employees in control. The most annoying problem is the increasing number of conflicting observations in case and sample studies. So many different results may finally mean that the studies did not control enough for country, sector and sample specificities or, more seriously, that something is wrong with the theoretical background of empirical studies, that is, principal–agent analysis.

Among the most striking results that confront the mainstream hypotheses, let us remember the following. Some studies have found that strategic restructuring has taken place in all ownership types, including SOEs and insider-controlled firms. Managers, under the pressure of new market conditions, unexpectedly initiated restructuring, even in not yet privatized SOEs (Pinto and van Wijnbergen, 1995). For the Czech Republic, Capek and Mertlik (1996) have not found significant restructuring in outside-owned firms, except in foreign-owned firms. Coffee (1996) has identified three problems in the Czech corporate structure: the securities market is neither transparent nor liquid, cross-ownership between banks obscures the governance structure of related investment funds, and the state still holds significant blocks of shares in the largest enterprises and banks. Another study (Lizal *et al.*, 1997) has established that, contrary to the most common picture of the Czech method (privatization first, restructuring thereafter), enterprise performance is favoured by pre-privatization break-ups of SOEs in 1990. Afterwards, it was easier to include better performing and smaller units in privatization programmes. On the other hand, many of the privatized firms continued receiving credits for non-performing projects, and state-owned limited liability companies dominated all domestic private firms in terms of the investment–production ratio (Lizal and Svejnar, 1998).

A survey of 200 Polish manufacturing enterprises has found that firms privatized to workers were relatively well performing and capable of adjusting more flexibly because worker ownership might reduce worker–manager conflicts (Earle and Estrin, 1996). Nivet (1997) finds that Polish employee-owned firms are among the best performers for the ratio of costs to revenues and profitability. However this result is doubtful because workers are more likely to have bought profitable enterprises (the selection bias again). A recent study, controlling for the selection bias (Earle and Estrin, 1997) shows that Russian firms privatized to managers have restructured more and performed better compared, not only to SOEs, but also to firms with dominant worker ownership.

We will not discuss the numerous interpretations of these conflicting results any further. The qualitative picture of corporate governance is less bright than the quantitative outcome of privatization. The relationship postulated by the principal–agent model between corporate governance and restructuring (profitability, productivity) is probably too restrictive and, in the real world, this relationship is affected by the macroeconomic development (see the previous section); moreover the relationship is not stable owing to frequent changes in the ownership of each individual corporation (sales of shares, takeovers, acquisitions) and, finally, the same agent may unpredictably[3] modify his or her economic behaviour depending on macro and micro circumstances, including the threat of a takeover, the election of new members to the enterprise boards, the emergence of a financial industrial group, loopholes in the corporation law and so on (a non-exhaustive list of unheeded factors in the principal–agent model). More or less regular bonuses, premiums, perks and bribes can link insiders to outsiders, especially in not yet fully-fledged institutions, in a way unpredictable by the theoretical model, so that profitability remains a meaningless variable, not to speak of profit distortions under imperfect competition. A lower profit may reflect the existence of a coalition between outsiders and insiders, which is fairly frequent in the transition countries, involved in an efficient strategy of hiding profit for tax evasion purposes.

Corporate governance issues are even more tricky in the case of mass privatization methods. In the Czech Republic, voucher privatization was assumed to trigger enterprise restructuring by new private owners, to be more transparent and fairer than asset trade, and to gain popular support for privatization and for the government in the next elections. In 1998, the Klaus government was gone, financial non-transparency and embezzlements linked to privatization were among the determinants of its fall, and restructuring does not seem to have been boosted any more than in other transition countries. On the other hand, some expected shortcomings of the Czech method have actually not materialized: even though voucher auctions had been a rather daunting administrative or even 'central planning' (Andreff, 1994b) task, the emergence of investment funds has prevented a wide dispersion of ownership and weak corporate governance structures. Studies of Czech enterprises show that, in many firms, one investment fund holds 20 per cent of the shares, and in other privatized firms two to four investment funds together hold a controlling minority, sometimes a majority of shares. The Czech funds probably concentrate a sufficient share in many privatized firms to control their management and strategy and ensure effective corporate governance. The problem is to know who controls the controllers. In particular, the system of cross-ownership among state-owned banks and investment funds (Mertlik, 1996) that has emerged leaves the management of these institutions insulated from external control, and this can explain why restructuring is often considered to be lagging behind in the Czech Republic.

In the case of Russia and most NIS, mass privatization has turned into a mass asset sale to insiders, both incumbent managers and employees, while investment funds have played only a minor role. The entrenchment of incumbent managers, survival strategies and defensive restructuring have characterized the first stage of mass (non-monetary or free) privatization. Where the managers were either competent or in a position to bargain on their own terms, ownership went from insiders to outsiders. But there are two problems. One is the emergence of coalitions of managers and outside owners (see next section). Another is the illegal, if not corrupt or criminal, means of transferring shares to outsiders. In

Russia, numerous typical violations of (small) shareholders' rights have blossomed during the second stage of privatization (Blasi and Shleifer, 1996), as well as financial industrial groups (FIGs: Freinkman, 1995). The latter were generally built up by new private banks buying shares of industrial enterprises, but some FIGs resulted from the transformation of former ministerial branches or associations into joint stock companies which had diversified into finance and trade. All FIGs are now challenging the insider ownership in Russian industry. Even though they solve, to some extent, the corporate governance problem, FIGs reconcentrate monopoly powers and industrial structures that prevailed under central planning.

A final qualitative limitation of privatization in transition countries is the residual state property that results from non-standard privatization methods and joint ventures with private or foreign capital, leaving the state with a share in the firm (Mihályi, 1996b). The least extensive residual state property is due to the state keeping a 'golden share' in the stock of a privatized enterprise. The most extensive occurs with public enterprises that the state is not able to sell or give away at the moment, so that they remain in full (or majority) state ownership. More often we observe a midway situation: either the state is willing to withdraw from shareholding but is finally stuck with a minority share, or the state keeps a blocking stake in order to discourage an unwanted foreign takeover. Then privatization is not completed because of an illiquid capital market or is postponed until the next political (governmental) change.

Residual state shareholdings may become an obstacle to effective corporate governance. When the state adopts 'hands off' management of non-strategic enterprises, private owners do not commit themselves to governance because they are waiting for full state divestiture. When the state remains the only or a majority owner in strategic enterprises, the situation is even worse and leaves room for incumbent managers to behave as stakeholders. The problem is usually due to the behaviour of the state representatives on the board of directors or the supervisory board. They are hardly committed, or even encouraged by the state (or some state body), to play an active role in enterprise management and, when they are, they could even vote against the decisions suggested by the representatives of private owners (for investment instead of dividend payouts, against increases of foreign capital in total stock). Furthermore the state representatives on corporation boards are often civil servants, academics or teachers – not professional experts in management, accounting, finance, marketing business law, skills which are thus still rather rare in transition countries. After sitting for some time on boards, they may even turn into an autonomous category of stakeholders, and then start lobbying from one board to the other, as described for interlocking directorates in the West (Dooley, 1969). One basic purpose is to maintain the status quo (profitable to them) to the detriment of further privatization.

On the other hand, when the state keeps a share in the stock of strategic enterprises, a big issue appears to be the possible constraints thus imposed on enterprise management. These constraints are usually derived more from macroeconomic and social policies (sustaining economic growth, cutting prices, hiring or not firing excess manpower) than from microeconomic criteria of efficient management, adjustment and restructuring. The risk here is one of inertia, favouring the survival behaviour of insiders and their pressures for getting state subsidies and bail-outs. Such a risk may delay further privatization and the transition countries might well be stuck with residual state ownership for a while. The French story shows that the privatization of management – with the government imposing profit-seeking and market-oriented behaviour on managers under the threat of being fired – is the best springboard for a further transfer of the resultant profitable state assets to private owners (Andreff, 1992).

## Corporate governance and beyond

'When "privatisation" became the word of the day in Eastern Europe, most policy makers and external observers made a number of rather simplistic assumptions which have since become increasingly hard to maintain [and] assumptions underlying the initial approach became increasingly inadequate' (Frydman and Rapaczynski, 1994, p. 168). This statement obviously applies to the principal–agent model, the mainstream approach that had mushroomed following the influential articles by Jensen and Meckling (1976) and Fama and Jensen (1983). In giving it up, we are not left without alternative or, better, complementary analyses of who makes decisions in privatized corporations in transition countries. First, there is the theory of corporate control that prevailed after the work of Berle and Means (1932) and before the emergence of the agency costs analysis. Second, we can dwell upon the literature on coalitions within economic organizations and, third, on a recent renewal in the theory of corporate governance. To some extent, an attempt to initiate a new analysis is present in the recent work by Earle and Estrin (1997). The authors argue that the peculiarities of ownership structures in Russia require a 'reconsideration of conceptual approaches to the analysis of corporate ownership, control and behaviour' (ibid., p. 4). Ownership structures are quite peculiar in all transition countries when compared to Western market economies. As rightly emphasized by Earle and Estrin, what matters is not only the concentration of ownership, but also the identity of owners. Let us go further and cross the Rubicon: who are the new owners and what is their number of seats in different corporate boards? Do they behave as shameless tycoons? How many shares do they personally own, through legal or illegal manoeuvres? Do they belong to alliances or interest groups? Such information, if available, can be analysed with tools which were up to date in the West some time ago.

The theory of corporate control developed either as a reaction against the idea of managerial capitalism (Marris, 1964) or as a consequence of empirical studies of corporate control (Kotz, 1978). It contended that governance had not become utterly independent from ownership in corporations operating in Western market economies, a fact that was exemplified by existing 'hard cores' of monitoring shareholders, cross-shareholding among several corporations and 'locked up' companies; the latter are meant to be corporations whose capital is owned by their own affiliates in a significant (majority) proportion and which consequently cannot be taken over by raiders. The whole issue was based on distinguishing majority and minority control of shares. The basic hypothesis was that corporate control structures are not static or stable forever, and that they are transforming as a result of mergers, acquisitions, tenders and proxy fights over electing the firm's boards. Thus the financial capital structure is interlocking a number of industrial firms and banks, through cross-shareholdings, into so-called 'FIGs' with a 'mother company' (a bank or a non-financial firm) at its core. This is a valuable approach for transition countries today.

After mass privatization in Russia, various interest groups, gathered around a new tycoon and/or a handful of managers, and often with the cooperation of one bank, started collecting privatization certificates or shares. The result is both an increasing weight of outsiders in the new emerging FIGs and the coordination of strategies among the firms linked by cross-shareholding. Then, after some delay, the Russian government began to sell its remaining shares in some most prominent enterprises through a 'loans-for-shares' scheme launched in 1995. Tenders and auctions for these shares became a battleground between rival FIGs leading to changing boundaries between their networks of cross-ownership. Since 1995, acquisitions and takeovers have developed in Russia. Just to mention a few recent examples, Oneximbank took over Norilsk Nickel and Sviazinvest by buying shares through monetary privatization, Yukos and Sibneft merged into Yuksi and, as regards foreign firms, ARCO acquired 10 per cent of Lukoil's capital, BP took a 10 per cent share in Sidanco and Elf-Aquitaine bought 5 per cent of Yuksi's stock equity.

We now have to study the networks of these financial stakes linking firms and banks together in order to detect which interest group, possibly associating various outsiders, or outsiders with insiders, controls each FIG. With a FIG structure, the assumed relationship between profitability and the nature (insider/outsider) of corporate governance may well be disrupted in many cases. Corporate governance is not stable and moves with mergers, takeovers, redistribution of shares and possible new alliances or coalitions between insiders and outsiders. The interest groups backing the FIGs are going beyond the theoretical cleavage between outsider and insider governance, so that it is no longer realistic to assume that outsiders (and which group among them?) must have, as residual claimants, the last say on firm's boards.

When one deals with economic situations that fall between market and hierarchy, namely the observed resilient networks of managers in many transition countries and the newly emerging FIGs, a glance at the literature on interlocking directorates is a must. The market relationships between the interlocked firms are not nullified, yet interlocks impose some hierarchy (Pennings, 1980). Multiple interlocks usually indicate a common interest group governing, controlling or, at least, coordinating the strategies among the interlocked firms. The basic idea underlying interlocking directorates is that corporate control cannot be studied for a firm in isolation, contrarily to what is done in principal–agent analysis. A well-established result based on graph theory is that in Western market economies, interlocked firms are clustered around 'linkers' or 'big linkers', that is, managers or owners who simultaneously belong to the boards of several different firms and who increasingly link firms of different origins and sectors; some banks are usually interlocked in each cluster (Fennema, 1982, Koenig and Gogel, 1981).

Could we expect some interesting results from a similar approach applied to firms in transition countries? Let us consider Russia, for example. It would be interesting to check whether industrial firms and banks are connected to FIGs through interlocking directorates. The problem is that finding interlocking directorates requires information as published (in the West) by *Who's Who, Kompass, Moody's, Fortune Directories* and so on. Such information is not yet fully available in the transition countries. However a first step would consist in examining in how many enterprise boards some business high-flyers such as Yevgeny Ananiev (MAPO Bank), Piotr Aven (Alfa), Boris Berezovsky (LogoVaz), Mikhaïl Fridman (Alfa, Sidanco), Vladimir Gusinsky (Most Bank), Mikhaïl Khodorkovski (Menatep, Yuksi), Vladimir Potanin (Oneximbank), Alexandr Smolenski (SBS-Agro), Rem Viakhirev (Gazprom) and Vladimir Vinogradov (Inkombank) have a seat. Detecting clusters of firms through interlocking directorates might also be helpful in the case of recombinant property in Hungary (Stark, 1996a, 1996b) or for the study of links and alliances between the directors of Czech enterprises (McDermott, 1997) that survived the privatization process.

Another case in point is the exercise of residual state property rights in partially privatized enterprises, particularly in the transition countries where the same state representative can be appointed to the boards of more than one enterprise. A first attempt at elaborating on this kind of analysis is already provided in recent research on enterprise–state relationships following mass privatization in Mongolia (J. Anderson *et al.*, 1997). The authors present data on board membership in order to detect how many representatives sit on the boards of privatized corporations, and conclude that the state is not a disinterested owner. Indeed 63.7 per cent of Mongolian enterprises have some state representation on one or both of the board of representatives and the auditing board. In order to reinforce another conclusion of this research, namely that 'the picture that emerges is of a cohesive public sector that has arisen after the privatization process' (ibid., p. 83) due to state representation on firms' boards, further research may be suggested: it should consist in checking whether we can find among state representatives some 'linkers' or 'big linkers' who link the boards of different firms.

The theory of economic organization focuses on coalitions. Among the participants in a firm, some subsets or groups can coalesce around a common target. At any moment, some coalition dominates the enterprise but can be removed by another in the making. The type of coalition in power and contingencies of the economic environment determine the kind of target which must reach a satisfying level in the firm: efficiency, survival, autonomy, growth, profit, asset value and so on (Mintzberg, 1983). The emergence of a new dominating coalition within the enterprise can obviously change the prevailing target. Even though survival usually characterizes insider coalitions and profit making outsider coalitions, the real picture in a corporation is often more blurred –

all the more so when managers are shareowners (and vice versa), when employees own shares, when there is discord within the management team or the corporate boards or (pretty often) alliances between some managers and core shareholders. Other elements can stabilize a coalition, according to Mintzberg: enterprise ideology, resource slack and the coordinating role of the chief executive officer. Once all these factors are taken into account, the objectives of insiders and outsiders might well overlap in many respects and in many firms. Less simplistic than the distinction between the profit-seeking behaviour of residual claimants as opposed to the rent-seeking behaviour of managers, this seemingly old-fashioned analysis is of peculiar interest in a nascent market capitalism such as in today's transition countries.

An internal coalition can of course encompass shareholders as well as stakeholders; in fact the latter are also, to some extent, shareholders, if we consider that a firm needs both finance capital and human capital to function, and thus both are residual claimants, and must be rewarded as such out of the firm's revenue. In a nutshell, this is the core argument of an attempt to renew the analysis of corporate governance (Blair, 1995). To Blair, most Western modern corporations do not fit the Easterbrook–Fischel model of corporate governance and the underlying principal–agent analysis, because in practice shareholders are rarely the only residual claimants. Residual claimants occur whenever there are parties other than shareholders who make investments specific to a given corporation, such as employees with specialized knowledge or skills. If assets such as finance capital and human capital are dependent on each other, then by definition neither has much value without the other. Neither has a more legitimate claim for residual revenue than the other. Thus the mainstream model fails. The firm (that is, shareholders) must share with employees some of the economic rents (or quasi-rents) from their common enterprise. This is because specific human capital is extremely important to the firm and thus worth being paid extra, of course out of the economic surplus generated by the firm. Therefore the emphasis of the mainstream model on the potential conflict between shareholders and managers is wrong. It is the stakeholder–management nexus that is important, whoever the stakeholders (managers, employees, shareholders) are. The modern corporations should be run in the interests of all the stakeholders, rather than just for the shareholders. In the same vein, Nuti (1995) argues that, in employee-owned privatized enterprises, each employee should own a share in the stock equity of the same value as his or her share in the total wage bill. If the wage is assumed to reward specific skills and training, then each employee will share in the residual revenue in proportion to his or her stake among all stakeholders.

A last issue is the legal or illegal behaviour of stakeholders and shareowners in the transition countries. Embezzlements, pressures on small shareholders, law violations, exploitation of legal loopholes and so on are partly a legacy of the informational cheating inherited from the former system (Andreff, 1996b). Such distortions call into question the legitimacy of ownership and of sharing the residual revenue with (or among) economic criminals. Beyond the moral concern, it is an issue of economic efficiency. Organized crime, illegal transactions and protection rackets impose economic costs on the transition countries (the more easterly, the higher the cost) in the form of a distorted resource allocation, a heavy 'private tax' burden, limited competition and capital flight abroad. Corruption also threatens the development of a market economy. The average corruption score, obtained in the World Bank survey of 3600 entrepreneurs in 69 countries, is higher for the transition countries than in any other region of the world (EBRD, 1997). In many transition countries, in particular in NIS, it seems that, after the collapse of the planned economy, managers continue to develop networks of personal relationships with government officials and with other firms (Rizopoulos, 1997). Corruption is often the fuel for such networks. This obviously means that managers involved in corrupt networks either are not under the control of supposedly honest owners or collude with new shameless or somewhat criminal tycoons, in Russia and points east. Privatization is then turned into its opposite, business corruption, which is not a step ahead on the path to a true market economy. Being the more dangerous challenge for the future of NIS, illegal economic behaviour should not remain uncriticized and unrepressed; only a stronger state could crack down on economic criminals with a chance of success (Andreff, 1998). After the first stage of transition, when prominent neoliberal assertions associated state minimalism with market efficiency, closer analyses now re-evaluate the role of the state in a market economy, and influential economists like Stern, Stiglitz or Malinvaud (Malinvaud and Sabot (eds.), 1997; Malinvaud *et al.* (eds.) 1998) emphasize the importance of cooperation and partnership between public and private activities.

## Conclusion: where has privatization gone?

'Rather than an unquestioned boon, privatization thus becomes an ambiguous, open-ended process that might lead to bad as well as good consequences' (Frydman and Rapaczynski, 1994, p. 176). Indeed the overall picture of privatization also contains a lot of deviations from the initial objectives. Many of these distortions reflect some kind of path-dependence in the privatization process. Some readers will regard these concluding remarks as a piece of economic semantics. Transferring assets out of state hands is defined as privatization. What about this label when ownership falls into the hands of employees? Of managers? Of municipalities? Or when it partly remains in state ownership? In the old times, we would have concluded that the privatization process in transition countries has resulted in some privatization as well as some socialization and municipalization of ownership, in mixed property and managerialism. In the first years of transition, it was probably taboo to put it this way. The unveiled economic reality is that transition countries have got from the privatization process a 'motley crew' of ownership structures.

## Notes

1. The literature on enterprise performance and restructuring has become considerable. Our comments are primarily based on surveys and studies with a wide coverage, namely R. Anderson *et al.* (1997), Barberis *et al.* (1996), Carlin *et al.* (1995), Commander *et al.* (1996), Grosfeld and Nivet (1997) and Lastovicka *et al.* (1995), as well as Wendy Carlin's contribution to this volume and the references quoted further in the text.
2. The two last mentioned findings are less mainstream than expected by the authors.
3. Within the strict model of principal–agent relationships.

# 9
# Corporate Governance during and after Privatization: the Lessons from Hungary

*Péter Mihályi*

## Introduction[1]

This chapter traces the evolution of enterprise governance over the past 10 years. Using the language of Stark (1992, 1996b) we reject the 'starting from scratch' approach in which privatization is portrayed as a new world being built on the ruins of communism. For us transformation resembles more a *bricolage* of rebuilding with the ruins. Instead of thinking about organizational innovation only as a replacement, we see reconfigurations and rearrangements of existing institutional elements. Thus the analysis below takes as its point of departure that the changes in enterprise governance – as well as in privatization and transition in a broader sense – are marked by path dependence.

The five sections of the chapter will give the reader a historical perspective pertaining to the pre-privatization debates (first two sections), the privatization process itself and its impact on both the privatized and not-yet-privatized state-owned enterprises (remaining sections).

## The controversial assessment of SOE managers prior to 1990

After 1956, many Hungarian economists earned fame with empirical studies. This research led to the accumulation of facts and thoughts about the SOEs in general, but above all about the management of the SOEs. With hindsight, it is clear that these results were biased in favour of the management. SOE managers appeared to be more progressive than the state party bureaucrats. In conflicts the economics profession tended to support the managers against planners, ministers and politicians.

Though the overall perception of the SOE management was positive, dissenting voices were also heard. Authors like Bauer (1976), Sárközy

(1986), Bod and Hall (1992), Csillag and Szalai (1985), Szalai (1982, 1990) and others looked at managers with a certain ambiguity. While acknowledging the management's right to fight against the irrationalities of central planning, they discovered in the managers' behaviour a dangerous tendency to maximize managerial autonomy: empire building, managerial opportunism, self-dealing and shirking. In the same way, as managers resisted the control of the state party bureaucracy, they were reluctant to accept the control of market institutions. As Bod (1988, p. 839) put it, 'slower expansion or forgone profits weighed much less for them than the threat that a creditor bank or a supporting state body would be able to see the cards in their hands'.

Among the influential minds only Kornai (1990) turned sharply against the management: 'Those who spend state funds cannot claim the same rights as those who have to rely on their own sources' (ibid., p. 68). Kornai argued, not for more, but for fewer control rights for SOE managers.

## Suggested 'privatization' models prior to 1989

In the section head above, the word 'privatization' was put between inverted commas because, prior to 1989, privatization per se was never seriously contemplated, either in Hungary or elsewhere. But the reform proposals themselves were suitable for privatization alternatives, when the political situation was ripe.[2]

The leasing model is associated with Tibor Liska's life work, stretching from the mid-1950s to 1989 (Liska, 1988). In 1966, he proposed leasing-type contracts between individual entrepreneurs, on the one hand, and the state, on the other. He planned to build this relationship on a periodically recurring auction process, where the incumbent lessee could always be removed, if somebody else offered a better deal for the state. The economics profession knew Liska's views, but he remained marginalized. Although incompletely, Liska's ideas were finally turned into reality in the late 1970s, when shops, cafes and restaurants were leased to private entrepreneurs. By 1988, about 11 per cent of the shops and 44 per cent of restaurants operated in such schemes.

The roots of the holding model go back to the preparatory discussions of the 1968 reform (Hoch, 1991). Already in 1968, written – though not published – proposals were made to create state-owned holding corporations in which a free flow of capital could have been allowed between companies, as long as both belonged to the same holding. A few years later, the same suggestion surfaced in a seminal article by Tardos (1972). His idea was to create a small number of profit-maximizing financial institutions, as a personification of state ownership. In this model, the existing SOEs would have been randomly distributed among the holdings.

Self-management, resembling the Yugoslav model, was also advocated. But even its advocates (Bauer, 1984) viewed it with great reservations. Nonetheless the favourable experiences of the Hungarian agricultural cooperatives suggested that, if industrial SOE employees were allowed to elect their managers, the firms would improve their performance in the same way as happened in the agricultural sector between 1965 and 1975. To some extent, this proposition was realized as part of the 1984–85 enterprise reform, when most SOEs got an elected board-type leadership, the Enterprise Council.

The cross-ownership model was the brainchild of Matolcsy (1990). Chiefly banks were identified as good candidates for cross-ownership, but some role was also envisaged for local authorities, pension funds and so on. The advantage of this model was seen in helping to create a market for capital, where ownership rights and management rights are separated. In 1988, the two-tier banking system came into being when departments of the central bank were turned into commercial banking corporations. The new banks were burdened with bad loans, thus a debt–equity swap was a tempting 'quick-fix' solution. With the swap the bankers achieved two objectives. First, they wiped clean the balance sheets in a technical sense; second, they gained a dispersed ownership structure. Prior to the swap, the banks were controlled by the state as a founder and a 100 per cent owner. After the swap, the banks were owned by a multitude of stakeholders which were individually all dependent on the management of the banks themselves.[3]

With hindsight, it seems fortunate that thorough theoretical discussions on various ownership models had been already held prior to 1989. When history put privatization on the agenda, the economics profession was prepared. This was important, since the protagonists of the academic debates soon went into politics or joined the government machinery.

It was easy to identify the similarities between the Liska model and the voucher method of mass privatization. Both concepts assume that everybody can become an entrepreneur, thus it is possible and desirable to turn a large segment of the population into capitalist owners without a track record and 'up-front' payment. Since the Liska proposal had been widely discussed earlier, the flaws of the voucher proposal were already known: in every society, entrepreneurship is a rare talent (Schumpeter,

1943), therefore government decision makers should not transfer assets to anyone by simply assuming that the candidate will be a good owner. Another shortcoming of the voucher proposal is the weakness of the Liska model: if assets are transferred to a new owner gratis, this will encourage rent seeking through reselling to a third party.

The holding model of the 1970s closely resembled the investment fund model advocated by the Polish large privatization programme. Hungarian economists disliked it and argued that the state-created holdings would decrease rather than increase the transparency of market relations. Once the possibility of profit redistribution is allowed, neither the shareholders nor stakeholders – banks, clients, potential investors, state supervision and so on – will be able to see through the smokescreen generated by the holding's management. Thus it was feared that the holdings would become a convenient channel for the political parties to intervene.[4] Furthermore the question of legitimacy was raised. As Soós (1990) pointed out convincingly, there was a paradox here. If the holding management is not independent, that is bad economics; if the managers are truly independent, that is unfair. How can they enjoy the freedom of action equal to the freedom of an owner, if they are nominees, just like any government bureaucrat?

Similar arguments were raised against the cross-ownership model. Among other worries, Mihályi (1989) recalled the weaknesses of the German ownership model. Though the (West) German economy was much envied, warning shots were fired by saying that cross-ownership between banks and large industrial conglomerates was risky, especially if a precise and strong legal system was not present to minimize abuse.

## Privatization and the new owners

### Strategic investors

From the outset, the Hungarian privatization policy has been focused on strategic investors[5] for large and medium-size SOEs. The most frequently applied divestment method, public tenders, did precisely this. Usually majority ownership was offered on these tenders, but there were important exceptions as well.

Speaking about foreigners, the term needs to be qualified. For well-known historical reasons, Hungary had a fairly large diaspora living abroad. Interestingly several generations are represented in the diaspora: pre-1945 émigrés, refugees of 1956, young 'adventurers' escaping from Hungary during the 1970s, and so on. After 1990, these people returned in large numbers, either as self-made businessmen or as resident representatives of foreign companies. Because of the generosity of the citizenship law, it is almost meaningless to make a division between these Hungarians and foreigners still without a Hungarian passport. In fact, dual citizenship was one of the tricks people used to become rich: depending on the situation, they showed the passport which promised more favourable treatment.

### Financial investors and the role of capital markets

At the beginning of privatization, financial investors[6] were expected to play a major role in the process. The Budapest Stock Exchange was reopened in June 1990 in great haste in order to prepare the ground for such deals. However the plans to use initial public offerings (IPOs) as the main avenue for sell-offs did not materialize. Until 1995, the stock exchange meant only a colourful spot on the privatization palette.

After the 1994 elections, the situation changed. Since the new government was determined to speed up the sell-offs of very large SOEs, managers turned their eyes toward the stock exchange. They understood two things: first, that dispersed ownership leaves a lot of power in their hands, certainly more than a strategic investor would do; second, they discovered an arbitrage possibility. The trick was to buy shares of their own company at a discount and to resell to the company immediately at the market price.

From 1990, lawmakers permitted the different state asset management agencies (SAMAs)[7] to sell 5–15 per cent of the equity in a divested company to employees of the company at a 50 per cent discount. Obviously the idea was to make the staff interested in privatization. Legally speaking, this was a possibility only. If the investor insisted on acquiring 100 per cent of the shares, the SAMAs were not obliged to sell shares to the employees. Gradually, however, the possibility has become an informal 'acquired right' of the staff. Since about 1995, it has also become accepted that managers of the SOE are entitled to a larger amount of shares than ordinary employees. In 1996–7, when commercial banks were privatized, some managers obtained much larger discounts and a much larger number of shares than the law permitted. With such incentives, managers stopped opposing privatization and worked chiefly on pushing down the issue price.[8]

For understandable reasons, every major sell-off reopened the discussion about the merits and flaws of the two privatization strategies: whom to choose, one strategic investor or several financial investors? As experience showed, the difference between the two methods is huge (Table 9.1).

*Table* 9.1   Comparison of two privatization strategies

|  | Strategic investor | Financial investor |
| --- | --- | --- |
| Equally suitable for large and small companies | Yes | No |
| Additional cash flow, capital increase | Yes | Yes |
| Opening up of additional markets | Yes | No |
| Independence from the influence of Hungarian party politics | Yes. Western managers at place cannot be easily influenced | No. There are several ways to influence the local Hungarian management |
| Higher privatization revenue | Yes. Strategic investors are ready to pay a 'future-oriented' price | No. Financial investors buy shares at a price, which allows them to sell within 24 hours – if needed |
| Helps the enhancement of capital markets | No | Yes |
| Potential conflicts between the management and the new owners | Yes. The new owners are present | No. The new owners never present themselves. In worst case they vote with their feet |
| Potential danger of transfer pricing | Yes | No |
| Neutral from sequencing point of view | After a strategic investor, financial investors are welcome | After financial investors, strategic investors seldom appear |
| Privatization can be phased in in several tranches with rising revenues | No. Once the strategic investor controls the firm, he cannot be forced to pay more for the second equity package | Yes. If the general mood is favourable at the stock exchange, prices of later trenches can easily go up |
| Helps to integrate Hungary into the NATO and EU | Yes | No |
| Loss of national sovereignty | Yes | No |

## What happened to cross-ownership?

As noted earlier, cross-ownership appeared to be a widespread phenomenon around 1990–91. The five large commercial banks had significant blocks in industrial firms, while these very same firms became coowners of the banks. Though it was not a deliberate government policy, for three independent reasons, the ownership links between banks and SOEs were cut drastically after 1992. By 1996, cross-ownership had become the rare exception in both the state and the private sectors.

- As the financial stability of many SOEs shattered, the position of their creditors – the banks – shattered as well. By 1992–3, the five large state-owned commercial banks were on the verge of bankruptcy. The government had to recapitalize them. In this way the Ministry of Finance became 80–90 per cent owner of such banks. Those industrial companies which had held previously large equity positions lost their investments.
- The SAMAs found cross-ownership links between banks and SOEs increasingly inconvenient. Since minority shares were traded on the over-the-counter markets (OTC) at considerable discounts, there was a threat that the privatization sell-off price would be negatively influenced by the OTC price. The corporatization of banks and the SOEs was a good opportunity to 'collect' the outstanding shares. If it was too late to confiscate, the SAMAs bought the shares from the banks or the industrial companies at going market prices.
- After 1991, the new banking and accounting laws (and their amendments) introduced stricter prudential rules. Through the burden of provisions, it became costly for banks to hold equity in financially unstable companies. By 1996, banks understood that direct participation in industrial companies was a low-profit, high-risk business.

## Quasi-owners

From the begining, there was a strong political commitment to create a diversified ownership structure in which local governments, the social security funds, employees and private households would play some role. Though it was never formalized in a theoretical model, let alone in any act of legislation, the idea was to forge such coalitions within all major companies through multi-stage privatization (Table 9.2). To promote this objective, Parliament has built tax concessions and procedural privileges into the new laws.

*Table 9.2*  The idealistic model of multi-stage privatization

| Stages | Type of investor | Expected results |
|---|---|---|
| 1 | A single strategic investor (foreign or Hungarian, depending on the size of the firm) | 'Real' ownership control, new technology, new markets, PR and marketing skills; privatization revenue |
| 2 | Financial investors (e.g. multilateral agencies, banks, pension funds, municipalities) | Privatization revenue plus capital increase; strict financial control over the strategic investor |
| 3 | Small investors (households, compensation coupon holders, individual speculators) | Privatization revenue plus capital increase; public control over the companies; 'people's capitalism' |

First, the country's more than 3000 municipalities had four different titles to acquire company shares in the privatization process.

(1) In all corporatized SOEs, municipalities were entitled to receive a certain percentage of the newly issued shares as compensation for the land upon which the company was built.

(2) The 1990 Act on Municipalities guaranteed that in those enterprises where the business activity was chiefly locally oriented service – local public transport, water management, funeral services, wholesale pharmaceutical distributors and so on – the local self-government bodies would become 100 per cent owners.

(3) Since the above-mentioned Act failed to define precisely the term 'locally oriented service', a sharp controversy rose between the SAMAs and the municipalities about the regional electricity and gas distribution companies. After long – and still not fully resolved – constitutional disputes, the SAMAs gave a certain percentage of the gas and electricity company shares to approximately 600 municipalities.[9]

(4) One of the particularities of the Hungarian privatization is the use of compensation coupons. These coupons were distributed among citizens who suffered personal or material injuries of certain kind, under fascist and communist rule. In proportion to these damages, a fixed number of coupons (or vouchers) were given to them. The coupons were accepted as a means of payment by the municipalities if the owner of the coupon was a tenant in a municipality-owned apartment and wished to buy the apartment. Though this was only one of the options in the usage of the coupons, munici-

palities have accumulated large stocks of coupons. There were two markets for these coupons. The municipalities could sell them for cash on the secondary market, or use them as a means of payment in purchasing company shares from the SAMAs. In order to encourage the second option, the SAMAs were ordered to give several kind of preferences to the municipalities at the tenders.

Second, the social security funds (health and pensions) were created in 1991 by an Act of Parliament. Since the government was short of cash and had no intention to raise contributions, the funds started operation in an undercapitalized state. To compensate this, Parliament committed company assets worth HUF 300bn from the SAMAs' portfolio. In reality, this transfer process was postponed year after year. Finally, in 1996, about a fifth of the promised amount (HUF 65bn) was transferred. This meant that the funds acquired minority blocks in about 40 privatized companies.

Third, employees and managers of former SOEs had four major ways to acquire stakes in privatized companies.

(1) As early as 1988, SOEs had the right to issue quasi-shares (non-voting fixed income papers) to their employees at the expense of profits. This door remained open until 1993, so that the SAMAs were forced to convert the quasi-shares to normal shares once the company was corporatized.

(2) The 1989 Transformation Act created an obligation for the SAMAs to finance employee ownership from the privatization receipts. After a company was sold, the SAMAs were obliged to return 20 per cent of the sales price to the company for financing the issuance of employee shares.

(3) The successive privatization laws prescribed that, in the course of corporatization and/or privatization, employees may be given 5–15 per cent of the company shares at considerable discounts. Depending on the size of the company this meant different absolute amounts, therefore a second limitation was built into the laws: as a general rule, employees were entitled to buy shares up to the level of their annual salaries.

(4) Employees and managers had the right to acquire 100 per cent ownership in SMEs through employee stock ownership plans (ESOP).

Finally, ordinary citizens and individual compensation coupon holders – or 'small investors' as the Hungarian privatization jargon calls them – have also been granted preferences. In the case of an IPO, 3–5 per cent of the shares were set aside. Between 1993 and 1997, there were more than 60 transactions where compensation coupon holders were entitled to swap their coupons for a predetermined number of company shares (for example, two coupons for one share).

As the reader will have guessed, it was impossible to accommodate all these ownership ambitions simultaneously. To make things worse, these claims were often in direct conflict with the interests of the strategic investors. The SAMAs as sellers also became hostile to these preferential ownership forms. They were revenue maximizers; thus for them the dissatisfaction of the investors was equal to forgone revenue.

Soon a modus vivendi was found. The above-listed quasi-owners realized that their acquired rights – the discounts, the tax concessions and the procedural privileges – could be translated into an arbitrage opportunity. Gradually, this practice became so widespread that the arbitrage was implicitly built into the first stage of the privatization transaction. Deals had multiple tranche structures, where different classes of shares were issued to different owners, but a couple of days/weeks/months later these shares were purchased by the strategic owner at a pre-negotiated price.

Needless to say, such complicated deals are time consuming and carry high transaction costs that go into the pocket of investment bankers, advisers, law firms and so on. This is a net loss for taxpayers. Another point worth mentioning is the lack of transparency. In the case of major deals, the structure was so complicated that the educated newspaper reader could hardly follow it. From a corporate governance point of view, however, the involvement of these groups of quasi-owners has proved to be almost harmless, thanks to their early exits. Although, in some cases, the municipalities did retain their stakes, their role in corporate governance was usually limited to discussing such matters as where bicycles should be kept.[10]

## The behaviour of SOEs after 1990

This section provides an overview of the changes in the behaviour of those SOEs, which – for any reason – remained fully, or partly, under state tutelage for some period between 1990 and 1998. The collapse of Soviet-type socialism as a political system brought many changes in the life of SOEs, even if no ownership change took place. The nature of these changes is complex and contradictory. We shall attempt to describe and assess them in three analytical dimensions. First, it will be shown that some changes brought improvement for all SOEs; a second group of developments had a mixed impact – some firms gained, other suffered; and a third batch of changes were detrimental for all state owned firms. Let us consider these three dimensions in turn.

**Positive developments**

Prior to 1990, Hungary was not only a socialist country with predominant state ownership, but it was part of the Soviet world empire. Socialist ownership and adherence to the Soviet political system were two inseparable aspects of the same historical situation. With the collapse of communism, the situation changed. Many features of the former regime disappeared almost overnight, while property relations remained unchanged for years. With the collapse of the communist system, there was no longer any need for

- conducting an industrial policy with a strong defence bias,
- keeping SOE managers and the population at large under police surveillance,
- keeping up artificially close trade relations with the Soviet Union and other members of the Council for Mutual Economic Assistance (CMEA),
- controlling imports from the West,
- securing full employment at the expense of efficiency, and
- suppressing wage differentials.

The disappearance of employment, wage and import control rules had far-reaching consequences. On the one hand, the efficiency of production shot up immediately as surplus labour was shed and performing employees were better paid. The liberalization of imports meant a better supply of inputs, although the appearance of new competitors made the life of many Hungarian firms very difficult. On the other hand, trade liberalization has brought about a fundamental change in the bargaining position of SOE managers – something, which was not foreseen.[11] Historically managers had had a relatively strong position *vis-à-vis* the state/party bureaucracy, because it was the managers' responsibility to organize supplies. As imports became easily accessible, the state/party bureaucracy became cynical about supply responsibilities: 'We don't care about the supply of milk (bricks, telephones or guns). If your company cannot produce it, somebody will import all this stuff. We are not going to solve your problems.' Once the state tutelage had been reduced, self-reliance remained the only remedy for

SOEs. Tough decisions could be postponed no longer. And so it happened. Within a relatively short period, 'downsizing' programmes were introduced in all SOEs.

## Signs of differentiation

Between 1989 and 1994, the core of the Hungarian economy – the energy sector, public transport, the railways, telecommunication, some parts of the chemical industry and large segments of the banking sector – were deliberately left out of the privatization process. For some of these SOEs, the collapse of communism and the political changes came as a blessing also from a business point of view. Pent-up demand shot up in telecommunications, gas distribution, air travel and insurance, while constraints on competition still remained in force.[12]

This differentiation among SOEs arising from variance in size, market and product patterns has had further implications. Once privatization started, it became clear that SOE managers pursue fundamentally different strategies. In the case of larger firms, initially only Western investors were expected to show serious interest. This was financially attractive to the management, because they knew that foreign ownership would bring 'almost Western' salaries and perks, and more possibilities to travel.

For those very large firms whose internal structure was diversified both in a technological and in a geographic sense, people expected splits and other rearrangements. It was clear that privatization would lead to the emergence of several new companies on the ruins of the old SOE. This, in turn, was expected to lead to the creation of new managerial positions. Thus even the middle level of SOE management became committed to privatization.

Privatization appeared as a panacea for many troubled companies, for financial reasons. Many large companies drifted to the verge of financial collapse, in spite of a relatively good overall market situation. For these firms, privatization meant an immediate cash flow injection.

There were at least two groups of firms, however, where the management was, as a rule, hostile to privatization. In very large companies, where the management had been accustomed to the privileges arising from 'being big and important', privatization was expected to sweep away all this. Arguably, even the very large Hungarian firms were small by international standards, so, once privatized, the firm would become just a subsidiary of a worldwide conglomerate. Such fears were particularly strong in the 'sunset industries', such as electricity and metallurgy, where chances of dynamic growth were bleak anyway.

In small and medium-size firms, managers who themselves aspired to become the owners were against a public sell-off. The management had no resources at the beginning of the privatization process, but they hoped that within two or three years they would enrich themselves enough and/or the price of their own firm would drop.[13] A widely used method to achieve these two goals was the reorganization of the SOE into a holding with five, 10 or 50 subsidiaries. This had two interrelated consequences. First, the holding itself became financially opaque to outside inspectors. Second, the creation of subsidiaries and different joint ventures with private partners opened the way for different forms of self-dealing, whereby the management was able to 'bleed out' its own firm and redirect the profits into their private ventures (asset stripping).

### Deteriorating state control

State-owned firms did not have a single master. Between 1990 and 1998, there were several rounds of reorganizations of the SAMAs (see note 7). These reorganisations of the SAMAs meant new desk officers, long settling-in periods, lost papers and confused new ideas. Little wonder that, amidst the hectic changes, SOE managers viewed themselves as the bastions of stability and professional competence.

On the top of all this, the most important SOEs have remained under the control of politics. It is still true that the boards and the CEOs of the top 15–20 companies cannot be nominated without the informal approval of the prime minister and his office. To make things worse, these nominations have always been subject to bargaining among partners in the coalition, which makes the outcome even more unpredictable.

Responsibility for the prolongation of this unhealthy situation does not lie only with the politicians. SOE managers should blame themselves, too. First, it is a long tradition that these people overemphasize the weight and importance of their own companies. They view themselves as strategic companies, they try to sell themselves as the motor of technological progress, and so on. Second, the managers of these large companies quickly understood that contributions to party finances are a good personal investment. In many odd ways, these firms have become supporters of charitable foundations, and offered sinecures to party and government officials. This mechanism leads, of necessity, to replacements after every election. The leaders of the incoming government are angry with the 'old' SOE managers whom they see as corrupt and incompetent clients of the defunct government. New people are brought in, who then continue the purges at the lower levels of the SOE hierarchy.

Contrary to the letter and the spirit of the Company Act, state owned firms are run by the CEO alone. The board has a secondary role at best and the supervisory board has almost no power. This is clearly a continuation of the past, but not entirely. The boards are neglected, because they deserve to be neglected. The majority of the external board members are political appointees, others are government officials. In both cases the appointment is viewed as a compensation for the low salaries that parliamentarians, party officials and civil servants can receive. These people have neither the time nor the competence to exercise corporate governance. Among the external board members, of course, there are competent people as well. This is often the case when high-ranking civil servants of a ministry are appointed to the board of company which falls within the ministry's competence, but this creates a conflict of interest, since the ministry official becomes the extended arm of the company, rather than the representative of the owner *vis-à-vis* the state-owned company.[14]

The SOE managers are in trouble in many ways. Because of the competition from the fast growing private sector, it is difficult to keep ambitious people on the payroll. It is not only a question of salaries. The SOE managers are regularly criticized by their own staff and the trade unions for the wrong, or at least disputable, decisions they have to implement on the orders of the SAMAs. From this point, the debated issues become confused. The underdogs blame their bosses for incompetent decisions, for undeserved remuneration,[15] for corruption. In a rapidly changing economic and legal environment, it is almost impossible to agree on the borders separating short-term losses and long-term gains, pragmatism from cowardliness, generosity from corruption. Under such pressures, it is understandable that top SOE managers try to avoid harsh measures. They tend to buy peace for themselves through wage rises and toleration of weak performance, theft and corruption.

## Conclusion: measured performance

At the time of writing, there is only one study available in which the three most important aspects of the problem are handled simultaneously. The paper of Pohl *et al.* (1997) analyses ownership, labour productivity and investments in privatized and state-owned industrial firms in seven East European countries. Their results seem to support the main messages of this chapter. First, the data for Hungary show that productivity rose both in the privatized firms and in state-owned entities. Among the well-performing countries, the difference in growth rates is the smallest in Hungary. Second, privatized firms have a far larger capability to invest than state-owned ones. This, however, is not a reflection of the shift from state to private ownership; it is explained by the fact that privatized Hungarian firms are foreign owned and foreign owners have deeper pockets.

## Notes

1. Peter Mihályi served as Deputy Government Commissioner for Privatisation in the Hungarian Government in 1994/95.
2. In academic circles, there was general agreement that, after 40 years of socialism, capitalism could not be restored ('the wheels of history will not turn backwards').
3. When the 1991 annual reports became known, everybody was surprised to see that, in the five largest commercial banks, more than 50 per cent of the shares were owned by the clients of the banks.
4. References were made to the Austrian *Parteiwirtschaft*.
5. In the Hungarian literature, two terms are used in this context with no difference in meaning: trade investor or strategic investor.
6. Alternatively the term 'institutional investors' is also used in Hungarian parlance.
7. Between 1990 and 1992, the State Property Agency was the most important owner of Hungarian SOEs. Later a second privatization entity – the Hungarian State Holding Company – was called into being. From this moment on, the two agencies were jointly referred to in Hungary as state asset management agencies (SAMAs). In 1995, the two SAMAs were merged into the State Privatisation and Holding Company. Further changes can be expected.
8. This effort ran somewhat counter to the interests of the SAMAs, but not entirely. In principle the privatization agency was seeking maximum revenue; in reality it was even more interested in showing a good price performance *after* the IPO. In other words, SAMAs did no put up too much of a fight against a low issue price.
9. The agreed percentages were arbitrary: 40 per cent in gas, 12.5 per cent in the electricity distribution companies.
10. The situation is similar to the textbook illustration of Western corporations' annual shareholder meetings, where the plan for a nuclear power station is accepted without any dissent, but two or three hours are spent on a debate about the location of the bicycle shed.
11. It would go beyond the scope of the present study, but it is certainly deserving of thorough research, to find out how and why *shortages* could disappear so quickly in an economy where shortages were so acute for decades.
12. Price control, licensing and other forms of state regulation were upheld or formalized, if they did not exist before.
13. The catering industry can serve as a clear, though not very important example. Prior to 1990, the city of Budapest had three or four top-notch restaurants, all state-owned. If they had been privatized right at the beginning of the process,

their prices would have been unaffordable for Hungarian investors. Between 1990 and 1997, the number of top-notch restaurants in Budapest increased to 20–25, almost all private by now. As the original three or four good restaurants were sold in 1997, their price was far below the 1990 level because of the increased competition.

14. From a legal point of view, this is an interesting situation. According to the Company Act of 1988, board members and other senior officers owe loyalty to the company itself, rather than to the owners. If they are found in breach of their duties, they are liable for any damage caused to the company. If these senior officers are external members of the board, their own employer – for example, the ministry – cannot give instructions to them pertaining to the office. In the case of conflict, of course, the owner or the appointing body has the right to ask for the replacement of 'his' board member at the annual shareholders' meeting.

15. From about 1992, severance payments became a widely discussed public issue. Prior to that, fired managers usually received three to six months' salary as compensation. From 1992, management contracts became widely used, with 24–36 months' salaries built in as compensation. There were also scandalous examples where SOE managers collected such huge compensation after only two or three months of service.

# 10
## Banks and the Privatization of Enterprises in Poland
*Robert Chudzik*

## Introduction

The privatization of the industrial sector is one of the major tasks governments in transitional economies are confronted with, but only a minority of countries have managed to pursue it successfully. There are many reasons that explain this sluggishness, with various political constraints standing at the top of the list, but the lack of large institutional investors is commonly mentioned next. This is why some experts point to banks as appropriate candidates to take an active stance in the privatization process (van Wijnbergen, 1994). In this chapter we address this issue with reference to the Polish experience. The first section discusses whether the banks as large equity holders are able to contribute to the process of restructuring enterprises. It takes a closer look at the problem of whether banks which hold both debt and equity can contribute to efficient corporate governance. In the present author's view the arguments presented in the literature raise serious doubts.

In search of an empirical corroboration, the second section explores the empirical data referring to enterprises which have entered bank conciliation proceedings in Poland in the course of the programme of bank and enterprise restructuring. An attempt is made to identify differences in the pattern of adjustment between firms which conducted debt–equity swaps (where the banks are large equity holders) and firms where only a debt write-off was implemented. The results do not indicate significant differences between these two groups of enterprises. They suggest a rather low capability or willingness of banks to play an active role in the process of firm restructuring. Thus the results can be considered as a support for the view that banks should rather concentrate on

155

the lending business whose disciplinary effect is conducive to establishing an efficient outside control over firm insiders.

## Bank equity holding and firm restructuring

The transition period is marked by firm insiders gaining a very strong position *vis-à-vis* other stakeholders. This process can be observed not only in SOEs but also in many newly privatized firms. In the pre-privatization phase the dominance of insiders stemmed from the inability of the state to monitor and control the companies under its jurisdiction. As a result the institutional void was occupied by better informed managers or employees. In some countries the managers gain a lot of discretion, whereas in others the legislation gives a wide range of powers to workers' councils, although these developments may lead to serious inefficiencies such as asset stripping or empire building activities in the former case and underinvestment in the latter.

The privatization of SOEs is seen as a remedy for the negative effects of outsiders' power being restricted. However the insiders aspire to playing an active role in the process of privatization as well. Thus the sale of a large portion of shares to outsiders seems to guarantee that firm insiders will be properly controlled and compelled to maximize the value of the firm.

There are two reasons why large stakeholders get involved in the monitoring and control of enterprises. Firstly, they have huge amounts of money at stake, so that losses ensuing from bad firm performance may easily exceed the costs of monitoring. Secondly, they are usually not able to withdraw their funds without incurring any costs (for example, in the form of a drop in share prices). Thus they make some kind of commitment to other stakeholders that outside monitoring will be performed and that agency problems will thereby be mitigated. This circumstance should then encourage small stakeholders to put up their money as well (Franks and Mayer, 1995). However large investments are also connected with non-negligible costs. In extreme situations large investors may enforce a decision which expropriates small stakeholders. And in certain circumstances this contributes to the softening of the budget constraint. According to Dewatripont and Maskin (1995) a forbearing attitude on the part of large investors can emerge ex post after the investment costs are sunk. The dispersed holding of claims will then be beneficial as the firm is not able to coordinate the process of renegotiation with many investors, and as a result this arrangement gives rise to hardening financial constraints ex ante (Hart,

1995). The advantage of large stakeholdings actually lies in the fact that, in order to implement efficient controlling devices, less effort is required for the creation of legal infrastructure than for the legal protection of small investors.

In the following sections we address the issue of whether a bank in transition should engage in controlling activities accomplished through taking an equity and debt stake in a company. We also explore the set of conditions to be fulfilled so that the banks are able to accomplish functions which are expected from large stakeholders.

The lack of legal protection for small investors calls for greater involvement of large equity holders in the process of firm monitoring and control. The major advantage of this form of corporate governance lies in the relatively low reliance on the outside legal system. It suffices for this system to be able to enforce such basic rights as voting at the general meeting, which guarantees influence on the composition of the board of directors.

However the wholesale resolution of the corporate governance issue through large equity holding encounters serious obstacles in transitional economies owing to the lack of large investors. Overcoming this impediment through intra-industry holdings will only worsen the situation as it leads directly to cross-shareholdings which only weaken outsider control. This is the reason why many observers propose a bank as a candidate to fill the institutional gap (Stiglitz, 1992; van Wijnbergen, 1994; Steinherr, 1993; Steinherr and Gilbert, 1994). The proponents of this idea adduce bank-oriented systems such as the German and the Japanese system where the banks directly hold large stakes of shares or control them through proxy rights. The major advantage which is attributed to large bank shareholding is the access to more information about internal affairs once the bank representative takes a seat on the supervisory board of the company (Steinherr, 1993; Saunders, 1994). Furthermore the bank gains influence over decisions passed by this body. In the context of transition one can expect that the bank, through its representatives, will detect potential firm distress at an early stage and will enforce the needed rescue action more easily.

However the evidence from the aforementioned countries provides a rather mixed picture in this respect. The authors writing about Japan stress the banks' active assistance in preparing appropriate workouts for distressed firms. Their involvement, however, generally ensues from the role they play as large stakeholders, irrespective of whether they are equity holders or debt holders. To the contrary, a similar case cannot be proved for Germany. Edwards and Fischer (1994) found, on the basis of a representative survey, no evidence that the bank representatives who sit on the company's board of directors play an important role in detecting distress cases. The main information sources are the bank accounts and regular visits by credit officers. Edwards and Fischer argue that the participation in supervisory bodies is of no advantage as the bank representatives get access only to limited information about the firms' operation and supervisory boards meet infrequently. Furthermore the evidence shows that German banks play a rather passive role in restructuring activities. Their common reaction to borrower's trouble is calling in loans or getting new collateral. They usually lack the capacity to send skilled specialists to work with the firm, nor do they have strong incentives to do so, as most lending is well collateralized.[1]

These results explain the low activity of banks in managing a firm despite the potential ability to play a more active role. The evidence from Germany thus suggests that the banks in Eastern Europe can hardly be relied upon as far as their involvement in firms' restructuring is concerned, since they have less expertise in this field than their German counterparts. Nevertheless the role of bank equity holding in the acquisition of information cannot be fully neglected, especially during transition, when information is quite a rare good.

There are, however, more fundamental objections to widespread bank involvement in equity holding. The most important one is that large equity holding makes the bank more subject to systemic risks, for the income base will depend not only on quite stable interest rate revenues and various fees, but also on capital gains which wildly fluctuate as a result of the overall instability and thinness of the capital market (Calvo and Kumar, 1993; Buch, 1996).[2] The banks in transition already have to cope with high systemic risks and suffer from a lack of capital. Thus industrial equity holding will only make things worse, as manifested in a greater susceptibility of depositors to bank runs and lower intermediation as a result of lower confidence in domestic depository institutions.

There are authors who even consider the combination of debt holding and equity holding as a supreme mechanism of control over management (Steinherr, 1993; Steinherr and Gilbert, 1994). They refer to the model of Dewatripont and Tirole (1994) which was designed for the case of the surveillance of bank management, but can be generalized to all kinds of companies. These authors point out that the combination of debt and equity is the optimal incentive scheme for firm management. It assumes that control over the firm remains with the equity holders who are considered more lenient in the case where firm earnings are high. However, once they drop beyond some pre-specified level, the control rights are shifted to the debt holders, who are commonly more prone to interfere with internal affairs, including calls for management layoffs. Thus the manager has a strong incentive to exert effort in order for debt holders' involvement in firm decisions to be avoided.

The supporters of the coupling of debt and equity finance in the bank emphasize the advantages which should come from the exchange of information generated by various sorts of finance (accounting data from debt holding *vis-à-vis* information from the supervisory board in the case of equity holding). However they miss the point as far as the incentives of financiers are concerned. The major factor which determines the incentives of financiers in the model of Dewatripont and Tirole is not the psychological characteristics of financiers, but the shape of their income functions. As the creditors receive a fixed amount and do not participate in 'up-side' profits, their payment function is concave. Hence they have a strong incentive to mitigate risk-taking behaviour of managers. This means greater interference in firm affairs once the bank takes direct control over the firm.

To the contrary, equity holders receive all 'up-side' profits and, therefore, become more lenient towards the management when it undertakes risky projects. The connexion of debt holding and equity holding in the bank's hands distorts this incentive mechanism. As the bank receives its share in the 'up-side' profits the concavity of the payment function will be attenuated. Thus the bank may show some forbearance to the management in the event that it fails to repay a debt. Once aware of this new bank attitude, the firm managers may be less reluctant to take greater risks or to behave imprudently. One can argue that this negative effect may be alleviated when 'fire walls' are established between these two lines of bank business, but the present author is rather sceptical as to whether such a wall will be sufficiently resilient in the case of large firms revenues from which constitute a significant percentage of bank income.

Bank equity holding raises serious doubts in the Western economies too. The main argument against widespread bank involvement in industrial ownership reflects some concerns about the danger that the banks may accumulate considerable power. This may even cause serious distortions in the allocation of goods and capital, as the banks face strong incentives to support the firms they are connected with by equity holding, even when these firms are not as efficient as their competitors. However it is argued that intense competition within the banking sector prevents most of the conceivable distortions (Saunders, 1994; Dittus and Prowse, 1996). But intense competition among banks does not exist in transitional economies where loan markets are highly segmented and some banks manage to take a dominant position in specific segments or regions. Thus it is quite possible for a well-managed firm to have problems getting credit when approaching the bank which holds some equity of its competitor.

Last but not least, banks simply lack skills in performing the function of an equity holder. Greater engagement in this field will exceed the capabilities of banks and withdraw too many human resources from much more important tasks, such as new lending (Long and Rutkowska, 1995).[3]

The above arguments thus support only minority stakeholding which enables banks to get better access to a firm's internal information, taking into account all reservations expressed above with respect to the usefulness of this source. But banks cannot be relied upon to perform functions which are attributed to, and expected from, large active shareholders. Thus governments should attempt to promote other institutions whose task it is to specialize in exercising active ownership control rights. Despite some scepticism, the idea of investment funds appears to be well-suited to transitional countries. First evidence from the Czech Republic and Poland shows that newly created funds eagerly take large equity positions that can be interpreted as a sign of prospective involvement in the management of companies under their control.

Despite reservations regarding bank equity holding, the role these institutions have the potential to play in exercising corporate governance is not negligible. Above we pointed to the model of Dewatripont and Tirole which emphasizes the strong inclination of debt holders to interfere with the borrowing firm's internal affairs in order to avoid excessive risk taking on the part of the firm. This intervention need not signify active involvement in firm management; it can also take on a passive form where lending is based on collateral which is foreclosed if the borrower defaults on the loan.

## The Polish experience with bank equity holding: the programme of bank and enterprise restructuring

### The outline of the programme

As a response to the bad debt crisis, the Polish authorities introduced a new conciliation procedure which was intended to facilitate the restructuring of distressed borrowers. The Bank Conciliation Proceeding (BCP) was created only temporarily, for the period of three years after the enactment of this law. The BCP diverged in many points from the traditional conciliation proceeding. The most important one was the replacement of the conciliation judge by the leading bank which organized the whole procedure. Another innovation was the inclusion of tax arrears in the negotiation, which was an important factor encouraging the borrowers to choose this restructuring path. The right to enter BCP was vested with the borrower. He could file for conciliation if he proved unable to service debt or if he envisaged doing so in the near future. However the group of borrowers falling under this regulation was confined only to (a) state-owned firms, (b) limited liability or joint stock companies where the state had more then 50 per cent of shares, and (c) former state agriculture companies being governed by the State Agency of the Agriculture Property.

The borrowers submitted the application for BCP to the bank or the group of banks (called the leading bank) whose claims constituted more than 10 per cent of all liabilities, provided the amount was not less than 100 000 PZL. If the bank claim was lower that the aforementioned amount it had to constitute more than 20 per cent of the total debt. The application had to be amended by proposals for conciliation, including a rescue programme for the borrowing firm. The leading bank was authorized to demand of the applicant that he make changes in his proposals. When these conditions were fulfilled, the bank could open the conciliation procedure and inform other creditors. The conciliation agreement included the conditions of debt rescheduling and, especially, the extent of debt write-off, prolongation or the debt-for-equity-swaps (DES). In exchange the borrower was obliged to implement the rescue programme which aimed at improving the operational performance of the firm.

The restructuring concept could also comprise the provision of new finance to the borrower from the bank. The conciliation agreement became legally valid if creditors representing more than 50 per cent voted for it. As far as the state-owned enterprises were concerned, the bank was obliged to submit an application to the Ministry of Privatization to transform these firm into limited liability or joint stock companies. The underlying idea was that the debt crises had originated in deficient corporate governance and so any rescue action should actually start with a decisive change in the ownership structure. Yet the proposed regulation certainly had no far reaching consequences, as the firm remained in state hands. What it achieved was only a weakening of the position of the workers' councils, as they were dismissed as part of the transformation into the new legal form.

In practice, the bank tried to achieve an understanding with the firm and the creditors representing half of the debt value before it organized the conciliation meeting where the arrangement was to be signed. The dominant position of the bank was additionally strengthened by two circumstances. Firstly, in many cases the tax arrears added to the bank credits exceeded the 50 per cent of total debt included in BCP, so that consultation with other creditors was redundant, and the tax office usually supported the standpoint of the bank as far as conditions of debt restructuring were concerned. Secondly, the bank controlled the information flow and limited access to it by other creditors so that the latter lacked orientation, for example, they did not know how big their claims were in relation to the firm's total liabilities or who the other creditors were. Therefore they were virtually unable to build a coalition of those not satisfied with the proposed conditions untill the general meeting of all creditors. The above circumstances suggest that in reality the negotiations took place only between the debtor and the bank. As has been noted, most strategic decisions in SOEs are taken by insiders or, more precisely, by managers.[4] Thus the decision to enter BCP could be taken only when it did not conflict with managers' preferences.

### The characteristics of the sample

Our research is based on two data panels of enterprises participating in the programme. The first one comprises 69 cases collected by the World Bank team and surveyed in the paper by Gray and Holle (1996). The second sample (Panel B) is smaller. It includes 37 firms with information from balance sheets and income statements for the years 1992–5. Sample A lacks detailed data covering 1995, thus we sometimes made computations for the separate panels, but, where it was possible, they were integrated into one group.[5]

Table 10.1 provides information about average financial indicators for both panels in 1992, before the programme started. In both samples the firms which had not only negative net profits, but also negative operating profitability predominated at that time. This suggests that firms' crises were not only rooted in a heavy debt burden, but had a deeper structural character. Thus restructuring which relies only on debt relief will not suffice to ensure future recovery. Looking at the two moments of the profitability distribution we can see no significant difference between the two samples. This applies also to the range of debt restructuring. Table 10.2 presents the average debt reduction for both samples.

*Table* 10.1   The main financial indicators for two samples in 1992

| | Sample of 69 firms (Panel A) | | Sample of 37 firms (Panel B) | |
| --- | --- | --- | --- | --- |
| | Mean | Standard deviation | Mean | Standard deviation |
| Operational profitability | –0.033 | 0.21 | –0.0375 | 0.196 |
| Net profitability | –0.47 | 0.98 | –0.279 | 0.378 |
| Revenues to assets | 0.77 | 0.355 | 0.7 | 0.395 |
| Revenues to receivables | 4.42 | 2.47 | 5.83 | 3.96 |
| The share of financial costs in revenues | 0.133 | 0.133 | 0.094 | 0.095 |
| Equity to assets | 0.223 | 0.36 | 0.48 | 0.23 |

*Table* 10.2   The share of write-off and debt–equity swap in total debt included in BCP

| Panel A | The average share of write-off in total debt | The average share of DES in total debt |
| --- | --- | --- |
| 45 firms without DES | 0.6 (0.17)* | |
| 24 firms with DES | 0.53 (0.23) | 0.32 (0.18) |
| Panel B | | |
| 11 firms without DES | 0.54 (0.2) | |
| 26 firms with DES | 0.44 (0.29) | 0.39 (0.28) |

*Note*:   * Standard deviation in parentheses.

Every panel is divided into two groups. The first includes cases where only write-off was implemented. In the second group a part of cancelled debt was exchanged for equity (debt–equity swap).

The average reduction ratio in both samples for firms without DES exceeds 50 per cent. The scope of debt reduction was even greater for firms where DES was implemented, and exceeded 80 per cent in both samples.

## Has DES facilitated the restructuring of distressed borrowers?

First we present the average financial indicators for both groups of enterprises. The numbers for the years 1992–4 refer to all firms in both panels whereas the information from 1995 is based only on the firms from panel B. Thus these numbers must be treated very cautiously in relation to the earlier indicators. Actually, we include them only to illustrate a potential difference between the two groups of enterprises within this panel.

At first sight (Figure 10.1), the firms with DES display greater improvements both for the whole sample in the period 1992–4 and for sample B in 1995 in terms of net profitability. This indicator, however, is misleading. Since the net profit includes extraordinary gains and losses, both debt write-off and DES led to significant improvements of net profits as the debt reduction was reported as an extraordinary gain. In addition, as already noted, DES led on average to greater write-offs.

*Figure* 10.1   The profitability ratios

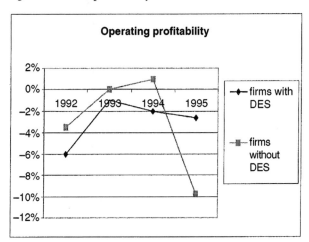

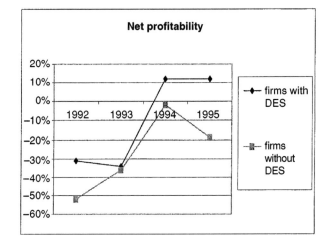

Thus it is not surprising that the increase in net profitability is greater for firms with DES than for firms without it.

A much better indicator for the economic performance, therefore, is the operating profitability. For the whole sample it displays an improvement during 1992–4 only for firms without DES. The other group only managed to perform better during the years 1992–3. Then the profitability ratio dropped to less than –2 per cent. As far as the

*Figure* 10.2    The turnover ratios

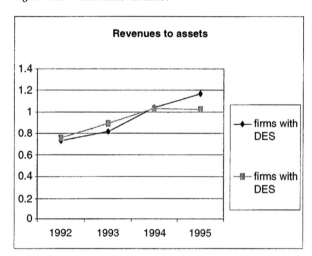

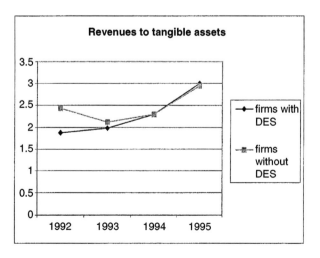

year 1995 is concerned, a reversed picture emerges where the group with debt–equity swaps performed much better than without DES. However, even this group displays negative operating profitability. Therefore it is not warranted to state that the bank involvement in equity holding caused a significant performance improvement.

On average, the bank conciliation proceeding proved to be an insufficient measure to improve profitability. However taking into account other efficiency measures such as turnover ratios leads to a more moderate view. (Figure 10.2). They provide some clues as to how efficiently the available funds are used in the firm's day-to-day performance. In contrast to profitability, both ratios under consideration improved significantly for both samples. So the claim that no restructuring in firms occurred at all should be rejected. The improvement of the turnover ratio means that managers managed to economize at least on available funds. They probably reduced inventories and collected overdue bills more efficiently. However this is insufficient to restore positive operating profits as these usually require more painful measures.

The two figures also fail to disclose a significant difference between the two groups of firms. The same conclusion can be formulated on the basis of a regression which controls the determinants of the profitability changes after the year 1992, when the programme of firms' restructuring had started. We examine whether the starting situation of the firm or the type of debt restructuring has an impact on its future performance. This relationship is controlled for by regressing the change in operating profitability between 1992 and 1994 (or 1995 for panel B only) on its value in 1992. We introduce also in all regressions the dummy variable DESDUMMY to examine whether debt–equity swaps and expected changes in ownership structure exerted an impact on the firms' performance. The detailed description of variables in question is contained in Table 10.3.

The results of the regression are contained in Table 10.4. They show that there is a strong negative relationship between the initial operating profitability in 1992 and its subsequent change. This means that relatively weak firms managed to improve their situation, whereas the stronger ones worsened their performance during the same period of time. At first glance, this outcome suggests that the BCP helped only the first group of firms while not being able to change the incentives of firms in a better starting position. So the programme was only partially efficient. Unfortunately this pattern of behaviour is similar to general attitudes of state-owned enterprises. It is well known that such firms started to think about restructuring only after their situation had

*Table* 10.3   The determinants of the changes in operating profitability

| Variable | Description |
|----------|-------------|
| OPPR92 | Operating profitability in 1992 |
| OP9492 | The difference between operating profitability in 1994 and 1992 |
| OP9592 | The difference between operating profitability in 1995 and 1992 |
| INPR | The change in production (between the years appearing in the name of the variable) in the industry to which the appropriate firm belongs |
| RELPR | The real change in the industry output prices between years appearing in the name of the variable |

*Table* 10.4   Regression on the profitability changes

| | Regression results | |
|---|---|---|
| Independent | Dependent variables | |
| variables | OPPR9492 for the total sample of 94 cases | OPPR9592 from panel B |
| CONSTANT | –0.955 (–1.66) P-value = 0.1 | –0.364 (–2.45) |
| OPPR92 | –0.474 (–3.147) | –0.75 (–3.51) |
| DESDUMMY | –0.064 (–1.11) | 0.045 (0.64) |
| RELPR | 1.38 (2.25) | 0.35 (1.91) |
| INPR | –0.2 (–0.71) | 0.006 (0.14) |
| F-statistic | 5.56 | 18.02 |

dramatically deteriorated. On the other hand, firms in quite a good position delayed the implementation of necessary steps to adapt to the changing market environment. Consequently their performance declined with time.

Looking at both panels from this standpoint one could concede that the programme allowed firms in a very bad situation to survive. However, at the same time, it weakened the financial discipline of firms with positive profits. As a result they did not modify their behaviour, as they were not forced to do so by sufficient financial constraints. The regression shows no significant influence of debt–equity swaps on performance changes. The resulting ownership change was insufficient to modify managers' incentives. According to the information provided by Gray and Holle (1996), DES usually failed to deprive the state of the dominant position among shareholders. Thus other outsiders may have problems with exerting pressure on firms' managers to implement more active restructuring strategies. As was to be expected, the increase of real prices is reflected positively in operating profitability. On the other hand, the changes in real output in the whole industry have no significant impact on dependent variables.

Summing up, the declining operating profitability suggests that enterprises signing a conciliation agreement did not have sufficient potential to adapt successfully to the changing market environment even after being granted a generous bail-out. In addition, debt–equity swaps and the ensuing control rights are not a powerful instrument in the hands of banks.

## Conclusion

The evidence available for the programme of bank and enterprise restructuring in Poland shows that equity holding by banks fails to contribute to greater restructuring efforts on the part of firms. The firms which decided to exchange their liabilities for shares were not performing better than those which only rescheduled their debt. An overall poor performance of both groups of borrowers testifies to a quite disappointing performance of banks as 'an agent of change'. As far as the aforementioned rescue programme is concerned, banks proved incapable of initiating and enforcing successful firm restructuring. Although BCP is not the only possibility for greater bank involvement in equity holding, there is no evidence that other means were widely used. The available data show that the 13 largest banks (without PKO SA, the former state savings bank, and BGZ, an agricultural bank) hold only 1 per cent of all assets in shares, which amounted to 14.3 per cent of their equity in 1993.[6] The amount is thus lower than the limits allowed by the regulatory norms.

The banks can also participate in the process of firm privatization, but there are only a few transactions in which the bank bought a controlling block of shares. Actually only one institution – Bank Handlowy – is visibly involved in this process and, even then, Bank Handlowy bought only a small number of firms, which were usually in a very good financial situation. After a relatively short time it attempted to sell most of the shares on the stock exchange. This strategy was highly profitable for the bank, but the profits originated in the right selection of the firm to be bought out rather than in the subsequent restructuring. The low bank involvement in equity holding shows that the banks are aware of their weak performance in corporate governance. Thus they were quite reluctant to accept debt–equity swaps in the BCP process.

Only two banks got more involved in these transactions, and it is interesting that they were the weakest ones in terms of capital adequacy in the group of nine commercial banks spun off from the central banks in 1989 (see Gray and Holle, 1996). These operations were probably treated by these banks as a means to tie the borrowers to the bank.[7] As these financial institutions were insufficiently endowed with equity they were hardly able to offer competitive interest rates to attract new good clients. The limited resources also impede introducing new services which are a significant factor in market competition as well. Therefore the weak banks may have realized that they had to make money on their old clients who had some chance of recovery in the future. It is necessary, however, to ensure that these clients will not abandon the bank when their creditworthiness improves. In order to avoid this, the banks engaged in equity holding which ensures knowledge of the firm's operations and allows influence over strategic decisions. The poor performance of the firms in question raises doubts as to whether such a strategy can be successful if there is no visible restructuring effort on the part of enterprises.

## Notes

1. Another reason why German banks play a subordinate role in exercising active influence over firms is the fact that banks have a controlling stake only in a minority of firms. Most companies in Germany are controlled by wealthy families and other enterprises (Nunnenkamp, 1995; Franks and Mayer, 1995).
2. It is argued that bank involvement in share trading will contribute to the development of capital markets (Dittus and Prowse, 1996). However the predominance of large shareholdings may actually jeopardize the liquidity of the market and contribute to great swings in prices following the banks' attempts to reduce their position in certain firms.
3. Sometimes it is argued that the banks which take both an equity and a debt stake in a firm are able to make use of economies of scope. However the research on this topic has failed to prove the existence of such effects between the two lines of bank business (Serra *et al.*, 1997).

4. This assumption does not exclude the possibility that the manager took into account the worker's preferences while making strategic decisions, especially when the workers may strongly oppose then.
5. 12 cases have similar financial figures in both panels and, therefore, they are taken into account only once in the integrated panel.
6. Source: 50 największych banków w Polsce, Miesięcznik Bank marzec 1997.
7. This view is based on personal interviews with bank officials.

# 11
# Manager Incentives and Turnover of Managers: Evidence from the Czech Republic

*Stijn Claessens and Simeon Djankov*

## Introduction

The association between corporate performance, managers and incentives is a much studied topic. One strand of literature has been motivated by the notion that financial incentives for managers, in the form of performance contracts, equity ownership and so on, could help align the interest of owners and managers: that is, reduce principal–agent problems, and thereby improve corporate performance and increase market valuation. This topic has been studied extensively (for example, see Murphy, 1985, for the effect of performance contracts on market valuation of firms in the United States, and World Bank, 1996b, for a review of performance contracts for state enterprises). The general finding is that these incentives do not work well for state enterprises, especially in developing countries (and the focus of improving state enterprises' performance has subsequently shifted to privatization), but work reasonably well for private firms in developed market economies (Jensen and Zimmermann, 1985). Recent theoretical models (Aghion *et al.*, 1994; Blanchard and Aghion, 1996) build on the existing literature and investigate the importance of incentive systems for executive performance in the context of transition economies. Some empirical evidence on the link between executive compensation and enterprise productivity growth during the initial transition period is becoming available (see Jones and Kato, 1996, for a study of Bulgarian firms).

Another strand of literature has studied the impact of changes in managers on corporate performance. The early contribution of Jensen and Meckling (1976) had highlighted the effects of managerial entrenchment and the accumulation of private benefits (rents) by managers on corporate performance. An active market for managers

171

and takeover (threats) by shareholders would help discipline and remove entrenched managers. A number of studies have since investigated the effect of changes in management on corporate performance, for example the effect of the unexpected death of chief executive officers (CEOs) on corporate valuation (Johnson *et al.*, 1985); the role of institutional investors in changing managers and the effects this has on corporate performance (Smith, 1996); and the role of manager turnover in the context of underdeveloped managerial markets (Djankov and Pohl, 1998). These papers generally find that changes in managers are associated with an improvement in corporate performance and market valuation (see Jensen and Zimmermann, 1985, for a review).

Both strands of literature are plagued, however, by simultaneity and selection problems. The studies of management changes in market economies may suffer from a selection problem as new managers may be better suited than existing managers to managing the firm currently. The improvement in corporate performance or market valuation associated with management changes occurs not because the old managers were entrenched, but rather because their skills mix has become outdated. The literature on the effects of changes in managers and financial incentives in transition economies often suffers from a simultaneity problem as either existing managers become owners or new owners replace existing managers, thus confounding the effects of incentives and management changes on enterprise performance. As a result, it is difficult to test whether the changes in equity ownership (that is, incentives) or the changes in management led to the changes in performance.

The Czech privatization experiment provides a unique opportunity to shed new light on the relationships between corporate performance on one hand and changes in managers and incentives, on the other. Two factors contribute to the uniqueness of the Czech experience. First, privatization of many firms occurred simultaneously through a distribution of voucher points to all adult citizens, followed by competitive bidding, and firms' ownership ended up determined largely exogenously to firm characteristics, including its management. While there was some equity ownership by managers, very few firms ended up with large insider ownership. As a result, we avoid the simultaneity problem of either the existing managers becoming the new owners or the new, outside owners replacing the existing managers. We are thus better able than existing studies on transition economies to separate the effects of incentives on enterprise performance from those of management changes. Second, immediately following the start of the transition and the implementation of the privatization scheme, there were few managers in the Czech Republic with skills suited to the new market economy. We thus avoid the selection problem – of the skill mix of new managers being better suited than that of the existing managers to manage the firm in changed circumstances – and can analyse the sole effects of management changes on performance and market valuation.

For the empirical part of the chapter, we use four enterprise performance parameters for a cross-section of 706 Czech firms over the period 1993–7. In particular, we study the effect of new managers and equity incentives on profitability, labour productivity, propensity to initiate new marketing efforts and Tobin's Q (ratio of market to replacement value). We control for initial conditions and sector-specific effects, and also study whether additional characteristics of general managers (age, years with the firm) help explain corporate performance. We find that all four measures of enterprise performance are positively related to bringing in an outsider as a new manager. Equity incentives of CEOs have an indeterminate effect on corporate performance. Indeed for three enterprise performance measures they have a negative effect, although only for new marketing departments is this effect significant. The results suggest that changes in managers are more important in bringing about improvements in performance than incentives in the form of equity shares. This finding is consistent with some recent theoretical models on managerial behaviour in transition (Roland and Sekkat, 1996; Roland, 1994).

The chapter is structured as follows. The first section briefly describes the Czech privatization scheme. The management changes resulting from the voucher scheme, valuation and profitability are documented in the second section, while the third section presents the results. Conclusions are summarized in the final section.

## The Czech voucher scheme and management changes

The Czech mass privatization scheme took place in two phases or 'waves': the first started in October 1992 and ended in June 1993; the second started in January 1994 and ended in October the same year. In total, 988 Czech enterprises participated in the first wave and 861 enterprises (of which 185 from the first wave) in the second wave. The process followed was similar in both waves. First, over a three-month period, firms were selected for privatization and managers had to submit privatization proposals, usually to the founding ministry. There were some differences in the selection of firms for the first and second wave. The first wave mainly consisted of manufacturing firms and excluded some large, vertically integrated industrial conglomerates. Those needed extra time to be split up into smaller, independent firms. The second wave included (along with a similar group of manufacturing firms) the newly created independent firms, as well as banks and utilities.

In the first wave, several dozen firms ended up with managerial or employee ownership; in the second wave, managers of many more firms acquired shares, although ownership stakes remained low. Further taking account of shares set aside for direct investors and for restitution, remaining shares were offered through a voucher scheme. All adult citizens could bid with points for shares on offer or, in a pre-bidding 'zero' round, could offer (part of) their points to investment funds, which could then bid for shares. A large number of such funds emerged (over 430 funds for the first wave and an additional 120 for the second wave) and many individuals offered all or most of their points to the funds. After the bidding rounds, points were exchanged for shares and secondary market trading started.

The authorities designed the privatization scheme to make the most use of information available among participants. General information on each firm was made available by the state prior to the start of the auction process, covering such items as business activity, number of employees, output and profit in preceding years and prior allocation of shares. To improve price formation, the scheme did not involve a single auction, but rather five sequential bidding rounds with price adjustments between rounds. The aim of the sequential bidding rounds was to reflect in the final prices the information gathering and analysis by individuals and institutions as well as any private and inside information. At the same time, restrictions on sales limited the effects of inside information and any linkages between preferred and final ownership.

Management changes were extensive. In 1990/91, prior to the first wave of privatization, the top management of all Czechoslovak companies was 'depoliticized' and general directors who were Communist Party members were removed from firms' management. In the majority of cases, the new general manager appointed at that time was the old technical director, that is, an internally promoted manager. Very few outside directors were appointed, in part owing to the limited supply of superior managers and a poorly functioning market for managers. In the years following privatization, however, further changes in top management occurred, in part dependent on the evolution of the ownership structure for each firm.

## Profile of Czech firms

We have data on Czech firms compiled from survey data. The data set is collected in two steps. First, financial and ownership information of 1191 firms listed on the Prague Stock Exchange (PSE) was collected by a private local marketing firm, contracted for the purposes of this study. All financial variables were defined using international accounting standards from the onset of the survey in 1992. A number of firms do not report PSE prices since their shares are not actively traded. We therefore exclude from our analysis firms whose shares trade less than four times in a given year. The 1992–7 data are complete for 371 firms which went through the first wave of voucher privatization. An additional set of 335 firms which went through the second wave report consistently after 1993, making altogether 706 firms for the period 1993–7. Once the base data set was collected, a second survey was performed in which interviewers visited all 706 firms that had previously supplied complete information and asked managers about their background and equity holdings. The second survey served as a basis for testing the hypotheses outlined in the previous section.

We use several variables to describe general managers (Table 11.1, Panel A). The average duration of general managers' tenure is four years, with less than 10 per cent of managers having been on the job for six or more years. This is a very short period when compared, for example, to the average of 13 years for US CEOs (Johnson *et al.*, 1985). The main reason, as explained earlier, was the dismissal of all general managers with Communist Party affiliation following the election of Václav Klaus as prime minister. Although general managers were changed, many of the new managers were internally promoted and the average tenure of general managers in any position with their firm was 15 years and 3 months. Approximately 8 per cent of all managers had worked with their firms for more than 30 years; 19 per cent of managers had worked for their firms for more than 25 years; and a third of all managers had 20 or more years of experience with their respective firms. Finally, the average age of general managers was 49 years – 10 years younger than their US counterparts (Johnson *et al.*, 1985, Morck *et al.*, 1989, McConnell and Servaes, 1990)[1] and a year younger than their Russian counterparts (Blasi *et al.*, 1997).[2]

The annual general managers' turnover rate in the sample was 12.0 per cent in 1991, 17.8 per cent in 1992, 15.2 per cent in 1993, 15.1 per cent in 1995, and 30.4 per cent in 1995. The comparable estimates for annual turnover for US firms range between 9.3 per cent (Denis and Denis,

*Table 11.1* Manager characteristics and corporate performance

### A. Management characteristics (as of 1 February 1997)

| | Mean | Std. Dev. | Minimum | Maximum | Median |
|---|---|---|---|---|---|
| Years as general manager (YCEO) | 4.052 | 2.471 | 0.5 | 16.0 | 4.0 |
| General managers with tenure of 6 or more years | 9.066% | | | | |
| Age in years (AGE) | 49.245 | 7.426 | 27.0 | 70.0 | 49.0 |
| General managers over 60 years of age | 6.233% | | | | |
| General managers under 40 years of age | 12.325% | | | | |
| Equity holdings % of total (SHARE) | 2.528 | 11.924 | 0.0 | 56.0 | 0.0 |
| General managers controlling 20% or more | 1.842% | | | | |
| General managers controlling 10% or more | 8.215% | | | | |
| Years with the firm (YFIRM) | 15.239 | 10.599 | 0.5 | 47.0 | 15.0 |
| General managers with 30 or more years in the firms | 7.791% | | | | |
| General managers with 25 or more years in the firms | 18.839% | | | | |
| General managers with 20 or more years in the firms | 34.278% | | | | |

### B. Corporate performance indicators

| | 1993 | 1994 | 1995 | 1996 |
|---|---|---|---|---|
| Tobin's Q (TOBQ) | 0.804 | 0.782 | 0.768 | 0.733 |
| | (0.502) | (0.441) | (0.465) | (0.508) |
| | 0.706 | 0.688 | 0.669 | 0.614 |
| Profitability (PROF) | 0.137 | 0.151 | 0.171 | 0.135 |
| | (0.116) | (0.113) | (0.126) | (0.138) |
| | 0.117 | 0.125 | 0.139 | 0.121 |
| Labour productivity (LABPRO) | 216.327 | 252.100 | 292.527 | 288.645 |
| | (192.056) | (210.821) | (256.991) | (244.816) |
| | 169.824 | 188.152 | 213.238 | 220.994 |
| Share of Firms with Marketing Departments (MKTDEP) | 24.8% | – | – | 61.1% |

Table 11.1  continued

### C. Control variables

|  | Mean | Std. Dev. | Minimum | Maximum | Median |
|---|---|---|---|---|---|
| Leverage (LEV), average for 1994–7 | 1.752 | 3.658 | 0.724 | 4.128 | 1.608 |
| Size (number of employees) | 1 100 | 2 897 | 9 | 49 701 | 382 |
| Excess demand of shares (EDEM) | 1.415 | 5.527 | 0.008 | 143.651 | 0.879 |

### D. Correlation matrix

|  | YCEO | AGE | SHARE | YFIRM | TOBQ: 96 | PROF: 96 | LABPRO: 96 | MKTDEP |
|---|---|---|---|---|---|---|---|---|
| Years as a manager (YCEO) | 1.000 |  |  |  |  |  |  |  |
| Age of the manager (AGE) | 0.315 | 1.000 |  |  |  |  |  |  |
| Share of equity by manager (SHARE) | 0.084 | 0.148 | 1.000 |  |  |  |  |  |
| Years with the firm (YFIRM) | 0.462 | 0.478 | 0.132 | 1.000 |  |  |  |  |
| Stock valuation (TOBQ:96) | 0.011 | 0.085 | -0.001 | -0.023 | 1.000 |  |  |  |
| Profitability (PROF:96) | -0.008 | 0.031 | -0.012 | -0.051 | 0.196 | 1.000 |  |  |
| Labour productivity (LABPRO:96) | -0.002 | 0.064 | -0.045 | -0.013 | 0.219 | 0.338 | 1.000 |  |
| Marketing efforts (MKTDEP) | -0.023 | -0.005 | 0.042 | -0.067 | 0.018 | 0.049 | 0.039 | 1.000 |

1995) and 7.8 per cent (Weisbach, 1988). The turnover rate for Russian CEOs was 8.4 per cent between 1992 and 1996 (Blasi *et al.*, 1997). The higher turnover rate in the Czech Republic was undoubtedly triggered by the dismissal of old managers by the Klaus administration in 1991–2, and the subsequent changes in management once privatization was completed. Neither event affected Russian firms where a 'depolitization' of industry did not occur and where insiders took over 58 per cent of all firms (Blasi *et al.*, 1997, Table 2).

The design of the Czech privatization, as discussed earlier, prevented managers from obtaining significant stakes in their respective firms. Indeed the average share of equity holdings of general managers was only 2.5 per cent of total equity, with only 1.8 per cent of managers holding 20 per cent or more, and 8.2 per cent of managers holding 10 per cent or more. This is low even by US standards: the average holding of US CEOs reported ranges between 11.8 per cent (McConnell and Servaes, 1990) to 9.5 per cent (Johnson *et al.*, 1985) and a lower bound of 2.7 per cent (Morck *et al.* 1989). This is comparable to the equity holdings in Russian firms, where general managers own 4.5 per cent on average (Blasi *et al.*, 1997, Table 4, 193). In both the Czech Republic and Russia, it may be that managers underreport their equity holdings. While we suspect that this is likely, it does not affect our benchmark specification where equity holdings are taken to be a discrete choice: 1 if a manager has any holding, 0 otherwise. It is difficult to argue that managers would not report small holdings.

To calculate Tobin's Q (TOBQ), we use the secondary market prices for firms traded on the PSE at the end of January following the year for which we use accounting and ownership data. This way we can be reasonably assured that the market has incorporated all available information. Using these prices, we calculate Qs as the sum of market valuation and total debt outstanding, divided by the firm's replacement value (net fixed assets plus inventory). Table 11.1, Panel B reports summary statistics. The mean Q is 0.804 in 1993, 0.782 in 1994, 0.768 in 1995, and 0.733 in 1996. There is a monotonic decline in mean Q over the period as the aggregate stock market went down after the initial surge in 1992. Typically in market economies firms in high skill-intensive sectors and with valuable intangible assets will have high Qs, while firms in physical capital-intensive industries and/or industries where the output prices are regulated will have low Qs. The sectoral dispersion of Czech firms' Qs is consistent with this: seven of the top 10 firms (highest Qs) are in services, while eight of the bottom 10 (lowest Qs) firms are in utilities. The values of Tobin's Q in 1996, for example, vary between 3.37 and 0.12. The Qs of most firms are stable over time: nine firms are in the top 10 over the whole period. These include three trading firms, two engineering and design firms, two beer producers, one construction firm, and one transport firm. Six of the bottom 10 firms are water utilities.

Profitability (PROF) is defined as gross (operating) profit over net fixed assets plus inventory. Table 11.1, Panel B shows that it increases over time, from 0.137 in 1993 to 0.171 in 1995 on average, with a decline to 1993 levels in 1996 0.5. Seven of the top 10 firms (highest profitability) operate in the engineering and architectural design, management and accounting sectors; six of the bottom 10 operate in the basic metals and the fabricated metal products (including armaments) sectors. The correlation between Tobin's Q and profitability goes up over time until 1995 (not reported here), which suggests that the market valuation becomes a better indicator of relative profitability as accounting data start to reflect the changes in firms' performance. This trend breaks down in 1996 as stock prices show increased dispersion.

Labour productivity (LABPRO) is defined as value added per employee. It is positively correlated with profitability. Previous studies of enterprise performance in transition economies treat labour productivity as a leading indicator of performance while profitability is a lagging indicator (Wolff, 1996). Labour productivity increases significantly over the 1992–5 period and declines somewhat in 1996. Finally managers of enterprises responded to the question whether there has been a new marketing department established after privatization (MKTDEP). They were given a discrete 'Yes/No' choice. This qualitative variable is complementary to the other three indicators. About 61 per cent of all firms had established a new marketing department by 1996, while only 24.8 per cent had marketing departments in 1993 (Table 11.1, Panel B, last row).

As control variables (Panel C), we use the firm's leverage (the ratio of assets to equity, LEV), the excess demand over supply of shares in the first round of the voucher scheme (EDEM) and sector dummies. A positive sign for leverage can be expected in regressions for Tobin's Q as leverage increases the value of the tax shield advantages derived from debt financing, thus increasing the relative value of a firm. Leverage may not, however, have a positive coefficient for the profitability regression since we use operating income as our profitability measure, which is not influenced by the tax advantages of increased interest payments. Alternatively, for both the Q and the profitability regression, leverage may have a negative coefficient as, according to some agency models, leverage can be negatively correlated with Q and profitability (see Harris and Raviv, 1991, for a review of the relationships between leverage and Q and profitability).

The excess demand variable in the first bidding round (EDEM) is used to control for other firm characteristics (favourable location, new machinery) which may have affected prices, firm performance and restructuring. Sector dummies (DSEC$_i$) are commonly used in studies on firm performance to capture sector-specific shocks (for example, increased exposure to international trade), growth opportunities and other sector-specific characteristics affecting firm performance and market valuation (see discussion above).

The average size of the 706 firms in the sample is 1100 workers. The dispersion is, however, very wide, with firms with as few as nine and as many as 49 701 workers. Few large firms account for much of the dispersion. The median size is only 382 workers, with approximately 7.8 per cent of firms with fewer than 100 employees, 26.6 per cent with fewer than 200 employees, 32.7 per cent with more than 750 employees, and about a quarter of firms (24.79 per cent) with more than 1000 employees.[3]

Table 11.1, Panel D reports correlation coefficients on manager profiles (YCEO, AGE, YFIRM) and the end-period values of profitability, labour productivity, Tobin's Q and the establishment of a new marketing department. All correlations of interest are relatively weak. The number of years as a general manager is positively correlated with the stock price, but negatively correlated with profitability, labour productivity and marketing efforts in the sample. Stock prices, profitability and labour productivity are all weakly correlated with the age of managers, while marketing efforts are weakly negatively correlated with the age of managers. Next, and in support of the hypothesis of managerial entrenchment, all corporate performance indicators are negatively related to the number of years that managers spent with their firms (YFIRM). Finally, with the exception of marketing efforts, all indicators have a weakly negative correlation with the share of equity holdings by general managers.

The hypotheses outlined in the previous section suggest a matrix structure with increasing positive correlation between corporate performance, on the one hand, and change of managers and equity holdings on the other. We provide some evidence for these hypotheses by presenting some descriptive statistics. Since the dependent variables vary greatly across sectors, we calculate the mean difference of each indicator by subtracting the mean value of the indicator for the whole sector from the individual firm's indicators. The results are reported in Table 11.2.

Table 11.2  Statistics on dependent variables (mean-differences)

| Variable | All managers 706 firms | All managers without equity 470 firms | All managers with equity 236 firms |
|---|---|---|---|
| MTOBQ96 | 0.000 | 0.004 | −0.009 |
| MPROFIT96 | 0.000 | 0.000 | 0.000 |
| MLABPRO96 | 0.000 | 0.127 | −0.253 |
| MMKTDEP96 | 0.000 | 0.001 | −0.002 |

| Variable | All Insiders 475 firms | Insiders without equity 307 firms | Insiders with equity 168 firms |
|---|---|---|---|
| MTOBQ96 | −0.008 | −0.011 | −0.002 |
| MPROFIT96 | −0.011 | −0.012 | −0.011 |
| MLABPRO96 | −20.336 | −23.695 | −14.196 |
| MMKTDEP96 | −0.021 | −0.013 | −0.036 |

| Variable | All outsiders selected by government 52 firms | Outsiders selected by government without equity 41 firms | Outsiders selected by government with equity 11 firms |
|---|---|---|---|
| MTOBQ96 | −0.210 | −0.182 | −0.295 |
| MPROFIT96 | 0.022 | 0.019 | 0.035 |
| MLABPRO96 | −28.596 | −29.324 | −25.894 |
| MMKTDEP96 | 0.041 | 0.027 | 0.099 |

| Variable | All outsiders selected by private owners 179 firms | Outsiders selected by private owners without equity 122 firms | Outsiders selected by private owners with equity 57 firms |
|---|---|---|---|
| MTOBQ96 | 0.081 | 0.106 | 0.026 |
| MPROFIT96 | 0.022 | 0.021 | 0.027 |
| MLABPRO96 | 62.264 | 69.969 | 45.789 |
| MMKTDEP96 | 0.046 | 0.029 | 0.074 |

The means for the dependent variables vary across managers' types in ways consistent with the hypothesis that outside managers provide additional value to the firm. Comparing the means statistics in the first column, we find that (relative to the average in their respective sectors) firms which are managed by insiders underperform on all four indicators; that is, the signs on the MTOBQ96, MPROFIT96, MLABPRO96 and MMKTDEP are all negative. The average labour productivity of insider-managed firms is almost 8 per cent lower than the sample average. Firms that have general managers appointed by the government during 1991–2 show higher than the (sector-adjusted) average level of profitability (MPROFIT96 = 0.022), and marketing efforts (MMKTDEP = 0.041). At the same time, the aforementioned firms show lower than the (sector-adjusted) average level of stock valuation (MTOBQ96 = 0.270), and labour productivity (MLABPRO96 = 28.596). Finally, firms who have outsiders (selected by the new private owners) as managers consistently outperform the other two groups on all corporate performance indicators. In particular, they have 20 per cent higher labour productivity than average in 1996 and their stock valuation is 10 per cent higher than the sample average.

The raw statistics are less supportive of the hypothesis on the role of equity incentives as we compare the indicators in the second and third columns of Table 11.2. We divided the sample of firms into those whose managers have (any) equity and those whose managers have no equity. For three measures (MTOBQ96, MLABPRO96, MMKTDEP96) firms whose managers have equity report lower than the (sector-adjusted) average values. For only one measure (MPROFIT96) is the value for equity holders higher than the value for managers with no equity holdings. F-test analysis (not reported) indicates, however, that in none of the cases is the difference between the two samples statistically significant.

The absence of support for the null hypothesis on equity incentives (namely, that equity incentives lead to improved corporate performance) may be due to problems with aggregation. In particular, it may be the case that insiders who hold equity do not perform better, but that the subsample of new managers selected by private owners shows different results. Hence we also test whether means differ according to equity ownership for each of the three type-of-manager groups. In each case, the results from the full sample are upheld: there is no statistically significant difference in the performance of firms led by managers with and without equity holdings (not reported). We also investigated the possibility of a selection bias, where new managers are appointed in certain type of firms, but we found no clear bias (not reported).

# Hypotheses testing

We estimate regressions using OLS specifications on all 706 firms in the sample (see Table 11.3). The benchmark specification uses dummy variables for both management changes and equity ownership by managers. The dummy SHOLDER for equity ownership by managers is always insignificant and positive only in the TOBQ regression. This confirms the evidence presented in the raw descriptive statistics that equity incentives are not sufficient to enhance performance. The dummy for manager change (OUTSIDER) is significant in three specifications and only marginally insignificant in the MKTDEP regression. It is always positive. Thus the hypothesis that appointing new managers brings about improved corporate performance is confirmed.

The coefficient on general managers' age (AGE) is marginally insignificant in most specifications, but positive in all cases. Older managers are (on average) more likely to lead their firms to better performance. A possible reason for this indeterminacy is the presence of old managers with experience in running Western firms (the 1968 Czechs). By 1997, such managers were in their late 50s and early 60s. Although a small group – only 22 of 706 managers (3.2 per cent of total) – are identified as 1968 Czechs, these managers have a large effect in the age distribution since they account for half of all managers above 60 years of age (compare to Table 11.1, Panel A). They do not appear to drive the results, however, since when we include a separate dummy for these managers the overall results are not changed (but the coefficient on this dummy is highly significant and positive).

The explanatory power of the regressions is good, with $R^2$s between 0.22 and 0.60, except for the marketing department indicator where the variables explain only 2 per cent of the variation. The lower $R^2$s for the TOBQ regression probably reflect the fact that the PSE prices largely reflect minority shareholder valuation. The low explanatory power of the MKTDEP specification may in part be due to the data available to us. In particular, although we know which firms have established their own marketing departments, we do not know which firms were part of an industry consortium which supplied them with marketing services. Thus we cannot distinguish between firms which had not opened a marketing department because their managers were not inclined to do so, and firms which were supplied with this service externally.

As expected, leverage has a positive coefficient for TOBQ in the estimation. However leverage has a negative coefficient for PROF, LABPRO, and MKTDEP. This may be because, under central planning,

*Table* 11.3   Estimation results on manager changes and equity incentives (OLS)

| Explanatory variable | TOBQ | PROF | LABPRO | MKTDEP |
|---|---|---|---|---|
| SHOLDER | 0.028 | −0.001 | −17.824 | −0.001 |
| | (0.964) | (0.146) | (1.452) | (0.296) |
| OUTSIDER | 0.082 | 0.037 | 44.223 | 0.065 |
| | (2.317) | (3.552) | (3.364) | (1.597) |
| AGE | 0.003 | 0.002 | 1.628 | 0.003 |
| | (1.618) | (1.695) | (1.938) | (0.128) |
| LEV | 0.021 | −0.001 | −7.041 | −0.002 |
| | (1.734) | (0.321) | (2.154) | (0.258) |
| EDEM | −0.001 | 0.001 | 0.431 | −0.002 |
| | (1.024) | (0.154) | (0.259) | (2.325) |
| TOBQ:BEG | 0.644 | – | – | – |
| | (9.523) | | | |
| PROF:BEG | – | 0.572 | – | – |
| | | (8.901) | | |
| LABPRO:BEG | – | – | 0.961 | – |
| | | | (9.931) | |
| AGRO | −0.010 | −0.023 | 22.319 | −0.041 |
| | (0.452) | (1.278) | (0.734) | (0.054) |
| WOOD | −0.148 | −0.014 | −11.223 | −0.023 |
| | (2.263) | (0.652) | (0.445) | (0.315) |
| TRA | 0.042 | −0.002 | 26.672 | 0.025 |
| | (0.596) | (0.142) | (2.141) | (0.406) |
| MIN | −0.176 | 0.043 | 29.632 | −0.084 |
| | (2.114) | (1.931) | (0.862) | (0.624) |
| CON | 0.105 | 0.020 | 5.362 | −0.136 |
| | (1.526) | (1.112) | (0.136) | (1.814) |
| FOOD | 0.209 | 0.006 | 20.957 | 0.012 |
| | (3.514) | (0.309) | (0.536) | (0.249) |
| APP | 0.016 | 0.014 | −23.541 | 0.057 |
| | (0.215) | (0.805) | (1.265) | (0.684) |
| CHEM | −0.074 | 0.024 | −23.249 | −0.024 |
| | (1.284) | (1.284) | (0.638) | (0.551) |
| MET | 0.021 | 0.010 | 12.624 | 0.051 |
| | (1.458) | (0.724) | (0.436) | (1.321) |
| MACH | 0.042 | 0.018 | 0.334 | 0.034 |
| | (2.421) | (1.985) | (1.365) | (0.664) |
| Constant | 0.031 | −0.027 | −17.331 | 0.332 |
| | (0.271) | (0.824) | (0.398) | (2.348) |
| Adjusted $R^2$ | 0.369 | 0.235 | 0.622 | 0.028 |

*Notes:*
All regressions are based on 706 observations.
Absolute values of *t*-statistics in parentheses.
The numeraire sector in all cases is Financial services.
Standard errors are heteroskedasticity-consistent.

Czech firms financed their long-term investment needs differently from their working capital. Their subsequent corporatization, including the determination of the book value of equity, may have led to a negative association between high leverage and profitability. The corporatization may have meant, for example, that firms which received more investment loans ended up more leveraged. Since during the transition these high capital intensive firms were generally less profitable, a negative association between leverage, on the one hand, and profitability and labour productivity, on the other, could have arisen.

The EDEM variable may be a good proxy for important but unobservable (to the econometrician) firm characteristics that help explain subsequent performance and valuation of firms. In all cases the coefficient is insignificant, however only in the LABPRO regressions is it positive. This suggests that either inside information was not important or that, as argued in previous studies on the Czech mass privatization (Hillion and Young, 1996; Hingorani *et al.*, 1997; van Wijnbergen and Marcincin, 1995), investors did not effectively discriminate between firms on account of any (inside) informational advantages. This may be because the strategy of most investors, and the large investment funds in particular, was to bid with all points in the first round. This was done for fear of not being able to use all available shares (the number of rounds was not established before the privatization started and investors thus did not know how many rounds were remaining) and because some of the investment funds had issued guarantees on their rate of return, which they could fall short of if too many points were to go unused.

The signs on initial conditions (the second group of coefficients in Table 11.3) are always positive. The coefficients are also highly significant, as expected. The sector dummies show some interesting patterns. Agribusiness has a negative coefficient in the TOBQ and MKTDEP regressions, which turns positive (but insignificant) in the LABPRO regression. The only sector where the coefficients are uniformly negative in all regressions is Wood, while Food, Metals and Machinery are the only three sectors with uniformly positive (albeit mostly insignificant) coefficients. F-tests for the joint significance of the sector variables show only statistical significance (at the 95 per cent level) in the TOBQ regression. We leave them in all regressions for comparability.

As discussed, we can distinguish three different types of managers: insiders, outsiders selected by the government and outsiders selected by the new private owners. In Table 11.4 we extend the analysis and

*Table* 11.4   Estimation results with separate dummies for different types of managers (OLS)

| Explanatory variable | TOBQ | PROF | LABPRO | MKTDEP |
|---|---|---|---|---|
| SHOLDER:OUTMOF | −0.305 | −0.146 | 225.869 | 0.917 |
| | (0.406) | (0.926) | (0.764) | (1.042) |
| SHOLDER:OUTOWN | −0.285 | 0.396 | 476.546 | 0.948 |
| | (0.315) | (1.418) | (1.394) | (0.452) |
| SHOLDER:INS | 0.236 | 0.004 | −239.651 | 0.405 |
| | (0.836) | (0.159) | (1.764) | (0.928) |
| OUTSIDER:GOV | −0.083 | 0.024 | 10.040 | 0.061 |
| | (1.705) | (1.468) | (0.527) | (0.769) |
| OUTSIDER:OWNER | 0.144 | 0.043 | 40.714 | 0.057 |
| | (3.045) | (3.326) | (2.649) | (1.148) |
| AGE | 0.003 | 0.001 | 1.659 | 0.003 |
| | (1.639) | (1.728) | (1.948) | (0.077) |
| TOBQ:BEG | 0.642 | – | – | – |
| | (9.532) | | | |
| PROF:BEG | – | 0.567 | – | – |
| | | (8.636) | | |
| LABPRO:BEG | – | – | 0.961 | – |
| | | | (9.764) | |
| LEV | 0.021 | −0.001 | −7.162 | −0.002 |
| | (1.746) | (0.374) | (2.176) | (0.248) |
| EDEM | −0.001 | −0.001 | 0.372 | −0.003 |
| | (1.012) | (0.094) | (0.218) | (3.024) |
| Sector dummies included | Yes | Yes | Yes | Yes |
| Constant | 0.044 | −0.027 | −17.957 | 0.344 |
| | (0.395) | (0.859) | (0.405) | (2.436) |
| Adjusted $R^2$ | 0.378 | 0.219 | 0.625 | 0.025 |

*Notes*:
All regressions are based on 706 observations.
Absolute values of *t*-statistics in parentheses.
The numeraire sector in all cases is Financial services and the numeraire management change is an internally promoted manager. Standard errors are heteroskedasticity-consistent.

study separately the impact of various types of managers using dummy variables.

The pattern of the effects of management changes and equity incentives on corporate performance is similar to that shown by the raw statistics (Table 11.2). Different types of changes in managers (insiders, outsiders appointed by the government, outsiders selected by the new private owners) affect corporate performance differently. In particular, managers chosen by private owners who were not internally promoted (OUTSIDER:OWNER) perform best, followed by managers chosen from the outside by the government (OUTSIDER:GOV), with internally promoted managers the worst. Equity incentives do not have a significant effect on corporate performance, even if one distinguishes between equity incentives held by internally promoted managers and equity incentives held by managers externally appointed (by the government or private owners).

One possible explanation for the insignificant results for equity holdings may be that, so far, we have not used the data on the size of manager holdings. As shown earlier, there is little variation across firms and the mean share of equity held by managers is very small (2.5 per cent). It is also unclear whether managers may have used other vehicles to invest in their firms. We nevertheless test the hypothesis that there exists a correlation between the size of each holding and manager performance by including the reported holdings instead of the dummy for holdings. The results (not reported) show no discernible pattern when the relative amount of shareholdings is included. Since it has been found that the relationship can be non-monotonic (Morck *et al.,* 1988, report that the relationship between Tobin's Q and CEO stock ownership is positive between 0 per cent and 1 per cent, negative between 1 per cent and 5 per cent, positive between 5 per cent and 20 per cent, and negative after that), we also run a piece-wise linear regression. We divide managers into groups who hold less than 5 per cent, less than 15 per cent, and more than 15 per cent and create a dummy for each group. Including these dummies in a similar regression as that of Table 11.4, we do not find any significant coefficients. An alternative hypothesis may be that the results are not supportive of the theory since holdings in small firms are less valuable than equal (in terms of share of total) holdings in large firms. We therefore run another set of regressions, substituting the value of each holding (defined as the number of shares the manager holds times their market value) for the share of equity the manager owns. Again the results are not statistically significant.[4]

In sum, we find that the results in Tables 11.2 and 11.3 are supported in subsequent refinements of the empirical specifications. The evidence for the hypothesis that new managers help the restructuring process is robust. The evidence on equity incentives, on the other hand, is indeterminate.

## Conclusions

The Czech voucher scheme provides a unique experiment for empirical research on the relationship between management profiles and corporate performance as it allows us to study the effects of management changes and incentives on performance with little concern for endogeneity or selection problems. We find that four measures of enterprise performance are positively related to the entry of new managers, especially those appointed by private owners. Equity incentives to general managers have an indeterminate effect on corporate performance. Indeed, for three enterprise performance indicators, they have a negative effect, although never significant.

The main conclusion for policy makers is that post-privatization enterprise restructuring in transition economies requires new human capital, which can only occur through management changes. Countries that opted for management buy-outs or countries with insufficient entry of new managers (either expatriates or newly trained managers) may have difficulties in achieving high corporate growth.

### Notes

1. Johnson *et al.* (1985) cover a sample of 172 US firms on the NYSE; Morck *et al.* (1989) cover 454 firms of the 1980 Fortune 500; McConnell and Servaes (1990) cover 1173 firms in 1976 and 1093 firms in 1986.
2. Blasi *et al.* (1997) report that between 1992 and 1996, for a sample of 332 Russian firms, 33 per cent of all general managers were replaced, with 19 per cent of new managers coming from the outside and 14 per cent being internally promoted. The average age of general managers in 1996 was 50 years.
3. In comparison, the sample used in Barberis *et al.* (1996) has an average firm size of 25 employees.
4. As an additional piece of sensitivity analysis, we use scatter plots to see whether the tenure (number of years associated with the firm) helps explain the relative performance of firms with insider managers. In particular, we divide the sample of insider-managed firms into firms with CEOs who had spent less than 10, less than 20, less than 25 and more than 25 years with the firm. The scatter plots (not reported) show a non-monotonic (but statistically insignificant) relationship where managers in the 10–25 years of experience groups perform better than managers with less than 10 or more than 25 years of experience.

# 12
# The Relationship between FDI, Privatization and Structural Change in Central and Eastern European Countries

*Gábor Hunya*

## Basic features of FDI in Central and Eastern European countries

FDI is a specific form of international capital flows, more long-term, more company-related than portfolio or other investments. By FDI foreign investors (basically multinational corporations: MNCs) establish a controlling position over their foreign affiliates. For these reasons costs and risks of investment are considered in a long-term perspective.

Factors determining FDI are summarized by Dunning (1993) under the headings of ownership, location and internalization. These terms relate to company-specific assets which, if utilised internally by the MNC and located internationally, result in the optimum utilization of these assets. FDI is motivated by the expansion to new markets, by increases of production efficiency via international relocation and by the acquisition of natural resources and of strategic assets including knowledge. The expansion to new markets appears to be a primary motivation of FDI worldwide, including the Central and Eastern European countries (Szanyi, 1998). Efficiency improvements and cost advantage of the location come second (Pye, 1997). Cost advantages in Central and Eastern European countries are mainly related to labour costs (Havlik, 1996) and in some countries also to energy and transport costs. Transactions costs, on the other hand, tend to be high in transforming economies (Dietz, 1991). The acquisition of natural resources and of strategic assets including knowledge appear to be secondary but important motives in some FDI cases. The primary objectives of investment change during the operation of affiliates and are modified by further investments.

The macroeconomic environment sets the general framework for the development of costs and risks and thus for the operation of foreign affiliates in a country (Baldwin *et al.*, 1997; Lizondo, 1990). In line with theory-based expectations, more advanced, stable and open countries have been the most attractive FDI targets also among the Central and East European countries in the 1990s. The Czech Republic, Hungary, Poland and Slovenia, as well as Estonia, have attracted considerable amounts of FDI either in volume or in comparison to their size. That this group of countries has been more attractive than others is the result of their better macroeconomic performance and stability, together with a faster pace of institutional transformation. The relative attractiveness within the group has mainly to do with the progress and method of privatization.

Eastern countries had a modest 4 per cent share in 1996 world FDI inflows, the four smaller countries among them (the Czech Republic, Hungary, Slovenia and the Slovak Republic) received 1.1 per cent and Poland alone almost 1 per cent. The seven East–Central European countries listed in Table 12.1 attracted some US$ 10.7 bn in 1995,

*Table* 12.1   Foreign direct investment in Central and Eastern European countries: Inflow 1994–7 and stock end 1997

| | Inflow US$ mn | | | Inflow 1997 | | Stock 1997 | |
| | *1994* | *1995* | *1996* | *1997* | *as % of fixed capital formation[1]* | *US$ mn* | *as % of GDP[1]* |
|---|---|---|---|---|---|---|---|
| Czech Rep. | 869 | 2 562 | 1 428 | 1 300 | 8.1 | 6 763 | 13.0 |
| Hungary | 1 319 | 4 571 | 2 069 | 2 307 | 22.5 | 17 529 | 39.3 |
| Poland | 1 493[2] | 2 511[2] | 4 000[2] | 5 678[2] | 19.7[2] | 15 305[3] | 11.5 |
| Slovak Rep. | 185 | 181 | 666 | 200[4] | 2.7 | 1 410 | 7.2 |
| Slovenia | 377 | 414 | 190 | 600[4] | 14.3 | 2 400 | 13.7 |
| Bulgaria | 214 | 164 | 303 | 510 | 51.0 | 1 252 | 12.5 |
| Romania[5] | 568 | 313 | 609 | 1210 | 18.0 | 2 800 | 8.1 |
| **CEEC–7** | **5 025** | **10 716** | **9 264** | **11 805** | | **49 859** | |

*Notes*:
1. Preliminary.
2. Projects with more than US$ 1 mn invested capital; in 1997 including small ventures: US$ 6600 mn.
3. 1997 stock including small ventures and adjusted to international methodology; stock measured by local method, US$ 20.7 bn.
4. Estimated.
5. Inflow based on FDI registration, stocks include only equity.
Flows do not add up to stocks in US$.
For a detailed description of methodology, see Hunya and Stankovsky (1997).
*Source*:   WIIW database, based on official data.

US\$ 9.3 bn in 1996 and almost US\$ 11.8 bn in 1997. The recent upswing is due to more privatization-related sales in Poland, Romania and Bulgaria.

In international comparisons the size of FDI inflow is usually compared to the gross fixed capital formation and FDI stocks to the volume of GDP (UNCTAD, 1997). The world average of FDI inflow compared to gross fixed capital formation is 5 per cent (1995) and there are only 20 countries where it exceeds 20 per cent. Hungary stands out with a rate of over 20 per cent FDI per gross fixed capital formation in each year between 1992 and 1997. The Czech Republic in 1995 and Poland in 1997 came close to this mark but also the others, except Slovakia, are above the world average. Extremely high rates can also occur as a result of a depression of domestic investment, as in Bulgaria. The world average for FDI stocks in GDP is about 10 per cent (1995) which is exceeded in 1997 by five countries out of the seven in Table 12.1. Only Hungary has relatively high stocks and is in the group of countries with the highest FDI penetration in the world.

The distribution of FDI by economic activities (see Table 12.2) reflects the opening up of individual sectors to foreign investment. Initially most FDI went into trade and manufacturing, later the share of finance increased. In countries where new sectors have been opened to foreign investment by the advance of privatization the share of manufacturing fell below 40 per cent. The most notable cases were telecommunications in the Czech Republic and also the gas and energy sector in Hungary. In Slovenia, where some activities are still closed to foreign investors and the manufacturing sector was privatized to insiders,

*Table* 12.2   FDI stocks by economic activities, 1996, per cent

|  | Czech Rep. | Hungary | Poland | Slovakia | Slovenia |
|---|---|---|---|---|---|
| Manufacturing | 37 | 40 | 62 | 47 | 39 |
| Electricity, gas, water | n. a. | 14 | n.a. | n. a. | 14 |
| Construction | 8 | 4 | 5 | 3 | n.a. |
| Trade, repair | 8 | 12 | 6 | 18 | 15 |
| Hotels, restaurants | n. a. | 2 | n. a. | 1 | n.a. |
| Transport, telecom | 22 | 9 | 5 | 2 | 1 |
| Finance, insurance | 8 | 9 | 21 | 25 | 17 |
| Real estate, renting | n. a. | 7 | n. a. | 2 | 10 |
| Others, incl. n. a. | 17 | 3 | 1 | 2 | 4 |
| Total surveyed FDI (US\$ mn) | 7 061 | 9 787 | 12 028 | 1 326 | 1 934 |

*Source*:   Hunya and Stankovsky (1997).

trade and energy have remarkable shares, the latter due to the atomic power station jointly owned with Croatia. Poland has a very high proportion of manufacturing FDI due to the imminent telecom and utility privatization.

## Privatization as a vehicle of FDI

The privatization of state-owned enterprises provided unique access to the productive assets and markets of Central and Eastern European countries. About half of the FDI in Central and Eastern European countries has come through acquisitions of, or capital increase in, state-owned enterprises. Some 10–20 per cent were greenfield investments, the rest being investments in existing foreign affiliates. With decreasing numbers of new ventures, this latter form is becoming more and more important in Hungary, the Czech Republic and Slovakia. Mass privatization by vouchers, sales to insiders, or to the management, have hindered foreign takeovers, whereas in direct sales tenders foreigners usually outbid domestic investors. The main method of privatization has boosted FDI in Hungary and hindered it in the Czech Republic, Slovenia and Slovakia. But foreign sales were allowed in all countries in specific individual cases. Capital increases through a foreign investor were an important means of privatization in the Czech Republic.

The efforts of Central and Eastern European governments to sell companies in the privatization process can be regarded as the most important incentive to attract FDI. The sale price was a matter of negotiation and took into consideration all risk factors. Foreign investors mostly competed with each other as domestic private investment capital was scarce. Post-privatization investment in restructuring was necessary even for the best central European companies. Therefore the often used argument that foreign investors picked only the best companies must be modified in so far as companies with a potential market were picked although they were mostly financially bankrupt or had no longer-term prospects without a big capital injection. The flagships of privatization, like Tungsram in Hungary or Škoda in the Czech Republic, were such cases.

At the outset of transformation most East–Central European governments believed in the rapid privatization of publicly owned productive assets. Many of them envisaged a fair redistribution of the wealth inherited from the former regime. Others, like Hungary and Estonia, cared more for the fast restructuring of state-owned enterprises and for budgetary revenues. It is quite evident after seven years of experience that improving corporate governance and profound restructuring matter more for future economic growth than the speed of divestiture or social justice, and that this objective has mostly been met by sales, especially to foreign investors.

The main privatization method and the chances of foreign companies participating in the privatization process depended in every country on

- the power of popular demand for fairness and justice,
- the budgetary and current account situation of the country,
- the expected restructuring effects, and
- the government's perception of national independence.

Conflicting expectations concerning the results of privatization gave rise to heated political disputes over privatization methods. As a result, the intensity of privatization fluctuated, and policy objectives and methods changed frequently. Although countries can be characterized by the dominant way of privatization, in fact all applied a mix of methods. (See Table 12.3 and 12.4.)

The mainstream approach would prefer the sale of public enterprises to strong and competent new owners able to restructure and develop the acquired company. Selling to foreign multinationals or to emerging

*Table* 12.3    Main methods and objectives of privatization

|  | *Fast, easy privatization* | *Improve corporate governance* | *Raise capital for restructuring* | *Raise government revenues* | *Social, political fairness* |
|---|---|---|---|---|---|
| Sale to domestic investor | – | + | = | + | – |
| Sale to foreign investor | – | + | + | + | – |
| Insider: |  |  |  |  |  |
| MBO, ESOP | + | – | – | = | + |
|  | (–) | (+) |  |  | (–) |
| Equal access voucher | + | – | – | – | + |
|  | (–) |  |  |  | (–) |
| Restitution | – | = | = | – | + |

*Note*:    Symbols for primary effects and (secondary effects): + positive impact; – negative impact; = neutral impact.
*Source*:    Own revision of Table 3.1. in World Bank (1996a).

*Table* 12.4   Estimated distribution of enterprise assets between privatization methods, up to 1997, per cent

|  | Sale to domestic investor | Sale to foreign investor | Equal access voucher | Insider: MBO and ESOP | Other* | Still state property |
|---|---|---|---|---|---|---|
| Czech Rep. | 10 | 10 | 40 | 5 | 5 | 30 |
| Hungary | 12 | 45 | 0 | 3 | 20 | 20 |
| Poland | 2 | 10 | 18 | 20 | 10 | 40 |
| Romania | 5 | 5 | 20 | 10 | 0 | 60 |
| Slovak Rep. | 3 | 7 | 25 | 30 | 5 | 30 |
| Slovenia | 3 | 7 | 20 | 20 | 20 | 30 |

*Note*:   * Other methods include restitution, transfer to social security funds and local organizations, liquidation.
*Source*:   Author's update and expansion of the table in World Bank (1996a, p. 3.13); Hungary: *APVRT Privatization Monitor*; Czech Republic: *Statistical Yearbook*, 1997, p. 513; own and WIIW specialists' estimates.

domestic entrepreneurs is the way to achieve this objective. But others may regard positive restructuring effects as being outweighed by short-term negative employment and price effects, loss of social equity and 'national control'. Equal access to public property by the population, or of the workers of a given company was a popular moral value and political objective satisfied either by voucher privatization or by ESOP programmes.

Hungary and Estonia came closest to the mainstream approach. As early as the 1980s, a foreign capital-friendly economic policy developed in Hungary as part of the reform process. This was later enforced by the expectation of positive restructuring effects and, last but not least, by financial necessity.

In initial discussions the speed of privatization was considered to be a primary objective, therefore voucher schemes were internationally praised. It soon turned out that the longer-term development potential depends to a more significant extent on the speed of restructuring. This correlates with the quality of corporate governance and access to new financing – conditions which are best in foreign investment enterprises. As a result, Hungary is ahead of other Central and Eastern European countries in terms of productivity improvements and the upgrading of export structures. The budgetary and balance of payments crisis of 1994 was able to be corrected and the country embarked on accelerating export-led economic growth fuelled by foreign affiliates.

Privatization policies based on vouchers or ESOP delayed micro-economic restructuring and finally led to macroeconomic imbalances. In the Czech Republic, the current account deficit triggered the devaluation of 1997, while economic growth slowed down. There are years of slow economic growth but also, it is hoped, of fast restructuring ahead. If the government wants to tackle the microeconomic foundations of the crisis and care more about corporate governance and restructuring in voucher-privatized companies, it will have to stimulate strategic investors to get more involved in the country. This would bring about a new privatization drive and an upswing in FDI in the coming years. Privatization in Poland progressed more slowly than elsewhere, but it gained momentum in 1996 and stimulated a surge in FDI.

## Foreign penetration in manufacturing in Central and Eastern Europe

The foreign penetration of manufacturing in Central and Eastern Europe can be expressed as the share of foreign affiliates in the economy as a whole by various indicators. Data are available for a somewhat larger group of companies than truly foreign-controlled affiliates. Companies with some foreign share in their nominal or equity capital, foreign investment enterprises (FIEs), were sorted out from national databases which contain data from the income statements of companies. For Hungary, Slovenia and Austria only very small ventures are excluded; data for the Czech Republic cover companies with 100 or more employees, data for Slovakia those with 25 or more employees.

Among Central and Eastern European countries only Hungary shows a high degree of foreign penetration (Table 12.5). In 1996, two-thirds of the equity capital was in FIEs, which produced more than 60 per cent of the country's manufacturing output. The openness of the Hungarian economy to foreign capital is thus higher than that of Austria, a small Western economy with a longer history of foreign penetration. FIEs in Austria employ one third of the workforce and produce almost half of the output in manufacturing. Rates are even higher in South European countries with lower development levels: about half of the Spanish industrial workforce is employed in companies with foreign capital, while more than 60 per cent of the Irish manufacturing output is from FIEs. Hungary is thus in the group of the most foreign-penetrated European economies. This position developed in the first half of the 1990s at a very rapid pace. The share of FIEs in manufacturing equity was only 13 per cent in 1991, increasing to

*Table* 12.5   Share of foreign investment enterprises (FIEs) in the manufacturing sector, 1996, per cent

|  | Equity capital | Employment | Investments | Sales | Export sales |
|---|---|---|---|---|---|
| Czech Rep. | 21.5[1] | 13.1 | 33.5 | 22.6 | |
| Hungary | 67.4[2] | 36.1 | 82.5 | 61.4 | 73.9 |
| Slovak Rep. | 16.9 | 11.7 | 24.3 | 21.6 | |
| Slovenia | 15.6 | 10.1 | 20.3 | 19.6 | 25.8 |
| *Austria*[3] | *24.8* | *32.9* | | *45* | |

*Notes:*
1. Own capital.
2. Nominal capital in cash.
3. 1995.
Czech Republic: non-financial corporations with at least 100 employees; Slovakia: non-financial corporations with at least 25 employees; Hungary, Slovenia, Austria: companies supplying tax declarations; Austria, Czech Republic, Slovakia: companies with any foreign share; Hungary, Slovenia: companies with at least 10 per ent foreign share in the nominal capital.
*Source:*   WIIW database on foreign investment enterprises, relying on data supplied by national statistical offices.

31 per cent in 1993 and doubling in the following three years. The sales policy of the privatization agency, the liquidation of state-owned companies and the weak domestic capital accumulation all played a role in this development.

The Czech Republic has a penetration rate of about one-third of Hungary's in terms of capital and employment. A doubling of the FIE shares in terms of most indicators occurred between 1993 and 1996: the share of FIEs in capital moved from about 11 per cent in 1993 to 21.5 per cent in 1996. In 1996, foreign investment enterprises provided almost 23 per cent of sales in manufacturing and 13 per cent of employment, both twice as much as three years earlier. In Slovakia, about 17 per cent of the equity capital in manufacturing companies is invested in FIEs, which employ 12 per cent of the labour force, but produce one-fifth of the output. Slovenia had stronger foreign penetration in 1994 than the Czech Republic and Slovakia, but in 1996 it was lagging somewhat behind the other two countries. Poland had in 1994 foreign shares similar to those of the Czech Republic.

FIEs have in all analysed countries higher shares in capital than in labour and even higher shares in output. This means that endowment with capital and also labour productivity are higher in the FIE sector than in the domestically owned enterprises. This confirms the expectation that foreign investors use more recent technology, but it also reflects the concentration of FDI in manufacturing branches with high capital intensity. FIEs in manufacturing pay, on average, higher wages than domestic companies in manufacturing. They can afford to employ the younger and better trained part of the workforce, which contributes to their high productivity.

The outstanding export performance relative to output indicates that FIEs are more export-oriented than domestic firms. This is confirmed by 1996 data for Hungary and Slovenia and by 1994 data also for the Czech Republic and Slovakia. Contrary to most survey results indicating that FDI in Central and Eastern European countries was mainly motivated by local market penetration, the activity of FIEs turns out to be somewhat different. In Hungary, FIEs provide about three-quarters of manufacturing exports and the difference in export intensity between the domestic and the foreign sector has been growing.

FIEs contribute more than proportionately to fixed investment outlays. This is a confirmation of the positive effect of FDI on economic growth and restructuring. Investment data also suggest that foreign investors rapidly restructure the acquired manufacturing firms. The rationalization of production generally means lay-offs, and new investments apply labour saving technologies even if they do processing for exports. Foreign penetration may thus increase unemployment in the short run. Stepped up investment activities of FIEs were confirmed by recent company surveys in Central and Eastern European countries (Szanyi, 1998) too. A continuous expansion of FDI can thus be expected as a consequence of the fixed investments undertaken by already existing FIEs. Investment by FIEs is mostly financed by retained profits, which may thus not be repatriated on a massive scale. Although the current account shows increasing profit transfers by FIEs, their profit reinvestment is also growing. As long as Central and Eastern European countries remain favourable locations for FDI in terms of future profit and risks, there is no reason why profits should be repatriated. Internationally competitive corporate tax rates like the 18 per cent practised in Hungary are certainly of advantage to keeping profits in the country. The allegation of widespread use of transfer pricing in MNCs in their relations to their Central and Eastern European subsidiaries has never really been confirmed.

## Exports of manufacturing FIEs

Higher than average export shares in sales indicate that FIEs are clearly more export-oriented than domestic companies, but the degree of export orientation across manufacturing industries only weakly correlates with the share of FIEs in total exports.

In the Czech Republic, exports represented 31 per cent of sales in the case of all enterprises and 41 per cent for FIEs in 1994 (no data for more recent years are available). The difference was present in all branches of manufacturing. An especially strong export orientation of FIEs was registered for wooden products, metals, furniture and clothes. FIEs' presence is not very pronounced in these branches, but investments were obviously made for the purpose of exports. Exceptions to the rule are office machinery, radio and television sets, paper and the almost entirely domestic-oriented printing and publishing industry. Weak export orientation of FIEs in these industry branches can be explained by the especially high suppressed demand before 1989 and rapidly expanding domestic markets. The branches where FIEs have a high proportion of total exports are naturally those where the invested capital is concentrated. These branches are not extraordinarily export-oriented: they sell about half of their products on the domestic market.

In Hungary, industries which are more internationalized worldwide and have a high penetration by foreign capital show a higher degree of export orientation. Of net sales of all Hungarian manufacturing companies, 24 per cent went for export in 1994; in the case of FIEs it was 30 per cent. The difference between the two indicators was similar in 1996: 30 per cent for all companies and 37 per cent for FIEs. FIEs provide more than three-quarters of manufacturing exports and the difference of export intensity between the domestic and the foreign sector has been growing. The share of export sales in FIEs' output in 1996 was above 80 per cent for motor vehicles, and above 70 per cent for electrical machinery. Export shares between 60 per cent and 70 per cent could be observed for the clothing and leather industries. Several companies in transport equipment and electrical machinery branches of industry have been established with a duty-free zone status and sell over 80 per cent of their products abroad. Export-oriented greenfield investments make up about 20 per cent of the total FDI stock of Hungary and contribute substantially to the improving foreign trade balance in 1995–6. Most of the greenfield projects have the status of a customs-free zone and produce one tenth of the industrial output.

As to Slovakia, the small size of the country makes sales abroad indispensable to most producers, so that the share of exports in manufacturing sales was 47 per cent in 1994 (the latest year available); in the case of FIEs, it was even higher, at 58 per cent. Apart from the car industry, also the shoe industry and wood processing FIEs have an export ratio of more than 70 per cent. The situation is similar in Slovenia, where FIEs in the manufacturing sector export 65.3 per cent of their net sales while the corresponding share for domestic enterprises is 45.9 per cent. Textiles, rubber and basic metals have higher export shares, but lower foreign presence, than the main foreign-penetrated and also export-oriented branches producing vehicles and machines. Major reasons given by foreign investors for their participation in Slovenian companies include a past record of successful cooperation with these enterprises, together with their export performance and established trade links (Rojec, 1997).

The outstanding export performance relative to output indicates that FIEs are more export-oriented than domestic firms. This is confirmed by 1996 data for Hungary and Slovenia and by 1994 data also for the Czech Republic and Slovakia. Export success can be attributed to the higher than average efficiency and quality of output and also to the advantages of international corporate linkages. Being integrated into the networks of a multinational enterprise, FIEs enjoy better access to foreign markets than domestic firms. The cost of exporting is lower for FIEs because they can receive cheaper and better marketing services, export financing and market information. On the other hand, the division of labour within multinational enterprises may prevent subsidiaries from entering certain markets in order to rule out competition with products from other subsidiaries of the same multinational enterprise.

Contrary to most survey results indicating that FDI in Central and Eastern European countries was mainly motivated by local market penetration, the export activity of FIEs turns out to be above average. There may be three reasons behind the diverging message of surveys on the motives of foreign investment and these findings. One reason is that the surveys usually do not differentiate between manufacturing industries, which usually have a positive trade balance, and other activities, including retail trade, which have almost no exports and a negative trade balance.

A second point is that the most widespread motive for all investment, not only of foreign investment, is an emerging new market opportunity. As pointed out above, the domestic market is the primary target of all companies, more in larger, less in smaller countries. FIEs do not need to be essentially different from domestically owned companies. The reason why they differ in their foreign trade intensity is that they are generally more intensely integrated into an international production network than companies without a foreign strategic investor.

Third, the entrance motive may be different from the later objectives of the foreign affiliate.

The specific features of FIEs suggest that they do not have only above-average export intensity but also above-average import intensity. This is especially true in the early stage of investment projects when FIEs import their own machinery and the supplier network is mostly foreign. While machinery imports are temporary, the import of inputs can only slowly be replaced by host country suppliers, many of which may themselves be foreign subsidiaries. The highly negative foreign trade balance of FIEs in the build-up period of projects contributed decisively to the extensive foreign trade deficit of Hungary in 1993–4 and most probably also to the 1996–7 Polish deficit.

## The upgrading of export structures

Changes in export patterns can be used to demonstrate progress in restructuring, the bulk of which is due to privatization and foreign investment. Increasing shares of engineering products in exports can be considered as structural upgrading. EU imports from the countries presented in Table 12.6 more than doubled between 1990 and 1996. The highest growth was shown by countries which registered the lowest EU share in exports in 1990 – the Czech Republic and Slovakia. Here the geographic shift of exports played a more important role than in Hungary or Slovenia, where a re-orientation of trade started already earlier.

The share of engineering in exports from Central and Eastern European countries closely correlates with the stock of FDI/GDP and the pace of structural upgrading of exports correlates with the FDI inflow per gross fixed capital formation. The most favourable export structure and the fastest upgrading can be observed in the case of Hungary. The increase in the share of machinery in Hungarian exports to the EU was 32 percentage points between 1990 and 1996, leading to a 52 per cent share. In the case of the Czech Republic, which started from a similar share in 1990, the improvement was 22 percentage points, and the result in 1996 was a 43 per cent share. There is no difference between the two countries concerning the change in the share of the group of labour-intensive light industry products. As for the other product groups, due to natural conditions, energy- and material-intensive goods are over-represented in the Czech industrial export structure, just as food is in the Hungarian.

Table 12.6 Central and Eastern European exports to the EU, share of commodity groups in manufacturing exports, per cent

| NACE code | Czech Republic* | | | Hungary | | | Slovak Republic | | | Slovenia | | |
|---|---|---|---|---|---|---|---|---|---|---|---|---|
| | 1990 | 1994 | 1996 | 1990 | 1994 | 1996 | 1990 | 1994 | 1996 | 1990 | 1994 | 1996 |
| DA | 6 | 2 | 2 | 19 | 11 | 8 | | 1 | 1 | | 2 | 1 |
| DB-DE | 29 | 26 | 18 | 29 | 26 | 19 | | 28 | 24 | | 31 | 26 |
| DF-DJ | 44 | 41 | 37 | 32 | 27 | 21 | | 45 | 39 | | 25 | 26 |
| DK-DN | 21 | 31 | 43 | 20 | 36 | 52 | | 26 | 36 | | 42 | 47 |
| Total volume ECU bn | 2.4 | 7.0 | 7.9 | 2.5 | 4.4 | 6.6 | | 1.8 | 2.7 | | 3.4 | 3.7 |

| NACE code | Poland | | | Bulgaria | | | Romania | | |
|---|---|---|---|---|---|---|---|---|---|
| | 1990 | 1994 | 1996 | 1990 | 1994 | 1996 | 1990 | 1994 | 1996 |
| DA | 16 | 7 | 6 | 15 | 7 | 6 | 1 | 2 | 1 |
| DB-DE | 29 | 38 | 28 | 27 | 32 | 34 | 60 | 58 | 50 |
| DF-DJ | 39 | 34 | 31 | 41 | 44 | 46 | 28 | 29 | 28 |
| DK-DN | 16 | 21 | 34 | 17 | 17 | 14 | 11 | 11 | 21 |
| Total Volume ECU bn | 4.0 | 7.9 | 10.1 | 0.4 | 1.2 | 1.4 | 1.2 | 2.3 | 3.3 |

Notes:
NACE codes: DA = Food, beverages, tobacco; DB-DE = Textiles, clothing, leather, shoes, wood, paper; DF-DJ = Chemicals, construction material, metals; DK-DN = Engineering (i.e. electrical machinery, transport equipment, machinery).
* Czechoslovakia for 1990.
Source: Eurostat, imports of the EU from Central and Eastern European countries.

Slovakia stands out with a more backward export structures and slow structural change. Slovenia shows an advanced export structure, but very slow change. As a result, the machinery share in 1996 was already higher in Hungarian exports than in Slovenian exports. As to other Central and Eastern European countries, the share of engineering in Polish (34 per cent), Bulgarian (14 per cent) and Romanian (21 per cent) exports is clearly lower than in the three most advanced Central and Eastern European countries. While the Balkan countries show little improvement, Polish exports underwent rapid restructuring after 1994.

The share of machinery in Central and Eastern European exports closely correlates with the stock of FDI/GDP. The pace of structural upgrading correlates with the FDI inflow per gross fixed capital formation shown in Table 12.1. The export structure of Hungary and also of the Czech Republic has shifted towards branches where there is foreign presence. In both countries export shares increased most rapidly for transport equipment, which was the primary target of foreign penetration.

## Conclusions

The above observations allow a number of conclusions. First, fast privatization is necessary but the method matters. In particular, improving corporate governance and deep restructuring are more important than the speed of privatization while strategic owners are better for restructuring than dispersed or insider owners.

Second, FDI has had mainly positive effects. The penetration of FDI has improved the economic growth potential of Central and Eastern European countries and it has contributed to the upgrading of economic structures. The volume of FDI/GDP is an indicator of the advance of countries in terms of transformation and globalization. Problems emerging in relation to FDI, such as balance of payments problems or economic duality, are important, but may diminish under proper policies. The basically positive results of FDI encourage governments to allow more foreign acquisitions in their current and future privatization projects than was the case earlier. The shift in policy is most marked in Poland, Romania and Bulgaria, while this Czech Republic may join this group soon.

Third, FDI provides future opportunities for acquisitions in the privatization process. Countries with privatization almost finished and dominating foreign ownership (Hungary and Estonia) provide few new opportunities: only some problematic companies in industry, some public utilities and selected areas of services still await privatization.

But the high degree of foreign presence makes these countries attractive for future direct investments owing to agglomeration effects. A steady and high rate of FDI inflows will take the form of greenfield projects and of capital increases in existing ventures. Countries with almost complete but shallow privatization (Czech Republic, Slovakia and Slovenia) face a second drive of ownership changes. As the owners who received property rights in various distribution schemes will not have the means to restructure the companies, they may invite foreign investors to do the job. In addition, there are important activities, especially utilities and banks, where major privatization deals are still ahead. Countries with privatization in progress (Romania and Bulgaria) offer many opportunities for acquisitions in all economic sectors. Investment in these countries is still more risky than elsewhere, but equity prices are not high and the access to the local market can improve if a local supplier is acquired. But privatization can remain slow as the administrative capacity for tackling sales is limited. In this respect, Poland provides an interesting mixture of opportunities for FDI within the privatization process, in management-owned companies and as greenfield investments alike.

Fourth, EU accession will attract additional foreign capital. Foreign firms have integrated Central and Eastern European countries into the EU at the microeconomic level, but to varying degrees. The process is most advanced in Hungary and Estonia, followed by the Czech Republic and Slovenia. Poland is catching up. Slovak, Romanian and Bulgarian companies are generally less integrated, which adds to other transformation problems. It is in accordance with these results that the Czech Republic, Hungary, Poland and Slovenia, together with Estonia, have been selected to start accession negotiations with the EU ahead of other countries.

During the accession process investment risk will diminish as political and economic stability improves with the implementation of the acquis. New business opportunities will be offered by the expansion of local markets, GDP growth being ahead of the EU average, and by improving market access due to further liberalization measures. This will be a benefit for EU investors and host countries alike. The full implementation of the provisions in the Europe (association) agreements will come into force by 2001–2. In terms of market liberalization, Central and Eastern European countries are already more advanced than South European countries had been at the time of accession. But they may not be ready to join the EMU (economic and monetary union) at the time of accession. Further liberalization of financial markets and the service sectors will in many Central and Eastern European countries (for example, Slovenia) take place only during the accession process and suffer delays if this process should be too slow. FDI also supports the catching up of Central and Eastern European countries in terms of economic development and wage levels, which may accelerate during accession. But the gap will remain for a considerable time and attract labour- and skill-intensive production to Central and Eastern European countries.

# III

# Privatization and the Emergence of Markets

# 13
## Transforming Socialist Networks
*Michael Keren*

## Introduction[1]

Why look at organizations as networks? The network representation puts the structure of the organization, say the firm, in the limelight, focusing on the flows of messages, information and commands, as well as materials, in it. Thus firms cease to be black boxes, but become a series of PBXs (private branch exchanges) that interact. The manner of interaction of firms in alternative environments is the focus of this chapter. Firms' corporate culture, the set of routines which makes a firm, is shaped by their environment, and a culture that is successful in the capitalist market will not be viable in a socialist planned economy, and vice versa. What this chapter tries to do is to examine the forces that lead to the development of given modes of behaviour.

The view of the economy at large, and the firm inside it, as a giant network which follows certain environment-imposed rules, provides perspectives that are not easily obtained otherwise. There are two aspects of the *ancien régime* which may be easiest to analyse in this manner. The lateral ties between enterprises in transition proved to be quite durable, with the result that, in some countries, flows of inputs continued long after the collapse of socialism and the cessation of payments for these supplies. This is one of the origins of the build-up of inter-enterprise credits. The simplistic view of a planned economy, requiring the planner's imprimatur for any material flow, would have led to the proposition that these flows stop once the planner is out of the picture.[2] The second aspect is the very stability of the institutions inherited from the socialist past. Rather than adjust to the changing circumstances, the new profit-requiring environment, enterprises continued to maintain their old patterns of behaviour which, presumably, were no longer rational. The manner in which the firms' culture is embedded in their network explains why change requires an extremely strong pressure from without, a pressure that was not supplied in many of the putatively transforming countries.[3]

Networks have been in vogue lately, and it is important to clarify the sense in which the term is to be used below. The closest usage can be found in the writings of economic sociologists such as Granovetter (1995). In other words, it has little affinity with the network externalities or the neural networks literature, although quite a few of the results of these two lines of research may be transferable to the networks discussed below. This is not to say that the interests of the present chapter and those of the economic sociologist are identical. The latter are mainly concerned with informal networks, and stress their importance in economic life. They use them to show that the sharp divide between markets and hierarchies is bridged by network relations, which are neither. This chapter's contention is that both hierarchies and markets are networks, that the simplistic view of the market as a forum where a multitude of traders meet is a fiction. This fiction is quite harmless when used to simplify the analysis of properly functioning, that is, competitive markets, but quite inappropriate for the study of the bureaucratic socialist economy. For these reasons it is also quite inadequate to study the processes of *transition* from socialism.

An essential constituent of the culture of an organization is its incentive structure. It is the means by which the owners motivate the CEO to follow their objectives, and the means by which the CEO motivates all other agents in the organization to follow his aims. Incentives must conform to the environment in which the organization functions. A firm in a competitive capitalist market has no choice but to strive to be profitable, and its CEO must be rewarded for making it profitable because, if it did not, the firm would eventually be ousted from the competitive game. The same does not apply to a monopolist, even though in this case too the owners may induce the CEO to maximize profits (or the value of the firm). It will be argued below that maximization of profits will not work in a socialist economy, which will instead lead to the maintenance of very strong horizontal ties in producers' networks. Furthermore socialist firms will be much more set in their ways than capitalist firms, whose environment forces them to be flexible. These different characteristics will affect the process of transition from the socialist bureaucratic economy to the capitalist market. Unless forced to invest all they can in changing their mode of operation, enterprises will continue to hold on to the practices inherited from the past.

The structure of the paper is as follows. The first section introduces the actors who take part in the play and the section places them in their respective networks, while the third forms the basis of the corporate culture acquisition procedure. The two following sections analyse the capitalist and socialist firms, while the sixth section draws consequences from the transition process. The last section, a brief paragraph, concludes.

## Agents and organizations

Economic agents in the universe examined in this chapter are employed in organizations, firms or enterprises. They have their own interests and tastes. Organizations as such do not have interests, but their owners will have objectives, usually the maximization of the firm's value. A successful firm will find incentive schemes which will lead the agents employed in the firm to act in a manner consonant with the owners' interests. A common means is to tie their income to profits by bonus payments, or their net worth to the firm's success through share options. The threat of dismissal may be an important tool: if the organization pays efficiency wages, agents know that, when they lose their jobs, they suffer financially, and this they will try to avoid. Reputation, positive or negative, may be an important incentive: if an agent is believed to have been instrumental in the success of the firm, his value in the market for managers will rise, but if he is assumed to have caused the demise of a firm, other firms may be disinclined to employ him. Unless there is some clear link between the interests of the agent and those of the organization, we cannot assume that the agent will follow the interests of the organization; indeed, often employees, when they cannot be fired, further their own agenda to the neglect of that of their employers.

In what follows we will be concerned mainly with one particular agent in each organization, the CEO. It is assumed that the CEO has the ability to impart the proper incentives to his own employees, so that they will follow his leadership. Suppose that his tastes are given by the utility function $u(s,v)$, where $s(.)$, his share of output, denotes the material benefit which his contract provides, and $v$ is his own agenda, for example, the avoidance of effort. Then a simplified representation of incentives which comprise, say, share options may be the following:[4]

$$s(v) = \beta(v) \times \Delta v, \ \beta' < 0, \ \beta'' > 0;$$

that is, remuneration is much more sensitive to the change in $V$ when the firm is in danger of bankruptcy than when sailing is easy. Consequently, when the firm is in danger of going under, for example going bankrupt or being (hostilely) taken over, the threat of a discrete loss of utility will force the CEO to give priority to the interests of the firm. At other times the private agenda may take over.

Suppose the CEO has a given endowment of one unit of effort for each discrete unit of time, of which he allocates $e$ to ensuring an increase of $v$ and the remainder $1-e$ to the furthering of his own agenda, $v$. Assume also that $v$ can either increase or decrease by a given amount, where the probability of an increase rises with his effort. In Figure 13.1 $\Delta s$ represents the expected marginal gain from a marginal addition to effort. The figure illustrates the effect of the fear of bankruptcy on firm value maximization. When $v$ is high, as in $v_1$ and there is no danger of bankruptcy, $\Delta s$ is relatively low, with the effect that the CEO may permit himself to spend a lot of energy on his pet projects $v$. Not so at $v_0$, where a bad draw may plunge the firm into bankruptcy. Here $\beta'$ is very high and so is $\Delta s$. Consequently all the CEO's exertion is channelled into saving the firm.

What is true of capitalist firms is true of organizations in general: when there is fear for an organization's demise, all efforts may be

*Figure* 13.1  Firm value maximization

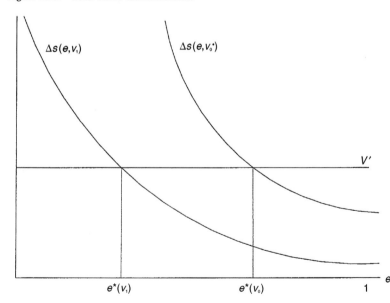

channelled into its salvation. At other times the private agenda may receive preference.

## Organizations as networks

A network model allows us to tie explicitly each agent to specific players, each sitting in her own node. Both goods and services as well as information flow along the lines which connect these nodes and, as is common in neural networks, the friction which hinders these flows will decline as use is made of the line.

Consider first the capitalist market network. There are two firms, firm 1 and firm 2, where firm 1 is dependent on firm 2 for an input. Both firm 1 and firm 2 have alternatives: there are, it is assumed, several potential suppliers and takers of the input, and if the two firms have created a habitual link between them we have to assume that each side has no better alternatives. The next section discusses the evolution of habitual links. Figure 13.2 illustrates two capitalist firms in a simple network, where firm 2 supplies firm 1.

It is the firms themselves that determine the shape of the network. They are the ones that decide who are to be their suppliers or to whom they are to sell their output. They also have the ability to switch partners, assuming they have not precluded this option by an agreement freely entered by them with their present network mates. In this they differ from the enterprises in the socialist network: there the links are designed by the planner and can be changed only by her.[5]

The socialist network is hierarchical: above the two producing units, here called enterprises, we have the planning hierarchy, and the game between the enterprises is strongly affected by the interplay between enterprises and the hierarchy, represented here by the planner. To examine the incentives the planner imparts to her subordinates, we have first to understand her constraints. The planner runs the monofirm, of which the two enterprises are a small part, for the principals, her political masters. A simplified structure of the monofirm,

*Figure* 13.2   The capitalist market network

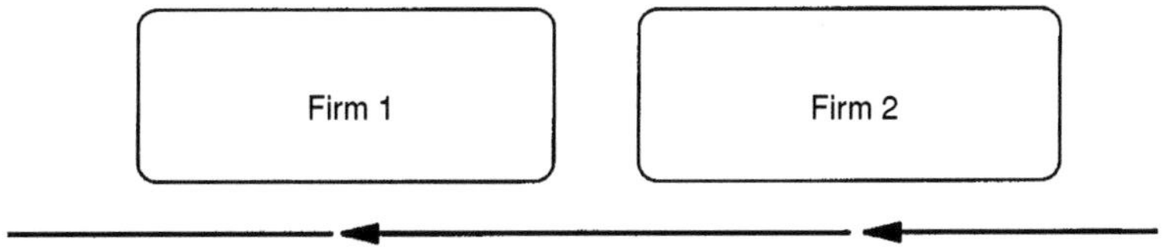

*Figure* 13.3   The socialist network

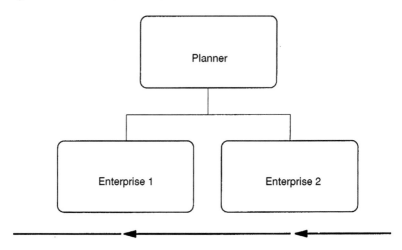

the planner and the two enterprises, is presented in Figure 13.3: the material flows in both figures, 13.2 and 13.3, are identical, but the organization differs.

The planner is the architect of the network, responsible both for the creation of the nodes – the enterprises – and the lines which connect them, that is, the supply relations which link enterprises together, and for the smooth running of the economy. For reasons that lie beyond this chapter, the planner cannot use the market to help her in either of these functions. She therefore has to coordinate the activities of the subordinate productive units, and instruct them how to act during a specified period. These orders we call a plan.

The planner's time is one of the constraints of the system. First, the elaboration of the plan is a very laborious process. Next comes the implementation stage: since the environment is uncertain, the plan has to be revised and adjusted to changing circumstances. The need to save the planner's time affects the organization of the planned economy and the structure of incentives.

As regards organisation, the architecture of the industrial network has to minimize the demands on the planner's time. This is one of the roots of the high degree of concentration of Eastern European industry: competition among enterprises may be useful in the information it provides the planner, but the fewer units the planner has to deal with, the easier her task. At least as important is the need to delegate as many of her chores as possible to subordinate enterprises. Monopolist suppliers (or, at times, buyers) can be made responsible for balancing their output.[6] This is also the root of the 'responsibility to supply' of the Hungarian New Economic Mechanism (NEM). Furthermore, when the planning task became too complex in the 1970s and 1980s, industry was reorganized vertically in some of the countries in combines and trusts. This meant that the material supply was internalized inside these huge enterprises, relieving the planner of the need to secure many of their inputs. One of the effects was to split up the intermediate suppliers, with serious effects on the transition.

To ensure the smooth running of the economy, the planner has to see to it that the coordinated plan is followed. The incentive system remunerates the enterprises for plan fulfilment: when the planner determines that the targets have been fulfilled, the manager receives a bonus, and the planner's lifelong career receives a boost. This is because the incentive contract between planner and manager is not a contract freely entered by equals: in this relation the planner is the unmistakable superior, and it is she who decides whether the plan has been fulfilled. There is a lot of sense in this: everybody is aware of the fact that production will take place under changeable circumstances, and the planner reserves the right to amend the plan as these will dictate. Since she will not be excused by her political superiors if production or supply breakdowns occur because of the failure by one of the subordinate enterprises to adapt to unforeseen events, she will insist that her subordinates obey her ever-changing instructions. In fact, she will expect them to try to adjust to any breakdowns by mutual help among themselves. She will judge, ex post, whether any deviations from the original plan have violated its spirit. As a result the enterprise manager considers the decision whether the plan has been fulfilled as a random variable, related to the constraints faced by the planner.

The expected target depends on the 'legitimate' needs of the customers, and these can be established through the lateral links between the enterprises. Each manager knows that what is important to his boss, the planner, is that his suppliers cooperate with him when the need arises. Likewise, when his customers need his help the supplier has to be cooperative because, if a breakdown in production occurs at one of his customer enterprises and the customer can prove that the supplier could have helped but did not, a black mark will be registered against him. Those parameters of the plan that have to do with the maintenance of the smooth flow of output have high priority; other parameters of the plan have lower priority, and their violation will be judged leniently.

Targets of quality and costs, and the introduction of new technology, need not be taken too seriously, unless their violation too may lead to breakdowns. But if too extreme a debasement of quality may mean that the customer can prove to the planner that the shoddiness of the supplies have caused a breakdown in production, the plan of the guilty supplier may be deemed not to have been fulfilled. The manager therefore has to maintain some minimum levels of quality.

The previous paragraph applies to civilian production. When it comes to defence and other priority sectors, the determination of the quality cut-off level is left to the customer; in other words, poor quality may disqualify a consignment from being accepted as output, and the producer's implicit incentives will be quite different. Defence and other priority sectors are ignored in this chapter.

## Routines, rules of thumb, evaluation and adaptation[7]

Why are some organizations adaptable, while socialist enterprises are inflexible? Decisions have usually to be taken in a hurry. Organizations therefore prepare decision rules ahead of time, to apply when foreseen events occur. These rules or routines are applied in real time, but after

*Figure* 13.4   Rule adaptation: choice of time to invest

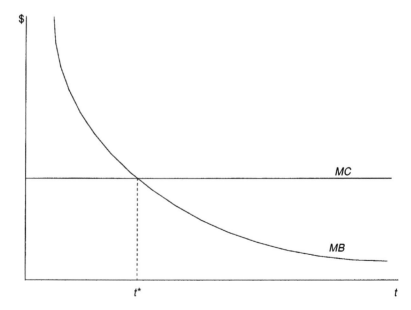

the event, when there is no pressure for fast decisions, the organization possesses options of re-evaluation and readaptation of the rule to the circumstances which were encountered. As more experience is collected over time, the organization learns to apply the rules more effectively. For stationary environments the need to adapt the routines may decline over time, and the need to evaluate past applications may subside. If there is disutility to re-evaluation, and its incremental utility declines, the organization may give up examining its past actions and settle into a rut of accepted routines.

If the organization evaluates and adapts the rule in the wake of its application, experience improves the application of the rule, the rule gets better adjusted to its environment and the expected benefits of its application improve over time. We can consider the continuous monitoring of the firm's decisions as a stream of investments that keep increasing its specific capital. Figure 13.4 illustrates the choice of rule adaptation in an organization: the declining *MB* curve represents the marginal expected improvement in the organization's value as a result of the investment of further monitoring time. *MC* is the marginal utility cost of monitoring, assumed to be fixed. Optimum monitoring is where $MC = MB$ at $t^*$.

*Figure* 13.5   Rule adaptation: the inflexible organization

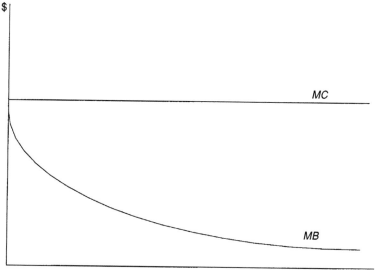

Should an organization continue indefinitely to monitor the application of its routines? If the environment is stationary, marginal improvements decline and, after a while, the cost of monitoring may exceed its benefits. The declining marginal productivity of the specific capital may lie below the costs of investment. As a result an organization functioning in a stagnant environment will become routinized and will cease to modify and adapt its rules of thumb. This is illustrated in Figure 13.5, which is identical to Figure 13.4, except that the $MB$ lies lower and meets the $MC$ at $t = 0$.

## The capitalist firm

Not all capitalist firms are dynamic, constantly monitoring their environment and adjusting their working rules to its evolution. Firms that function in a relatively stationary and secure environment, such as monopolistic utilities, may be as conservative and inefficient as socialist firms. But they may also be enterprising, because they benefit from taking initiatives. In a competitive industry with free entry, where each player has to be constantly aware of the strategies of his competitors, both existing and potential, the continuous monitoring of the environment and of past decisions is a condition of continued existence.[8] The maximization of firm value is imposed on the firm by fear of bankruptcy or takeover. Such a firm is a PBX, which, to be successful and ensure longevity, has to be constantly on the search for new links, new markets and new suppliers, constantly rethinking itself.

Consider the establishment of a link between two firms, firm 1 and firm 2. Firm 1 plans to introduce a new product, for which it requires an input which firm 2, as well as several other firms, is capable of supplying. Both firms require initial investments before the transaction can commence. Then a contract can be signed between the parties if their cooperation results in a larger annual gain than the combined costs of the investment. How the gain is divided between the parties depends on the alternatives: if there are many other firms that are capable of supplying the input at similar quality and cost, then firm 1 will pocket the larger share. If, on the other hand, the product of firm 1 has many potential alternative producers, all of whom require similar inputs, the winner will be firm 2. The contract between the sides will be for an extended period, but there will be provisions in it that permit changes in the agreed price when firm 2's costs and/or the price firm 1 can obtain change in a measurable manner. There will also be prescribed renegotiation dates, which enable the parties to change the provisions of the contract and to terminate it if no agreement is found.

Once production commences, the situation may change. Suppose the price firm 1 receives and firm 2's cost turn out to differ from the original estimate. Suppose firm 2's costs are higher than expected, and it is in fact losing from the contract. Then the firm will press for a change for an improvement, even if the original contract did not have an explicit provision to this effect. And, provided the price firm 1 receives is not much lower than expected, it may consent, to preserve good will. Alternatively firm 2 may threaten to break off the link if it finds alternative customers. Or suppose firm 1 discovers that firm 3 can supply the input at a lower cost, or at higher quality. Then, to paraphrase Dore, who characterizes Japanese networks, firm 1 will approach their suppliers and tell them, 'Look how [firm 3] has got [its] price down. We hope you can do the same because we really would have to reconsider our position if the price difference goes on ... If you need ... finance to get ... new [equipment] we can probably help' (Dore, 1983, p. 364). In other words, the sides continue to exert pressure on one another to maintain the best production practices, by keeping in reserve a hidden threat to break the link and establish an alternative one.

## The socialist enterprise

The socialist enterprise can be thought of as an old manual switchboard, where the operator has departed, leaving a small number of switches connected (because the planner–operator did not want too many alternative suppliers to exist: (see pp. 212–13). The connected lines will remain linked, while other lines, also potentially linkable, remain cut off. The reason is that the enterprise is functioning in a stationary environment, where no dramatic changes are to be expected. In particular, it need not be worried about a possible end of its existence. The planner, although the undisputed superior of the enterprise and its staff, is highly restricted in the sanctions she can apply.[9] The enterprise will hardly ever be closed down. The director may be removed, he may be promoted or demoted, but neither event is necessarily a direct response to the functioning of the enterprise, which the planner has very few tools to monitor. This does not mean that a better-run and more profitable enterprise is not a better working place for all its staff, but that the transformation of a poorly operating enterprise into a better one requires a heavy investment in the change of work routines, whose outcome is uncertain and which is not worth undertaking. As a result SOEs are extremely conservative organizations. When their environment suddenly changes with the start of transition, they find it very difficult to adapt to the new environment.

## Transition

To turn a conservative organization into an evolving one requires qualities of leadership that have alternative, and possibly much more remunerative, avenues. Furthermore, certain skills are required in order to change the firm's strategy, its production profile and the mix of goods produced, and these are unlikely to be found among the staff of the organization. And, lastly, any attempted change is a gamble whose outcome is uncertain. It is therefore not easy to bring the enterprise to undertake a serious attempt at transformation, as long as alternative paths to survival exist. Thus, as long as an agency can be found that is ready to soften the budget constraint, be it through subsidies or soft loans, the enterprise is unlikely to start trying to change.

For each enterprise, the factors that determine the difficulty of transformation are partly objective, related to the environment in which the particular firm is functioning and to its own endowment, and partly subjective, to do with the characteristics of the agents that make up the firm. The objective ones can be divided into two groups, technological factors and institutional ones. Consider the technological ones first:

- **Product design**   Process industries do not have to worry about the basic design of their product. The definition of the product is usually standard, and all the enterprise has to correct is possibly the quality of its output, the next item on the list.
- **Product quality**   Though usually poor, qualities of output in Eastern Europe do differ considerably. In some lines of production, such as metallurgy, Russian techniques are extremely advanced, while for most consumer goods shoddiness prevails.
- **Distance from the final user**   Enterprises which produce for the final consumer are dependent only on their own actions, their own reforms. Those that are suppliers to other enterprises depend on the cooperation of those that follow them in the network. Hence a possible measure of the difficulty of restructuring may be the number of links in the network that separate the enterprise and the final consumer.

- **Marketization of the suppliers and customers** An enterprise whose customers have restructured may find that it is forced to follow and restructure itself. If its customers have not restructured, it may find it much harder to restructure itself. Likewise, if its suppliers have restructured it may be much easier for it to concentrate on its area of relative strength and not to spread out, Soviet fashion, and supply itself with all its needed inputs.
- **Industrial branch, or market conditions** The heavy industry-biased structure of industry and the paucity of services means that the initial market conditions differ for different categories of firms. Firms in heavy industry have a lower probability of survival if left to fend for themselves in the market, while new service firms should find it easier to discover a niche for themselves.

As for the institutional factors, they have mainly to do with the ability to continue to exist in the absence of restructuring and reforms. The question, essentially, is whether the enterprise management believes that the budget constraint is soft, or can be made soft. Can directed loans be found, can taxes be deferred, are there suppliers (such as electric companies) who will supply inputs on open credits?[10] If the answer is 'no', then the need for reform is pressing. If it is, 'The possibility remains, but it is unlikely to persist', then one has to start planning a restructuring strategy, provided one believes there is a chance of success. If it is believed that there is no real danger to the enterprise's existence, regardless of what is done, then there is no pressure for reform and change.

Finally there are the subjective factors: the character and skills of the enterprise staff, particularly of the manager and the leading cadre, will affect the strategy selected. An enterprising manager may load the dice in favour of change, while a conservative one may tip the scales in favour of the status quo. Thus these factors provide a stochastic answer to the question, 'Will enterprise *i* try to reform itself?' This is illustrated by the parallelogram of forces in Figure 13.6.[11] The horizontal axis in the figure measures the ease of transformation, that is the various technological dimensions that determine whether attempts at adjustment – of routines, product mix and costs – to the demands of the market have a high chance of success. The vertical axis measures the *lack of need* to change: if the environment does not threaten the enterprise with extinction even if it does not change its mode of operation, it gets a high reading on this dimension. The four points *A–D* in the figure illustrate the forces which act on different enterprises. The enterprise at

*Figure* 13.6   The parallelogram of transformation forces

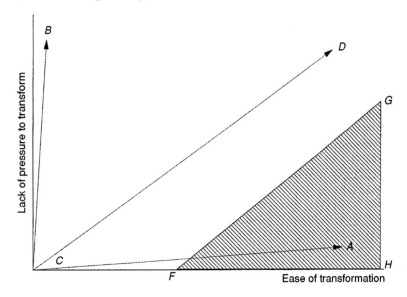

*A* may be close to the market and under strong pressure to transform, because the chances of survival without change seem to be low. There may be a threat of an imminent hardening of the budget constraint. Thus there is a high probability that CEO *A* will make the utmost efforts to transform. The enterprise at *B* is in the exact opposite pole of attraction: its objective characteristics make the success of transformation very unlikely, and it has a very good chance of success in the old routines. Its CEO is not likely to reform; instead he will strive to maintain links with the powers that can assure the enterprise of continued support. An enterprise in situation *C* is in a harder position: it has no chance of continued existence, even if it exerts itself to the full to adjust to market conditions. As a result its CEO is likely to expend all his efforts on his own agenda, for example on attempts to strip the enterprise of all its useful assets into satellite enterprises, which may enable substantial parts of the workforce to continue to exist as a working unit. As for the enterprise at *D*, here the CEO has a free hand: he may, at will, either continue as before, or lead the enterprise into a more secure and affluent existence as a transformed enterprise. We surmise that the status quo ante will be the victor here, because the CEO will find it extremely difficult to enlist the cooperation of other stakeholders, whose acquiescence if not active support is required for transformation to succeed. Without the immediate threat to continued existence, the forces of inertia and dislike of change are likely to prevail.

The triangle *FGH* summarizes the arguments of the previous paragraph: an enterprise in this triangle will probably embark upon a course of change. The two conditions have to coexist: transformation has to have a high enough chance of success, and it has to be accepted as the only available alternative for survival, for the CEO to be sure that he can overcome all the forces which anchor the enterprise to its accepted routines.

The characterization of socialist networks on pp. 211–12 is relevant here. Consider the effects of the reorganization of enterprises into vertical combines, usually grouping a firm producing a marketable good with a variable number of tiers of suppliers, in a network which is relatively insulated from the remainder of the economy. Combines were often broken up after the collapse of the socialist system, and for good reasons, the principal one being that the supplying industries were chopped up arbitrarily into relatively low-technology, non-competing enterprises, while in the West, for instance in the automotive industry, one often finds suppliers that have become specialized hi-tech firms, supplying several competing producers. Often the final producer can be saved: being close to the market it may find it relatively easy to adjust and transform, provided it has a reasonable line of products and a reservoir of good human capital. Not so the suppliers: they are isolated from the market, having lost their main customer, with low technology, often low-quality human capital, and are much too small for modern market conditions.[12]

Figure 13.6 can be used to examine transition policies of the various Eastern European states. Take, for example, German reunification. In the vertical dimension of the figure, it was quite clear to enterprises in Eastern Germany that their budgets have hardened, and that they are not going to be saved from extinction unless they reform themselves. On the horizontal axis, the sale of enterprises to westerners, who undertook to invest in them and continue employing at least a part of the existing staff, meant a push to the right, the positive aspect of the Treuhand's policy. The negative part, the shift to the left, was the overvaluation of East German wages that priced the bulk of ex-GDR industry out of the market. Thus the very firms that were to be tested for survivability faced impossible hurdles which they had little chance of surmounting. Instead of temporary wage subsidies, which might have

helped surmount these hurdles, the East was offered capital, or investment, subsidies. These offered no relief to labour-intensive firms, probably the only ones worth saving. The case of some successors states of
the Soviet Union is the exact opposite: here there is no danger to existence without reform, and consequently hardly any transformation.

## Conclusion

The network model has enabled us to shed some light on the nature of
the socialist system and on transition to capitalism that would not be
forthcoming under conventional analysis. In particular it enabled us to
go a step beyond the statement that enterprises in transition economies
are inflexible, tend to stick to old routines, old products and old customers and suppliers, and explain the origins of this resistance to change.
This new tool deserves further development and application, until it
becomes a regular constituent of the economist's arsenal.

## Notes

1. I am grateful to the participants of the conference for valuable comments
   and criticism, which were very useful in the revision of the original paper.
2. Compare Blanchard and Kremer (1997).
3. A very different view of corporate culture can be found in Kreps (1990).
4. It may seem that options are asymmetric, of value only when $\Delta V \geq 0$. It is
   argued below that $\Delta V < 0$ may have reputation costs that, in the longer run,
   entail a loss of income, that is, an income stream that is proportional to the
   negative $\Delta V$.
5. Essential unofficial networks also exist, but they are disregarded here.
6. Compare Keren (1973).
7. This section draws on a paper by W. Bentley McLeod, presented at the
   Chicago meetings of the AEA and ACES in January, 1998 (McLeod 1998).
8. See, for instance, the *Economist*'s story of the near collapse of IBM in the
   mid-1980s, when it did not react to the change in the PC (personal com-
   puter) market, which it helped to engineer (6 June 1998, pp. 97ff).
9. See Keren (1993).
10. See Schaffer (1997).
11. The figure has been inspired by Gaddy and Ickes (1998), although it is not
    identical to theirs. They measure the distance from the market in terms of
    needed capital on the horizontal axis (and a large distance means that
    transformation is not easy) and relational capital on the vertical axis (and
    this translates closely to the lack of pressure to transform). Rather than ask
    about the likelihood of attempts at transformation, they consider the likeli-
    hood of viability.
12. See Meyer (Chapter 15 in this volume) whose example of the changed
    structure of Škoda's network is an excellent illustration. Hunya, in Chapter
    12, is also relevant.

# 14
# Towards a Theory of Markets: Networks, Communication and Knowledge

*Eckehard F. Rosenbaum*

## Introduction[1]

Economists have devoted little attention to the analysis of the market concept, even though the concept is virtually omnipresent in many policy recommendations. If a market economy is to be built in Central and Eastern European countries (cf. Lavigne, 1995), for instance, the task assumes an as yet insufficient degree to which markets were present prior to 1989. Consequently (a) markets have to be built anew or, at least (b) conditions have to be created which induce their development. However both objectives presuppose an understanding of what markets are and how they emerge. This is self-evident as far as (a) is concerned, but it also applies to (b), for the latter assumes the existence of a causal link between the preconditions of markets and their emergence.

In previous work we have argued for an understanding of markets in terms of three broad empirical characteristics: specified and voluntary exchange, regularity and typification, and competition (cf. Rosenbaum, 1998, and, similarly, Brezinski and Fritsch, 1997; Fourie, 1991). Against this background, a theory of markets should be able to explain what sort of mechanism *produces* market phenomena. Its scope is thus broader than, and on a conceptual level different from, price theory. For price theory already presupposes the existence of markets while examining different market *forms* in terms of their implications for the formation of relative prices and the allocation of resources.

The present chapter argues that a market phenomenon can be understood as being created by a communicative network whose mode of operation is contingent upon the knowledge agents possess about this network. The chapter then suggests that, in view of the many obstacles network building has to face, the development of markets is more complicated than the literature assumes. At the same time, building markets does not necessarily start from scratch because informal networks which are the remainder of central planning (see Grabher, 1995; Grabher and Stark, 1997) may in fact form the nucleus of markets to be.

## Background: markets and networks

The literature on the relationship between markets and networks is rather ambiguous. Some authors treat 'network' and 'market' as distinct concepts,[2] sometimes regarding networks as a particular organizational form *within* markets (cf. Beije and Groenewegen, 1992). For a second group, markets are essentially *constituted* by a network of exchange relationships.[3] Given this state of affairs, we begin by explicating how the approach adopted here is related to the literature.

### The received view

The equivocal relation between network and market has its roots in the fact that the notion of a network can accommodate a wide range of social phenomena. Indeed network theory appears to make few theoretical claims in its own right that would help to place the approach firmly within a specific field of inquiry. And although the literature has mostly drawn a sharp line between networks and markets, authors differ with respect to the essential characteristic(s) of both networks and markets. Some authors, for instance, understand networks metaphorically as 'complex arrays of relationships among firms' (Johanson and Mattson, 1987) while others regard networks as 'managed economic systems' (MacMillan and Farmer, 1979). Unless the nature of the relationships is clarified, however, the first characterization fails to distinguish networks from long-term contractual relations, while the second obscures the decentralized and spontaneous nature of networks. Finally the suggestion of placing networks on a continuous scale between contract and organization (Williamson, 1985) makes one wonder how to deal with intraorganisational contracts. Because organizations, too, form contractual arrangements (Grossman and Hart, 1986), organizations and markets can be distinguished, not by the presence or absence of contracts, but at most by the relative weight of contractual arrangements, and by the frequency with which arrangements are renewed and hence subject to competition.

Against this background, Teubner has suggested a trichotomy of markets, organizations and networks. He argues that networks of firms have to be conceived as emergent collective actors which are the outcome of an 'autopoietic process' (Teubner, 1992). In this process, market elements (competition) are incorporated into organizations, and organizational elements (contracts) fuse with markets, thereby forming organizational and market networks, respectively. The two types have in common that events within such networks are doubly attributed to both contractual relations within the network and to the network as a whole, and actions have to conform with both individual and network interests.

Other authors also differentiate between markets, networks and hierarchies, albeit for different reasons (cf. Håkansson and Johanson, 1993; Powell, 1996). For Håkansson and Johanson, markets and networks are characterized by general and specific relations respectively, while networks and hierarchies differ according to the degree to which behaviour is guided by norms or individual interests. For Powell, markets, networks and hierarchies can be differentiated along eight dimensions which include, amongst other things, the normative basis as well as the degree of flexibility and the type of communication. Summarizing the organization research literature on markets and networks, Mayntz also supports a trichotomy, suggesting that the logic of interaction in networks differs from both the market logic of competition and the logic of authority and obedience that dominates hierarchies (Mayntz, 1993).

The above summary highlights the point that networks are perceived as reactions to market and organizational failure, in that networks are supposed to share a number of beneficial properties that are allegedly absent in both markets and organizations. But the appeal of network theoretic considerations rests to a considerable extent on an understanding of markets that is but a caricature of real markets. By equating markets with competitive exchange (cf. Mayntz, 1993, or Teubner, 1992), the revealed understanding is unduly narrow. Most seriously, competition and the common metaphor of intersecting demand and supply curves do not make intelligible how market phenomena are generated in the first place.

## Networks in centrally planned economies and market economies

To assess the potential role of the network approach for a better understanding of markets, it is helpful to recall the formal definition of a network. Accordingly, two claims can be identified. First, networks are seen as 'patterns or regularities in relationships among interacting units' (Wasserman and Faust, 1994, p. 3), often referred to as social structures. Second, such relations cannot be analysed by examining individuals (or organizations) in isolation. Two questions then have to be addressed: first, what is the nature of the said relations in the case of a market and, second, what is it that makes these relations inaccessible as it were to an individualistic type of analysis? Let us begin by addressing the first question.

As argued elsewhere (cf. Rosenbaum, 1998), one of the essential elements of markets as empirically discernible phenomena is precisely a certain degree of regularity and typification in exchange. It has to be emphasized, though, that regularity is a criterion that applies at the aggregate level but does not generally hold for exchanges between specific actors. The latter may indeed be singular or at most irregular events, whose relative frequency depends on the kind of good or service that is exchanged and on the degree of competition. In particular under conditions of (intense) competition, even buyers with a technologically induced constant demand for a commodity are likely to switch between various sellers as no seller is able to maintain competitive advantages for long. It thus seems hardly justified to regard recurrent encounters of specific buyers and sellers *which result without exception in exchange transactions* as the core of a market (for example, Snehota, 1993; Mattson, 1995). Stock markets, for instance, and thus the purest form of market activity (Marshall, 1938), would have to be excluded if persistent exchange relationships were to be regarded as the core of a market. Besides, by focusing on stable exchange relationships, centrally planned economies (CPEs) too can be described in terms of networks, for 'patterns or regularities in relationships among interacting units' were pervasive in CPEs, more so in any case than in market economies. At the same time, both the range and the nature of interactions between agents differs on various counts in centrally planned and market economies (see also Michael Keren, (Chapter 13, in this volume), and only some types of interaction in market economies exhibit pattern-like features.

First, note that the actual exchange in a market economy is only the final stage of a much more comprehensive and decentralized process of making offers to buy or sell, formulating counter-offers, haggling about the price, setting up a contract or an informal agreement, evaluating the fulfilment of the contract, sorting out conflicts arising from this evaluation, and so on (Richter, 1996; Mises, 1961). Importantly the subject matter of transactions during the initial and final stages of this process is not goods or services but information and knowledge. And more actors are usually involved than those (two) between whom the final deal is struck. Thus prospective buyers gather or elicit offers from various sellers, while sellers may direct offers at a variety of potential buyers or respond to buyers' inquiries. In this process, information can only be confined to price quotations in the case of completely homogenous products. In other cases, the material exchange is necessarily preceded by the exchange of information about the commodity and buyer's preferences so as to interlock and coordinate the activities of market participants (Snehota, 1993). Moreover, unless product innovation is slow or absent, this process of exchanging information is likely to turn into a dynamic process of mutual learning and adaptation when firms attempt to compete through innovation and thus have to learn about the needs of their customers. Customers, on the other hand, acquire information about the characteristics of new products or services, thereby modifying the cognitive component of their preferences (cf. Lundvall, 1993; Mattson, 1995; Teubal and Zuscovitch, 1994).

Second, market economies and CPEs differ in terms of the relative importance of formal (contractually or legally regulated) and informal (non-contractual and sometimes illegal) interaction among agents. Generally, formal relations appear to dominate exchange transactions in CPEs, whereas informal relations (as exemplified above) prevail in market economies. Clearly this is not to play down contractual relations, nor is it to ignore the relevance of informal contacts that helped to overcome the deficiencies of plans while, at the same time, undermining them. The point is that many important processes that are part and parcel of exchange transactions in market economies (but absent in CPEs) are not formalized in contractual relations but unfold on the basis of non-codified agreements, habits, norms and rules which are underpinned by mutual trust and shaped through prior experience and practice.

Third, centrally planned and market economies differ in so far as in CPEs the structure of interaction and the nature of the relations between agents are largely hierarchical and, in any case, mediated through central planning agencies and the party–state hierarchy. Consequently certain relations, notably those between producers, retailers and wholesalers, have remained underdeveloped (Bateman, 1997; Keren, 1997; Swaan, 1997). In market economies, by contrast, the economic relations have a decentralized structure which is mostly the result of locally initiated interaction. Moreover, being demand rather than supply-constrained, retailing and wholesaling relations figure more prominently.

Given these considerations, a network-theoretic analysis of markets can be justified by the role of largely informal but patterned relationships among agents, as exemplified above. To be more specific, what takes place on a regular basis is the exchange of information rather than the exchange of goods or services. Note, though, that the exchange of information differs from the exchange of goods or services in fundamental ways. Being a form of (verbal or non-verbal) communication, it follows rules which, on the part of actors, constitute roles, such as speaker versus listener. These roles invariably require a counterpart such as another agent without whom the role could not be played and thus would remain meaningless. This implies that communication is directed, in that it takes place between specific (types of) actors, and that it must be guided by a form of rationality which differs fundamentally from the means–ends rationality of orthodox economic reasoning because instrumental abuse of the opponent would be adversarial to successful communication (cf. Ulrich, 1987). Taken together, these considerations show in turn that communicative relations cannot be conceptualized purely individualistically, hence constituting a type of relationship which belongs to the province of network theoretic reasoning as outlined above.

How, with whom and what is communicated now and in the future depends on the history of previous and the structure of current exchange transactions as well as on the location of agents within the network of communicative relations as perceived by them. Hence in order to explain action within existing networks as well as to analyse the development of communicative networks and markets, one has to examine what agents actually know about their environment, that is the kind of *structural knowledge* they possess.

## Networks as the source of market phenomena

In the previous section, it was argued that recurrent patterns of communication rather than stable exchange relationships form the core of market phenomena. And because structural knowledge determines the benefits agents can draw from a communication network, in particular if the network exhibits a low degree of connectedness (few direct links relative to the total size of the network), the form of communicative patterns as well as their development over time is likely to depend on the structural knowledge agents possess. In the following we look at these issues in more detail.

## Communication, structural knowledge and competition

Structural knowledge consists not merely of a map of the *actual* communication relations of an agent. Nor can structural knowledge be restricted to the history of exchange transactions. Instead three further elements have to be taken into account. First, even if two agents do not communicate with each other at present, and even if they are not engaged in any kind of exchange transaction, they may know each other *as potential and trustworthy sources of specific information* that is relevant for future exchange transactions. Structural knowledge thus constitutes a distinct type of knowledge whose subject matter is not factual information about, say, the characteristics of a specific commodity, but knowledge about who may be a *source* of information concerning this commodity.

Second, an agent's structural knowledge cannot be reduced to a map of the communicative (and possibly exchange) relations of this agent. Nor is it a map of all relations within a networks. The second point is an immediate consequence of agents' limited cognitive capacities, whereas the first point highlights the possibility that an agent may know and make use of the fact that two other agents are engaged in market communication and exchange transactions. Knowing a relation is therefore different from being part of a relation. The latter implies the former, but not vice versa. And while knowing a specific agent may still be conceptualized in term of a (possibly asymmetric) relation with this agent (she may not know me, nor may she know that I know her, and so on), the knowledge of relations between her and other agents in the network is not necessarily part of my knowing her (or part of my knowing any of the agents with whom she is related). This follows from the fact that relations are located between agents, as it were.

Third, structural knowledge varies with the size and the complexity of the underlying communicative network. The bigger and more complex the network, the lower is the likelihood that agents know all that can be known about the network. Size and complexity depend in turn on the degree to which the network is decentralized. In highly centralized networks, that is networks that exhibit a star-shaped design, the structure is relatively simple and thus poses few cognitive problems for agents. In decentralized networks, by contrast, the structure is more complex, and by implication unlikely to be known *in toto*.

The last remarks emphasize the importance of structural knowledge for understanding competition. For competition is not only, as Simmel has put it, a parallel effort, attempting to surpass an opponent by offering opportunities for exchange which are preferred by other buyers or sellers (Simmel, 1903). Nor can competition exclusively be regarded as an attempt to take advantage of structural holes in networks in terms of access to, and timing of, information, and referrals to other people, and in terms of control (Burt, 1992). Both elements are important; and their significance results not least from the fact that the notion of perfect competition denotes a situation in which, to all intents and purposes, competition is absent. Still, for competition to occur, agents must have some idea of what the communicative network and the structure of exchanges it supports look like. This is obvious as far as Burt is concerned, since agents can only take advantage of *known* structural holes. But it also applies to the Simmelian understanding of competition. Not only does it make a difference whether attempts to surpass an opponent are undertaken in a situation that is perceived as being of strategic nature,[4] it also matters whether, and to what extent, the opponent's past actions have been observed and thus incorporated in the formulation of one's own course of action. On both accounts of competition, therefore, agents have to figure out what could be an appropriate starting-point for competitive action.

The argument can be summarized as follows. If competitive exchange of the kind envisaged by Simmel or Burt is an essential element of markets, then the most basic network required for market phenomena to occur is a communicative network. Potential buyers and sellers have to send and collect information about offers to buy and to sell prior to any regular trade activity (exchange). Once a communicative network has come into existence, agents can decide to engage in transactions on the basis of the received information, while the exchanges themselves (their price, location and time) will become the source and subject matter of further exchanges or transmissions in the communicative network. Thus not only do exchange transactions presuppose prior communication, but the terms of these transactions and the agents involved in them also constitute the subject matter of future communication, thereby providing information that can be used to modify agents' structural knowledge.

### Specified transactions and uniform prices

For market prices to function as an allocation mechanism, they not only have to be relatively stable over time, they also have to be uniform, taking into account transactions costs, throughout the economy during economically relevant time periods. Without a certain degree of uniformity, it would simply remain unclear what the relevant market price is. But if exchange transactions take place in a decentralized manner, there is no central agency which collects and posts information about individual exchange transactions. This raises the question of how decentralized interaction can produce an interconnected outcome in the form of a uniform market price.

For the conventional approach to markets, the problem constitutes a conundrum which is only overcome at the cost of conceptualizing markets in a way that leaves out reality, namely as the intersection of (fictitious) demand and supply curves. The network approach outlined above helps to solve the puzzle. For communication between agents can now be seen as the mechanism by which price information is channelled through the economy. Communication of prices and communication about individual exchange offers lead thus to the interrelation of decentralized transactions. Only if prices are communicated from agent to agent throughout the whole economy, therefore, can this information be available even for distant agents as an input for their decision on future exchange transactions and thus lead, via communicatively expressed competitive pressures, to the convergence of the prices of various decentralized exchanges to a uniform market price.

In a similar vein, a high degree of connectedness (a dense communicative network) may prevent producers from making extensive innovation and thus encourage typified exchange in that the type of product producers offer has to conform to previously established standards (to maintain comparability for instance). Alternatively it may prevent innovation in that information about such innovation is quickly dispersed and then adopted by competitors, thereby limiting the benefits from innovation. All in all, these considerations underpin the point that stronger ties among actors (and a denser network) narrow the latitude for autonomous action (Sedaitis, 1997).

## On the development of markets: incremental growth, path-dependence and structural knowledge

This section will examine a number of factors that are likely to influence the development of markets *qua* networks over time. To begin with, note that network changes are likely to occur incrementally because, in each period of time, agents can only sever and establish a limited number of contacts. Important constraints that come into play here are indivisibilities, sunk costs and limited resources. It is safe to assume, for instance, that establishing and maintaining contacts is costly, which implies that agents cannot maintain or establish an unlimited number of contacts. Nor can they easily switch between contacts if invested resources are sunk. Finally the 'fine-tuning' of one's network relations may be hampered by a minimum input of resources required for establishing certain relations, thereby precluding modifications at the margin.

How, and to what extent, incremental changes are undertaken depends on the knowledge agents possess about the structure of the network in which they are located. In other words, in order to understand which contacts are severed and which contacts are newly established, it is not sufficient to know agents' objectives against the background of the current network. One has also to examine what agents know about their network environment. Structural knowledge is thus not only necessary for competition, as discussed above, it also influences the development of a network over time. The underlying supposition is in both instances that the benefits agents can draw from a network or from changes in the network depend in large measure on what they know about the network. Competition and network dynamics may therefore simply be two sides of the same coin in so far as competition may alter the structure of the network when some relations are newly established and others severed in a move to exploit structural holes.

Another important cause of incremental growth is bounded rationality. Agents do not only possess incomplete knowledge of potential contacts and the benefits accruing from additional contacts; even if they possessed this knowledge, they would not necessarily be able to make use of it, owing to their limited computational resources (Simon, 1986). Hence agents cannot remodel the network they happen to be located in *in toto* but have to consider links one at a time. The role of trust is of particular relevance in this context because of a possible trade-off between the fixed costs of a network (many contacts leading to high fixed costs) and the running (or transaction) costs (many direct – high-trust – links lower transaction costs). Trust may thus reduce the transaction costs in a network while increasing the (fixed) costs of maintaining the network. The latter means that trust-based (communicative) networks are more expensive to build than networks which require a low input of trust. In addition, one should expect networks involving a large degree of trust to be more stable than networks which can easily be remodelled since investment in trust cannot be shifted from one contact to another.

Whatever the specific cause of incremental change may be, if modifications occur only in a stepwise manner then a large part of the prior development of the network is preserved over time. Thus incremental change can be regarded as a source of path-dependence. Another source of path-dependence results from externalities among contacts. Knowing a group and being known and trusted by a group is often more than knowing individual members and being known by them. What comes into play here is a kind of common knowledge effect, in that trust may be conferred on common acquaintances on the basis of their being known to all members of a group or even the network as a whole.

Incremental change and path-dependence then imply that the creation of a market is a process that necessarily takes some time. How fast this can be achieved depends of course on the available resources. Among intangible resources, it is in particular the amount of structural knowledge relative to the complexity of the existing situation which is likely to determine the speed with which agents can modify communicative networks and the exchange relations that develop on this basis.

## Some implications for economic transformation

The literature on transformation often insinuates that the abolishment of one coordination mechanism (the plan) implies the automatic emergence of another, the market. Yet abolishing the plan means first of all that there is no coordination mechanism whatsoever. At least in part, the transformational recession has therefore to be explained by a *lack* of coordination (Kornai, 1994) and hence by a lack of markets. The point may be obscured by the prevailing understanding of markets, but it becomes clearer if it is acknowledged that the allocative function of markets requires network structures to occur. As was argued in the previous section, however, building such networks is necessarily incremental, characterized by path-dependence, and hence is time consuming.

The task of building networks is especially acute in the case of heterogeneous commodities which are not traded on organized marketplaces such as stock or commodity exchanges. While, in the latter case, communicative networks can sometimes be reduced to (relatively simple) star-shaped networks of auctioneer and traders, in which exchange partners may be largely ignorant of each other, markets for heterogeneous commodities have a decentralized structure which is (re-)produced through the interaction of participants and thus contingent upon their knowledge and expertise. To interpret, as is sometimes done, the reopening of stock exchanges in transition countries as a major step towards a market economy is besides the point. A stock exchange is a relatively simple type of market from the perspective of network theory, in that the structure of the related communicative network exhibits only a limited degree of complexity.

In contrast to an established market economy, network building in transition economies is complicated by a number of factors. First, in addition to the widespread absence of appropriate tacit skills (Swaan, 1997), the creation of new markets does not take place against the background of an established system of markets but under conditions characterized by the widespread absence of input and output markets. Hence the simultaneous creation of several networks can be expected to put a particular strain on agent's resources and capabilities. Second, 'entry' of former centrally directed firms does not occur step by step but, provided there are several producers, largely simultaneously as soon as the planning system is abolished. Initially this is likely to lead to confusion and subsequent mistakes, as stable communication (and exchange) relations among agents have not yet evolved. At the same time, the benefits resulting from weak relationships are scant, thus offering few incentives to maintain or strengthen these relationships. Third, the emphasis on communicative networks highlights the importance of communicative skills and the need for an affine ethic which guides communicative processes.

The development of communicative networks is also likely to be influenced by initial conditions. For transition countries, this means, that for lack of alternatives, pre-existing networks will be used at the beginning. Only in the course of time are these networks likely to be reconfigured so as to accommodate the changed needs of economic agents. This is not to glorify 'alte Seilschaften' as the importance of personal connections is bound to decrease over time, but to suggest that building new communication (and exchange) networks is facilitated if there is some basis from which the process can take off rather than a sort of *tabula rasa* situation. Pre-existing structures are thus a kind of resource in at least two senses. They are a source of variation (cf. Grabher and Stark, 1997) and, epitomized in structural knowledge, a basis upon which new communicative networks can be built.

What impact are transformation policies likely to have on pre-existing networks? Consider for instance privatization and restructuring. Since structural knowledge and, to a somewhat lesser extent, communicative networks are invariably tied to individuals, the method of privatization, and in particular the extent to which restructuring is undertaken by insiders and outsiders, respectively, may influence the degree to which networks continue to exist. For instance, if firms are largely sold to foreigners, and if restructuring is mainly in the hands of foreign managers as well (in contrast to so-called management buy-outs or employee-owned firms), informal networks are likely to be destroyed and structural knowledge is likely to be lost.

For the firm to be restructured this may be of little relevance since its foreign owner will connect it to new international networks, especially if little more than branch plants with few local links are to be established. And since these networks do not suffer from any legacies from the past, they may even be advantageous from the viewpoint of the firm in question. But for firms not (yet) privatized, the remaining network is now less beneficial and its value decreases with more and more firms being privatized or closed down. In the end, losing customers, suppliers or both means that the value of firms to be privatized at a later stage will, *ceteris paribus*, be lower. At best, revenues from privatization fall short of expectations, while, at worst, firms have negative value and have to be closed down.

## Conclusions

The present chapter has laid particular emphasis on the role of structural knowledge for understanding the emergence and development of competitive markets. Nevertheless, the present account is only the first step towards a more comprehensive theory of markets and a number of questions await further investigation. Consider the dynamics of networks. Does the assumption of common structural knowledge undermine competition (as understood by Burt, 1992) as well as attempts to remodel a network? As we have seen, some structural knowledge is necessary for both competition and network change. However, if structural knowledge is common knowledge, the possibility arises that other agents react to the attempt at modifying the network and that this possibility is again taken into account by those who consider modification first.

Further, under which conditions do prices converge in decentralized markets? Communicative networks are clearly necessary but they are not sufficient for convergence since it has also to be considered how agents react to price signals. In the most general sense, this question is concerned with the problem of whether local (or partial) interaction leads to an equilibrium (cf. Berninghaus and Schwalbe, 1996, for further discussion). Another question is whether trust is equally important for communication between individuals and communication between firms. Whom are we trusting and why?

Finally how are the concerns that motivate other network-theoretic works (cf. Honohan and Vittas, 1996) related to the present chapter: network externalities, complexity and redundancy? As to network externalities, it is clear, that if network structures can be regarded as a kind of resource, then leaving or joining a network may impose costs on its remaining members which are neglected in individual decision making. Honohan and Vittas have made this point with respect to membership in payment systems, but it is likely to apply to markets, too, as losing potential customers or suppliers reduces the economic value of a firm. It is less clear how important the notion of complexity and the concomitant emphasis on unpredictable network phenomena are in the context of markets. Work on capital markets suggests that larger networks and hence more complex patterns of interaction can lead to more volatile and therefore less predictable prices (cf. Baker, 1984). On markets for produced goods, by contrast, many producers and sellers are likely to reduce the risk of some producers or buyers opting out of the market. Redundancy, finally, is closely related to competition since the latter presupposes exit and hence the possibility of transacting with somebody else, that is an economic agent whose existence as potential transaction partner has been redundant so far.

## Notes

1. I would like to thank participants of the conference and Herman van Hoen for comments on an earlier draft of this chapter. Financial support from the Deutsche Forschungsgemeinschaft (DFG) is gratefully acknowledged.
2. Cf. Albach (1993), Håkansson and Johanson (1993), Mahnkopf (1994), Mayntz (1993), Teubal and Zuscovitch (1994), Teubner (1992) or Williamson (1985).
3. Cf. Fourie (1991), Snehota (1993), Mattson (1995).
4. The analysis of strategic interaction in networks is the subject matter of recent work in evolutionary game theory (cf. Blume, 1993; Kirman, 1997). In contrast to the present chapter, however, this work takes the structure of the network as given.

# 15
## Direct Foreign Investment and the Evolution of Markets in Central and Eastern Europe

*Klaus Meyer*

> Compare the problem of establishing transactions after the disintegration of the party-state hierarchy with a hypothetical situation in which all consumers from Paris would be replaced by Londoners, while all producers, wholesale and retail companies from Paris would be replaced by companies from the Milan area. For quite some time Paris would be dominated by chaotic conditions and a serious fall in output as actors would lack any frame of reference to base their decisions upon. (Swaan, 1997, p. 65)

The essence of systemic transformation in Central and Eastern Europe is the replacement of coordination by central plan with coordination via markets, as reflected in the title of the 1996 *World Development Report*. The same study suggests that foreign investors have an important role to play in the transition process through their contribution to enterprise restructuring and through their transfer of capital and know-how (World Bank, 1996a). Yet foreign investors' impact on the development of markets has not been analysed systematically.

To start with, markets do not function as classic microeconomic models suggest. Perfect competition is the exception rather than the rule. This is particularly true when multinational companies are involved. Therefore the essential question is, 'What types of market relationships will evolve?' In important sectors, firms operate within, more or less, tight production networks of international partners, which are often dominated by one strong partner (see, for example, Borrus and Zysman, 1997; Rugman and D'Cruz, 1997). Foreign investors expand the networks to which they belong and, in an optimistic scenario, integrate Central and Eastern European businesses in global production networks.

This chapter first summarizes the recent literature on the impact of foreign direct investment (FDI) on enterprise restructuring in Central and Eastern Europe, and the evolution of markets in the process of economic transition. On this basis, the business-to-business markets in the automotive supplier industry are examined. The chapter concludes with a modified assessment of the role of foreign investors. The creation of business networks and the access to international production networks are stressed as major elements of enterprise transformation.

## FDI and enterprise restructuring

Transformation of former state-owned enterprises stands at the centre of the microeconomic debate in the transition economics literature. Empirical studies explore the determinants of enterprise performance in Central and Eastern Europe, both before and after privatization (for example Pohl *et al.*, 1997; Frydman *et al.*, 1997; Earle and Estrin, 1997). The evidence suggests that, if hard budget constraints were imposed, most firms initiated adjustment processes, even before privatization, in order to increase productivity. Post-privatization performance varies across countries, industries and, what is most important, depending on initial conditions in 1989. The evidence is, however, mixed with respect to the hypothesised effects of various forms of ownership (see, for example, Chapter 7 and 8 in this volume).

Foreign-owned firms, and firms with non-equity cooperation with foreign partners, outperform purely domestic firms, according to several studies (see, for example, Chapter 12 in this volume). Domestic firms progress in terms of defensive restructuring that may involve 'downsizing' of employment and assets. However they rarely develop corporate strategies that would enable them to compete in open markets in the long run. Foreign-owned firms are more active in strategic restructuring: development of new products, investment in new production facilities, development of marketing, entry into new markets, and so on.

However, the distinction between defensive and strategic restructuring is crucial to understanding which firms may prosper in the future. Based on empirical studies, it has been argued elsewhere (Meyer, 1998a) that the following barriers to strategic restructuring can be identified.

- The access to financial resources is inhibited by an underdeveloped financial sector and the high risk of investing in an uncertain environment.[1]

- Weak systems of corporate governance often lead to principal–agent conflicts between owners and management, and between different groups of owners, notably in the case of insider-owners (see, for example, Carlin, Chapter 7 in this volume).
- The local leadership lacks the kind of managerial knowledge – and latest technology – that is necessary to compete in an open economy of the 1990s. Leaders in the central plan system had different tasks to fulfil and developed other skills than managers in a market economy.

Foreign investors have crucial advantages over local owners: they have access to international financial markets, they can contribute human capital for managerial tasks and they can establish effective owner control over the organization. Furthermore foreign acquirers may be in a better position to overcome organizational inertia through convincing leadership. However investors face more serious obstacles to change than post-acquisition management elsewhere. The change process in the acquired firms is part of the overall transition process. It poses particular challenges for the management of change (Meyer and Bjerg-Møller, 1998).

- The adaptation to a new economic system often has to be accomplished simultaneously with the shift from Fordist methods of production to flexible, specialized forms of production, which require entirely different methods of organizing the business (Sorge, 1993).
- Success in a market economy depends on tasks, skills and performance criteria that are beyond the experience of individuals and organizations used to the central plan system. Advances in these areas depend on the acquisition of tacit know-how that requires an interactive and time-consuming learning process (Frydman and Rapaczynski, 1997; Swaan, 1997).
- In Central and Eastern Europe organisations, existing routines, attitudes and possibly even value systems often inhibit competitive behaviour. Awareness of the need to change is high, but this does not necessarily translate into willingness and ability to define and adopt appropriate new behavioural patterns (Sztompka, 1993; Michailova, 1997).

## Markets in transition

The changes within organizations are interdependent with changes in external relationships, and thus the development of markets. A market economy encompasses a variety of markets, both for consumer goods and for factors of production. Where foreign investors enter the markets, they influence the behaviour of local market participants. For instance, with respect to labour markets, foreign investors may introduce more competitive incentive schemes to attract highly qualified individuals, and employ more flexible hiring and firing policies. Other market participants observe such behaviour and, as a result, adjust their job search or recruitment strategies.

Labour markets are, however, unique in many ways, and thus merit a separate treatment. The same applies to markets for energy, telecommunications and other infrastructure projects. Investors in these industries, obviously, make major contributions to the development of the sector, and to the businesses using its services. The welfare effects for the local economy depend, however, on the regulatory framework established for natural monopolies (Canning and Hare, 1996; Carbajo and Fries, 1997).

On capital markets (another unique market) the contribution of non-bank foreign investors is limited.[2] Since the shares of foreign-owned firms are usually not traded on local equity markets, the foreign investors do not contribute per se to the evolution of local systems of corporate governance (Kogut, 1996). Nevertheless East European capital markets are developing under strong Western influence. Western businesses, investors or others may not raise capital locally, but they become involved as consultants to local firms, as traders of equity or as portfolio investors.

The present chapter focuses on business-to-business markets for manufacturing goods and business services. Eastern observers complain that Central and Eastern European firms cannot gain access to Western markets, or to foreign investors producing within the region, even though local suppliers assert that they can provide comparable goods at a lower price (for example, Sereghyova, 1995; Lorentzen *et al.*, 1998). Apparently, subtle 'barriers to entry' inhibit sales to large multinational manufacturers.

A supplier offering a product of the same quality as leading competitors but at a lower price would, under the 'usual assumptions', be able to sell his output. Similarly a producer offering a slightly lower quality product at a substantially lower price would find customers at the lower end of the market. Since Central and Eastern Europe has substantial factor cost advantages, economists would expect major export opportunities.

However, the assumptions of the neoclassical market model only hold for some markets. Where the standard assumptions do not apply, business networks play an important role. For instance, as far as most intermediate goods are concerned, firms buy from suppliers with whom they have had long-standing business relationships. Similarly sales are often customer-specific as a result of customization of products, for example in machine building or automotive supplier industries, or owing to marketing strategies and interdependence of production and sales activities. Studies have demonstrated that, to a large extent, exchange in business-to-business markets takes place within long-lasting business relationships (for example, Håkansson, 1982; Levinthal and Fichman, 1988; Ford, 1997) and that a limited set of customer firms and supplier firms account for a large share of each other's businesses (Cowley, 1988; Håkansson, 1989). Thus many inter-firm relationships are built on long-term relationships or business networks.

As a consequence, exchange relations with other firms are a defining element of the modern business firm and essential for the firm's capability-building process (Andersson *et al.*, 1997). In networks of established business relationships, firms economize on search costs and create a certain degree of stability. In addition, the social embeddedness of market transactions (Granovetter, 1985) eases the collection and verification of relevant information and, through reducing scope for opportunism, reduces contract enforcement costs.

In transition economies, market institutions are evolving gradually. With the dissolution of the central plan, administrators became economic agents. Yet few of the institutions supporting a market economy were in place. Swaan (1997) explores the transaction costs faced by agents without experience on the market: they need to become aware of potential types of business and respective preferences of consumers and other business partners. Thus agents have to engage in considerable search processes to set up transactions and to find the right price. The transaction costs of these search processes are so high that they may inhibit many transactions. As Swaan (1997) argues, this has been a major factor leading to the drop in output.

Apart from the cost of search processes, other transaction costs are also high. With weak information, accounting and legal enforcement systems, information asymmetries and opportunities for opportunistic behaviour are common and vast. As many firms are new entrants to the market, they have not yet had the opportunity to establish a reputation. Selection of partners with good reputation and self-enforcing contracts, therefore, have become essential for foreign business in Russia (Thornton and Mikheeva, 1996).

Networks have an important role to play in overcoming these transaction costs, because they establish relationships that reduce search, negotiating and enforcement costs. The emergence of markets is, therefore, interdependent with the transformation of business networks. In the central plan economies, informal networks between firms were often vital to negotiating barter deals that could overcome crucial shortages, yet the weak coordination between business units along the product chain has been a major source of inefficiency in the Soviet regime (Liefert, 1993; Chikan, 1996). With transition, personal networks permitted short-term adjustments for many firms, but only after a major transformation will these new networks be able to foster new production structures. Western businesses compete on the basis of supply chains that are often integrated across firms.[3] However inertia in the existing networks may in fact inhibit the creation of new, market oriented networks (Sorge, 1993; see also Rosenbaum, in the present volume).

Successful development of network relationships is a key factor in enterprise performance during transition. Having been separated from the global economy for 40 years, Central and Eastern European firms must now create new networks, gain access to global markets and integrate themselves into global business networks. The latter has high priority as benefits from international trade are expected to make a major contribution to economic development. The next section explores the nature of international networks in an industry of particular importance to Central and Eastern Europe.

## The automotive industry in Central Europe

The automotive sector accounts for a major share in FDI inflows and includes some of the most publicized industrial investment projects. Soon after 1989, all major producers of passenger cars in Central and Eastern Europe had formed joint ventures with, or were taken over by, Western partners. In addition to West European companies, two Asian firms use Eastern Europe to enter the lower end of pan-European markets: Daiwoo in Poland and Romania, and Suzuki in Hungary. The largest early investment has been the partial acquisition of Škoda by VW.[4]

The car manufacturers are followed by their suppliers. About 50 Czech and Slovak suppliers formed joint ventures or were acquired by established multinational automotive suppliers, while 20 foreign firms invested in greenfield sites. In this way, the automotive components sector received about 10 per cent of all FDI in the Czech Republic. Škoda pressured its local suppliers to link up with Western partners, while VW urged its global suppliers to invest in the Czech Republic. VW imposed tough requirements for costs and quality, and threatened to drop those unable to fulfil worldwide standards. At the same time, VW – as did other car multinationals – worked closely with suppliers to help them achieve the required standards.

In 1996, VW started production of the 'Octavia', a new model assembled in an entirely new production plant. It is based on a VW platform that is integrated in VW's global product development and product chain management. The product development and the production process are closely integrated and the development of components is in part delegated to suppliers. VW introduced this new production strategy on a worldwide scale in the early 1990s. The number of basic platforms in the VW group is reduced, and procurement is concentrated on a small number of first-tier suppliers who are taking extended responsibilities.

Many suppliers are setting up their production facilities in nearby supplier parks or, with Škoda, even within the plant itself. A small number of suppliers take full responsibility even within Škoda for the logistics, control and assembly of whole modules. Their integration enables close coordination, reduces logistics costs and facilitates product modifications and development.

The use of global platforms is optimized through a unified sourcing strategy that requires Czech suppliers aiming at supplying components to bid in a worldwide competition. This creates great opportunities for those local suppliers who can become global suppliers for the VW group. Other suppliers failed to secure contracts for the 'Octavia' but had undergone substantial modernization that enabled them to export supplies to other multinationals. Yet another group struggles for survival as second-tier suppliers.

The global sourcing and the globalization of the supplier industry reflect worldwide changes in the automotive industry.[5] Throughout the 1990s, car makers have transferred much responsibility for researching, developing and manufacturing of whole component systems to their major suppliers. This enables increased use of economies of scale and component-specific know-how. However this new 'modular production' requires high investments by the supplier, both with respect to the development of components and for the actual production facilities. Since many smaller Czech and Hungarian firms faced tight financial constraints during the transition period, they were unable to undertake such commitments. However those suppliers who did invest in the relationship with the car manufacturer are rewarded with higher value, long-term contracts.

In this process, the first-tier components companies are becoming powerful partners of the car industry. A wave of global consolidation has left three or four producers of parts such as brakes, transmissions and suspensions worldwide. These companies gain strength not only from market power but from their control over essential technology. Since the product development is in part delegated, they also possess crucial technological competences necessary for the final product. Long-term contracts should give suppliers security of demand and encourage further product innovation without fear of losing the sunk costs of development or of a monopsonistic exploitation of productivity advances by the manufacturer (Nishiguchi and Anderson, 1995). However relying on some single suppliers for key components and expecting them to deliver just-in-time creates a reverse dependency. Interruptions at a key supplier can lead to severe interruptions in the assembly.[6]

Apart from the increasingly global, and powerful, first-tier suppliers, there are a multitude of producers of small parts in the second tier. The production networks in the East European automotive industry follow the worldwide pattern, with one peculiarity: the first-tier suppliers are mostly foreign-owned, at least in part, while the second tier consists of those locally owned firms that failed to attract foreign investors (cf. Havas, 1997; Myant, 1997; Sadowski *et al.*, 1997). Second-tier firms are usually not involved in product development and, thus, benefit far less from technology transfer. They may specialize in products of lesser technological sophistication than that before 1989. Their markets are more price-competitive, and they have to bear a major burden of adjustment in cases where the multinational car manufacturer changes its strategy or its product design.

Most manufacturers of car parts in the Czech Republic, Slovakia and Hungary find themselves in the second tier, and in a weak bargaining position. The supply of intermediate goods in the second, or even third, tier to foreign-owned car makers in the region enables survival for many components manufacturers, but they have few opportunities to receive technology transfer that would enable them to develop their own capabilities.

## Operating within a business network

Major multinational manufacturing enterprises are reducing their in-house value-added and are focusing on the development, marketing and coordination of external business relationships. They organize transactions in new modes that bear characteristics of both markets and hierarchies.[7] They are embedded in a network of business relationships, which take, formally or informally, a long-term character.

The complex interactions of firms in a production network are managed by a lead firm. The disintegrated value chain is controlled by a firm that possesses key competences in the form of technology or brand names. The competitive advantage of the lead firm, or 'platform firm' (Rugman and D'Cruz, 1997), is shifting away from production-based competencies towards competences in managing a network of related firms (Borrus and Zysman, 1997). If the suppliers are subject to high asset specificity, the network is rather stable and thus requires at least partially non-market coordination mechanisms.

The lead firm identifies the most suitable suppliers, considering both their production costs and their innovation potential. The interfaces between firms are designed so as to reduce transaction costs. These two tasks are interdependent because production costs may vary for different agents. A supplier may be able to build his module into the car on the assembly line at lower cost than the car manufacturer himself. Transferring the task to the supplier, however, makes the market interface between the two firms more complex.

To keep transaction costs under control, both the selection of partners and the establishment of suitable contracts are essential.[8] Firstly, the agreed-upon transactions have to be enforceable. If alternative suppliers are available, the threat of supplier switching can be used to pressure weaker partners into compliance. However the high specificity of capabilities and investments in customized components leads manufacturers increasingly to rely on single suppliers. The specificity often evolves within the business relationship as suppliers develop customer-specific know-how and contract-specific technologies. To some extent, these capabilities are developed through experiential learning in the business relationship. Over time, the partners invest in relationship-specific human capital, which is a form of asset specificity and increases their interdependence (Nishiguchi and Anderson, 1995; Andersson *et al.*, 1997).

The relationship-specific learning process reinforces both the benefits from the continuation of the relationship and the advantages of relying on a single supplier. This requires mechanisms to manage the business relationship that do not rely on markets alone but include elements of hierarchy. To control the relationship, firms use self-enforcing contracts; that is, each partner, at all stages of the relationship, can gain more from a continuation of the relationship than from its cancellation, and the gains are of similar magnitude. For instance, multiple interfaces with the same supplier, for example in different countries, increase the mutual interest in the continuation of the relationship, and lead to the formation of global strategic alliances (cf. Hamel and Prahalad, 1989; Dunning, 1997).

For new partners to be admitted to a network, their reputation is essential, to control potential opportunism. Preference is given to firms who can be trusted, for example because of a long-standing relationship, and who have a proven ability to fulfil the requirement concerning, say, the innovative potential to develop components, and the financial strength to guarantee product quality. Both criteria favour incumbents over entrants and thus raise the entry barriers.

Thus the Czech automotive components industry faces an uphill struggle, despite the German investment and a special commitment to aiding local suppliers. Czech firms have to compete with multinational corporations with worldwide research and production networks. Secondly, they have to acquire the managerial know-how to provide the services, such as just-in-time delivery, expected in the industry. Thirdly, they have to offer complete modules ready for insertion on the assembly line, rather than traditional 'parts'.[9] It seems that being taken over was the only feasible way for many firms to gain, or retain, access to the key market.

## Conclusion

This chapter has explored business-to-business markets in transition economies for the automotive industry. The emerging patterns are strongly influenced by recent trends in the worldwide relationships between car manufacturers and their suppliers. Increasing specificity of components leads to tighter multinational business networks and in consequence raises barriers to entry in the industry. As most local suppliers in Central and Eastern Europe are weak, they cannot overcome these entry barriers on their own.

Further research is required to understand the impact of production networks on economic transition. Interesting research questions include the coordination mechanisms between members of the network, the role and development of second-tier suppliers and the extent of asset specificity in different industries.

The importance of network contacts has to be taken into consideration when analysing transition economies. Recent research focuses on enterprise transformation as a function of corporate governance. Our research suggests that it is also important to consider the structure of the markets and networks in which the firms operate. The evolution of business relationships is an essential element of enterprise restructuring in Central and Eastern Europe. Firms must establish international business contacts and integrate into international production networks. This is a crucial, though often neglected, barrier to enterprise restructuring in Central and Eastern Europe.

Economic policy advice often implicitly relies on a classical market model that is no longer appropriate. Industrial policy has to become aware of the network structures in important industries. This has consequences for the focus of policy measures. First, market access is in itself an important aspect of enterprise transformation in Central and Eastern Europe. Market access through a partnership can also ease other problems, for example in raising financial capital (lower risk) or in obtaining managerial and technological know-how (from the partner).

Second, the impact of foreign investment on the host economy depends upon the position of the investing firm in its own business network, as well as on the strategic role of the new affiliate within that network. Flagship firms have, at least potentially, an essential role in the evolution of industrial clusters (Dunning, 1998). The investment of VW in Škoda may be such a positive case.

Third, opportunities for local firms to participate in international production networks depend on the management of the network, and especially upon its openness (for example, v. Tulder and Ruigrok, 1997). Opportunities to enter a network depend on the strategy employed by the flagship firm, notably the degree of competitive bidding used. Special opportunities may arise if the institutional environment encourages the investor to seek local suppliers. For instance, local content requirements for the access to the EU market (Suzuki, Daiwoo) or obligations negotiated in an acquisition (VW), particularly induce more cooperation with local suppliers.[10]

However, if countries develop an industrial cluster around a single multinational flagship firm, the economy may, to a large degree, become dependent on this firm. This may expose the economy to external shocks affecting this particular firm, and it would increase the bargaining power of the multinational at the expense of local stakeholders. Suppliers in the cluster should, therefore, aim at diversifying their business relationships to prevent a dominant dependency.

## Notes

1. Financial markets in the region are unable to provide finance for small and newly established businesses because banks continue to provide finance for

non-viable (former) state-owned enterprises with soft budget constraints, and acquire government bonds. Hunya (in this volume) shows that foreign-owned firms indeed report more long-term financial sources on their balance sheets, which enables them to finance higher fixed investment outlays.

2. On transaction costs inhibiting the efficiency of new commodity exchanges in transition economies, see Davis (1998).

3. Firms in transition economies appear slow in adapting higher degrees of integration of supply chain management when compared to foreign-owned firms operating in the same country (Price, 1998).

4. For further details of this case, see Meyer (1998b). The most important primary sources on the case are Myant (1997), Dörr and Kessel (1997) and v. Tulder and Ruigrok (1997).

5. On recent trends in automotive supplier industry, see, for instance, OECD (1992), Dicken (1998), Nishiguchi (1994), and Griffiths (1998a).

6. Recent incidences include a stoppage at Saab in Sweden due to a strike affecting a Danish supplier and a major interruption of assembly by Ford in Germany and the UK after Kiekert, its supplier of door and boot latches, failed to deliver. Kiekert cited software problems as a cause, but the business press speculated about a bargaining game concerning new contracts (Griffiths, 1998b; *Süddeutsche Zeitung,* 1998a, 1998b).

7. Such intermediate forms have been discussed in the recent transaction cost literature (for example, Williamson, 1991; Hennart, 1993).

8. Japanese car manufacturers have been at the forefront of managing production networks. They build and maintain relationships with a number of principles, which are increasingly adopted in Europe too (Nishiguchi and Anderson, 1995). First, both parties practise win–win behaviour consistently. For instance powerful buyers institutionalize mechanisms to work with suppliers to achieve cost savings jointly. Second, suppliers and buyers share vulnerability, for example by limiting the number of trading partners to a handful, or by making investments in each other. Third, the more powerful party involves and rewards its counterpart, for example by sharing information to foster the suppliers' innovativeness. Finally, the system has a recognized leader, yet this leadership does not abuse oligopolistic power but ensures that various constituents within the networks do not operate at cross-purposes.

9. If rumours in the German press are correct, an additional entry barrier is created by a corrupt procurement network controlling certain sectors of the automotive supplier industry (*Spiegel,* 1997).

10. To export from Central and Eastern Europe to the EU, the value-added from EU plus Europe Agreement countries must exceed a certain benchmark to avoid import duties. Imports from the parent are thus counted for VW but not for Suzuki. Few efforts to develop supplier networks are made by firms aiming at local markets, such as Peugeot and Ford, who assemble semi-knockdown cars in Poland (v. Tulder and Ruigrok, 1997) or Opel in Hungary (Havas, 1997). However, under the Europe Agreement, as in the EU, local content requirements referring to a country or region are not permitted any more.

# References

Aghion, P., O. Blanchard and R. Burgess (1994) 'The behavior of state firms in Eastern Europe: pre-privatization', *European Economic Review* **38** (6): 1327–49.

Agrawal, A. and C. Knoeber (1996) 'Firm performance and mechanisms to control agency problems between managers and shareholders', *Journal of Financial and Quantitative Analysis* **31** (3): 377–97.

Albach, H. (1993) 'The transformation of firms and markets: a network approach to economic transformation processes in East Germany', Discussion Paper FS IV 93–1, Social Science Research Centre Berlin, Berlin.

Allen, F. and D. Gale (1995) 'A welfare comparison of intermediaries and financial markets in Germany and the US', *European Economic Review* **39** (2): 179–209.

Amihud, Y. and H. Mendelson (1986) 'Asset pricing and the bid–ask spread', *Journal of Financial Economics* **17**: 223–49.

Anderson, J., G. Korsun and P. Murrell (1997) 'Enterprise–state relations after mass privatization: their character in Mongolia', *MOCT-MOST* **7** (4): 81–99.

Anderson, R. E., S. Claessens, S. Djankov and G. Pohl (1997) 'Privatization effects in Central and Eastern Europe', *MOCT-MOST* **7** (3): 137–62.

Andersson, U., J. Johanson and J.-E. Vahlne (1997) 'Organic acquisitions in the internationalization of the business firm', *Management International Review* **37** (S2): 67–84.

Andreff, W. (1992) 'French privatization techniques and experience: a model for Central–Eastern Europe?', in F. Targetti (ed.), *Privatization in Europe: West and East Experiences,* Aldershot: Dartmouth, 135–53.

Andreff, W. (1994a) 'East European privatization assessed from West European experience', *Emergo: Journal of Transforming Economies and Societies* **1** (1): 21–33.

Andreff, W. (1994b) 'Comment: planning private ownership: is the Czechoslovak solution a model?', in *Privatization in the Transition Process: Recent Experiences in Eastern Europe,* Geneva: UNCTAD, 289–301.

Andreff, W. (1996a) 'Corporate governance of privatized enterprises in transforming economies: a theoretical approach', *MOCT-MOST* **6** (2): 59–80.

Andreff, W. (1996b) 'Facteurs inertiels et effet de sentier ("path dependency") dans l'analyse théorique de la transition', Documento de Trabajo 9624, Facultad de Ciencias Economicas y Empresariales, Universidad Complutense de Madrid, Madrid.

Andreff, W. (1998) 'Industrial transformation in Central–Eastern European and East-Asian countries: should the state wither away?', in J. Henderson (ed.), *Industrial Transformation in Eastern Europe in the Light of the East Asian Experience,* London: Macmillan, 41–63.

Antczak, M. (1996) 'Income from the Privatization of State Enterprises in Poland, Hungary and the Czech Republic in 1991–1994' Studies & Analyses, No. 80, CASE, Warsaw.

Aoki, M. (1994) 'The contingent governance of teams', *International Economic Review* **35** (3): 657–76.

Appel, H. (1995) 'Justice and the reformulation of property rights in the Czech Republic', *East European Politics and Societies* 9 (1): 22–40.

ÁPV Rt. (1995) *Éves Jelantés* (Annual Report), llami Privatizációs és Vagyonkezelö RT (Hungarian State Privatization and Holding Agency), Budapest.

Åslund, A. (1995) *How Russia Became a Market Economy*, Washington, DC: Brookings.

Åslund, A., P. Boone and S. Johnson (1996) 'How to stabilize: lessons from post-communist countries', *Brookings Papers on Economic Activity* (1): 217–313.

Baker, W. (1984) 'The social structure of a national securities market', *American Journal of Sociology* 89 (4): 775–811.

Baldwin, R. J., F. Francois and R. Portes (1997) 'The costs and benefits of eastern enlargement: the impact on the EU and Central Europe', *Economic Policy* 24: 127–76.

Barberis, N., M. Boycko, A. Shleifer and N. Tsukanova (1996) 'How does privatization work? Evidence from Russian shops', *Journal of Political Economy* 104 (4): 764–90.

Bateman, M. (1997) 'Industrial restructuring and supply chain development in Eastern Europe', in S. Sharma (ed.), *Restructuring Eastern Europe: The Microeconomics of the Transition Process*, Cheltenham: Elgar, 14–28.

Bauer, T. (1976) 'The contradictory position of the enterprise under the new Hungarian economic mechanism', *Eastern European Economics* 15 (1): 3–23.

Bauer, T. (1984) 'The second economic reform and ownership relations: some considerations for the further development of the new economic mechanism', *Eastern European Economics* 23 (3–4): 33–87.

Baysinger, B. and R. Hoskisson (1990) 'The composition of boards of directors and strategic control', *Academy of Management Review* 15 (1): 72–87.

Beije, P. R. and J. Groenewegen (1992) 'A network analysis of markets', *Journal of Economic Issues* 26 (1): 87–114.

Berglöf, E. (1997) 'Reforming corporate governance: redirecting the European Agenda', *Economic Policy* 24: 93–123.

Berle A. and G. Means (1932) *The Modern Corporation and Private Property*, New York: Macmillan.

Berninghaus, S. K. and U. Schwalbe (1996) 'Evolution, interaction and Nash equilibria', *Journal of Economic Behaviour and Organization* 29 (1): 57–85.

Blair, M. (1995) *Ownership and Control: Rethinking Corporate Governance for the Twenty-first Century*, Washington DC: Brookings.

Blanchard, O. (1997) *The Economics of Post-Communist Transition*, Oxford: Clarendon Press.

Blanchard, O. and P. Aghion (1996) 'On insider privatization', *European Economic Review* 40 (3–5): 759–66.

Blanchard, O. and M. Kremer (1997) 'Disorganization', *Quarterly Journal of Economics* 112 (4): 1091–1126.

Blanchard, O., F. Lopez-de-Silanes and A. Shleifer (1994) 'What do firms do with cash windfalls?', *Journal of Financial Economics* 36: 337–60.

Blasi J. and A. Shleifer (1996) 'Corporate Governance in Russia: An Initial Look', in R. Frydman, C. W. Gray and A. Rapaczynski (eds), *Corporate Governance in Central Europe and Russia. Vol. 2: Insiders and the State*, Budapest, London and New York: CEU Press, 78–108.

Blasi, J., M. Kroumova and D. Kruse (1997) *Kremlin Capitalism: Privatizing the Russian Economy*, Ithaca and New York: Cornell University Press.

Blaszczyk, B. and M. Dąbrowski (1994) 'The privatization process in Poland', in *Privatization in the Transition Process. Recent Experiences in Eastern Europe*, Geneva: UNCTAD, 85–117.

Bleckmann, A. (1992) *Zur verfassungsrechtlichen Sanierungspflicht der Treuhandanstalt*, Cologue: Heymanns.

Blume, L. E. (1993) 'The statistical mechanics of strategic interaction', *Games and Economic Behavior* 5 (3): 387–424.

BMF (1991) *Die Tätigkeit der Treuhandanstalt: schnelle Privatisierung, entschlossene Sanierung, behutsame Stillegung*, Bundesministerium der Finanzen, Berlin.

BMWi (ed.) (1991) *Probleme der Privatisierung in den neuen Bundesländern*, Gutachten des Wissenschaftlichen Beirates, Bundesministerium für Wirtschaft, Bonn.

BMWi (1997) *Wirtschaftslage und Reformprozesse in Mittel und Osteuropa*, Bundesministerium für Wirtschaft, Bonn.

Bod, P. A. (1988) 'A vállalat, a menedzser és a tulajdonos: avagy miért van ismét szükségünk vállalatelméletre?' (The enterprise, the manager and the owner, or why do we need management theory?), *Közgazdasági Szemle* (7–8): 830–43.

Bod, P. A. and J. Hall (1992) 'Toward an autonomy preference theory of the East European firm', *Eastern European Economics* 30 (4): 57–67.

Borish, M. S. and M. Noël (1996) 'Private sector development during transition: the Visegrád countries', Discussion Paper No. 318, Washington, DC, World Bank.

Borish, M. and M. Noël (1997) 'Privatization in the Visegrád countries', *World Economy* 20 (2): 199–219.

Borrus, M. and J. Zysman (1997) 'Wintelism and the changing terms of global competition: prototype of the future', paper presented at the workshop 'Will there be a Unified European Economy?', Kreisky Forum and BRIE, Vienna.

Boycko, M., A. Shleifer and R. Vishny (1995) *Privatizing Russia*, Cambridge, Mass. MIT Press.

Brada, J. (1996a) *Corporate Governance in Transition Economies: Lessons from recent Developments in OECD Member Countries*, Paris: OECD.

Brada, J. (1996b) 'Privatization is transition – or is it?', *Journal of Economic Perspectives* 10 (2): 67–86.

Breuel, B. (1992) 'Mandate and activities of the Treuhand', in Treuhandanstalt, Ostausschuß der Deutschen Wirtschaft and BDI (eds), *Privatisation: Together into the Social Market Economy*, Cologue: Deutscher Instituts-Verlag, 166–9.

Brezinski, H. and M. Fritsch (1997) 'Spot-markets, hierarchies, networks and the problem of economic transition', in H. Brezinski and M. Fritsch (eds), *The Emergence and Evolution of Markets*, Cheltenham: Elgar, 7–19.

Brom, K. and M. Orenstein (1994) 'The privatized sector in the Czech Republic', *Europe–Asia Studies* 46 (6): 893–928.

Brücker, H. (1997) *Privatization in Eastern Germany. A Neo-Institutional Analysis*, London and Portland: Cass.

Brücker, H. (1998) 'Treuhandanstalt postmortem: An assessment of the Eastern German approach to privatisation and reconstruction', mimeo, Deutsches Institut für Wirtschaftsforschung, Berlin.

Buch C. (1996) *Creating Efficient Banking Systems. Theory and Evidence from Eastern Europe*, Tübingen: Mohr.

Buch, C. and R. Heinrich (1997) 'The end of the Czech miracle?', Discussion Paper No. 301, Kiel Institute of World Economics, Kiel.

Bundestag (1994) 'Bundestagsdebatte über das Gesetz zur abschließenden Erfüllung der verbliebenen Aufgaben der Treuhandanstalt am 4. März 1994', in Treuhandanstalt (ed.), *Dokumentation 1990–1994*, Berlin, Vol. 15, 220–48.

Burt, R. S. (1992) *Structural Holes: The Social Structure of Competition*, Cambridge, Mass.: Harvard University Press.

Calvo G. A. and M. S. Kumar (1993) 'Financial markets and intermediation', Occasional Paper No. 102, IMF, Washington, DC.

Canning, A. and P. Hare (1996) 'Political economy of privatisation in Hungary: A progress report', paper presented at the conference 'The Institutional Framework of Privatisation and Competition Policy in Economies in Transition', London Business School, London.

Capek, A. and P. Mertlik (1996) 'Organizational Change and Financial Restructuring in Czech Manufacturing Enterprises, 1990–1995', in B. Baszczyk and R. Woodward (eds), *Privatization in Post-communist Countries*, Warsaw: CASE, vol. 2, 259–84.

Carbajo, J. and S. Fries (1997) 'Restructuring infrastructure in transition economies', Working Paper No. 24, EBRD, London.

Carlin, W. and P. Aghion (1996) 'Restructuring outcomes and the evolution of ownership patterns in Central and Eastern Europe', *Economics of Transition* 4 (2): 371–88.

Carlin, W. and M. Landesmann (1997) 'From theory into practice? Restructuring and dynamism in transition economies', *Oxford Review of Economic Policy* 13 (2): 77–105.

Carlin, W., J. Van Reenen and T. Wolfe (1995) 'Enterprise restructuring in early transition: the case study evidence', *Economics of Transition* 3 (4):427–58.

CBOS (1997) 'Świadectwa Udzialowe', Report 13/13/97, Centrum Badania Opinii Spolecznej, Warsaw.

Chew, D. (ed.) (1997) *Studies in International Corporate Finance and Governance Systems: A Comparison of the U.S., Japan , and Europe*, Oxford/New York: Oxford University Press.

Chikan, A. (1996) 'Consequences of economic transition on logistics: the case of Hungary', *International Journal of Physical Distribution and Logistics Management* 16 (1).

Coase, R. H. (1937) 'The nature of the firm', *Economica* 4: 386–405

Coffee, J. C. (1996) 'Institutional investors in transitional economies: lessons from the Czech experience', in R. Frydman, C. W. Gray and A. Rapaczynski (eds), *Corporate Governance in Central Europe and Russia. Vol. 1: Banks, Funds, and Foreign Investors*, Budapest, London and New York: CEU Press, 111–86

Commander, S. , Q. Fan and M. E. Schaffer (eds) (1996) *Enterprise Restructuring and Economic Policy*, Washington, DC: World Bank.

Corbett, J. and T. Jenkinson (1997) 'How is investment financed? A study of Germany, Japan, the United Kingdom and the United States', *The Manchester School* 65 (S): 69–93.

Corbett, J. and C. Mayer (1991) 'Financial reform in Eastern Europe: progress with the wrong model', *Oxford Review of Economic Policy* 7 (4): 57–75.

Cowley, P. R. (1988) 'Market structure and business performance: an evaluation of buyer/seller power in the PIMS database', *Strategic Management Journal* **9** (3): 271–8.

Csillag, I. and E. Szalai (1985) 'Basic elements of an anti-monopoly policy', *Acta Oeconomica* **37**: 65–78.

Czada, R. (1996) 'The THA in its environment of politics and interest groups', in W. Fischer, H. Hax and H. K. Schneider (eds), *Treuhandanstalt: The Impossible Challenge*, Berlin: Akademie-Verlag, 148–73.

Dąbrowski, J. M. (1996) 'Privatisierung der polnischen Wirtschaft: Fünf Jahre Erfahrung', *Vierteljahreshefte zur Wirtschaftsforschung* **65** (2): 235–47.

Davis, J. D. (1998) 'Russian commodity exchanges: a case of organized markets in the transition process 1990–96', *Economics of Transition* **6** (1): 183–96.

Denis, D. and D. Denis (1995) 'Performance changes following top management dismissals', *Journal of Finance* 50(4): 1029–57.

Dewatripont, M. and E. Maskin (1995) 'Credit and efficiency in centralised and decentralised economies', *Review of Economic Studies* **62**: 541–55.

Dewatripont, M. and J. Tirole (1994) *The Prudential Regulation of Banks*, London: MIT Press.

Dicken, P. (1998) *Global Shift. The Internationalisation of Economic Activity*, London: Chapman.

Dickertmann, D. and S. Gelbhaar (1994) 'Treuhandanstalt: Theoretische Deutungsmuster ihrer Privatisierungstätigkeit', *Wirtschaftsdienst* **74** (6), 316–24.

Dickertmann, D. and S. Gelbhaar (1997) 'Parafiski, Nonfiski und die Deutsche Treuhandanstalt Berlin', in K. Tiepelmann and G. van der Beek (eds), *Politik der Parafiski*, Hamburg: Steuer- und Wirtschaftsverlag, 291–320.

Die Wirtschaft (ed.) (1993) *Kombinate: Was aus ihnen geworden ist. Reportagen aus den neuen Ländern*, Berlin: Die Wirtschaft.

Dietz, R. (1991) 'The role of Western capital in the transition to the market: a systems' theoretical perspective', in L. Csaba (ed.), *Systemic Stabilization in Eastern Europe*, Aldershot: Dartmouth.

Dittus, P. and S. Prowse (1996) 'Corporate control in Central Europe and Russia. Should banks own shares?', in R. Frydman, A. Rapaczynski and C. W. Gray (eds), *Corporate Governance in Central Europe and Russia. Vol. 1: Banks, Funds, and Foreign Investors*, Budapest, London and New York: CEU Press, 20–67.

DIW, IfW, IWH (various years) *Gesamtwirtschaftliche und unternehmerische Anpassungsfortschritte in Ostdeutschland*, Kiel Institute of World Economics, Kiel.

Djankov, S. (1997) 'On the determinants of enterprise adjustment: evidence from Moldova', Mimeo, World Bank, Washington, DC.

Djankov, S. and V. Kreacic (1998) 'Restructuring of manufacturing firms in Georgia: Four case studies and a survey', mimeo, World Bank, Washington, DC.

Djankov, S. and G. Pohl (1998) 'Restructuring of large firms in Slovakia', *Economics of Transition* **6** (1): 67–86.

Dooley, P. (1969) 'The interlocking directorate', *American Economic Review* **59**: 314–23.

Dore, R. (1983) 'Goodwill and the spirit of market capitalism', *British Journal of Sociology* **34** (4): 459–82.

Dörr, G. and T. Kessel (1997) 'Das Restrukturierungsmodel Škoda-Volkswagen: Ergebnis aus Transfer und Transformation', Discussion Paper FS II 97–603, Social Science Research Centre Berlin.

Dunning, J. (1993) *Multinational Enterprises and the Global Economy*, Wokingham: Addison-Wesley.

Dunning, J. (1997) *Alliance Capitalism and Global Business*, London: Routledge.

Dunning, J. H. (1998) 'Location and the multinational enterprise: A neglected factor?', *Journal of International Business Studies* 29 (1): 45–66.

Dyck, I. (1997) 'Privatization in Eastern Germany: management selection and economic transition', *American Economic Review* 87 (4): 565–97.

Earle, J. S. and S. Estrin (1996) 'Employee ownership in transition', in R. Frydman, C. W. Gray and A. Rapaczynski (eds), *Corporate Governance in Central Europe and Russia, Vol. 2: Insiders and the State*, Budapest, London and New York: CEU Press, 1–61.

Earle, J. S. and S. Estrin (1997) 'After voucher privatization: the structure of corporate ownership in Russian manufacturing industry', Discussion Paper No. 1736, CEPR, London.

Earle, J. S., R. Frydman *et al.* (1994) *Small Privatization*, London and Budapest: Central European University Press.

Easterbrook, F. H. and D. R. Fischel (1991) *The Economic Structure of Corporate Law*, Cambridge, Mass.: Harvard University Press.

EBRD (various years) *Transition Report*, European Bank for Reconstruction and Development, London.

Edwards, J. and K. Fischer (1994) *Banks, Finance and Investment in Germany*, Cambridge, UK: Cambridge University Press.

Egerer, R. (1995) 'Capital markets, financial intermediaries and corporate governance', Policy Research Working Paper No. 1555, World Bank, Washington, DC.

Eisenberg, T. and S. Takashira (1996) 'Should we abolish chapter 11? The evidence from Japan', in J. Bhandhari and L. A. Weiss (eds), *Corporate Bankruptcy. Economic and Legal Perspectives*. Cambridge, UK: Cambridge University Press, 501–30.

Fama, E. (1980) 'Agency problems and the theory of the firm', *Journal of Political Economy* 88 (2): 288–307.

Fama, E. and M. Jensen (1983) 'Agency problems and residual claims', *Journal of Law and Economics* 26 (2): 327–49.

Fennema, M. (1982) *International Networks of Banks and Industry*, Dordrecht: Nijhoff.

Fischer, W. and H. Schröter (1996) 'The origins of the Treuhandanstalt', in W. Fischer, H. Hax and H. K. Schneider (eds), *Treuhandanstalt: The Impossible Challenge*, Berlin: Akademie-Verlag, 15–39.

Fischer, W., H. Hax and H. K. Schneider (1996) 'Preface', in W. Fischer, H. Hax and H. K. Schneider (eds), *Treuhandanstalt: The Impossible Challenge*, Berlin: Akademie-Verlag, 1–12.

FNM R. (various years) *Annual Report*, Fond Národního Majetku eske Republiky (Fund of National Property of the Czech Republic), Prague.

Ford, D. (1997) *Understanding Business Markets: Interaction, Relationships and Networks*, San Diego: Academic Press.

Fourie, F. C. v. N. (1991) 'The nature of the market: a structural analysis', in G.M. Hodgson and E. Screpanti (eds), *Rethinking Economics: Markets, Technology and Economic Evolution*, Aldershot: Elgar, 40–57.

Franks, J. and Mayer C. (1995) 'Ownership and control', in H. Siebert (ed.), *Trends in Business Organisation: Do Participation and Co-Operation Increase Competitiveness?*, Tübingen: Mohr, 171–96.

Franks, J. and C. Mayer (1997a) 'Corporate ownership and control in the U.K. Germany and France', *Journal of Applied Corporate Finance* 9 (1): 30–45.

Franks, J. and C. Mayer (1997b) 'Ownership, Control and The Performance of German Corporations', mimeo, Said Business School, University of Oxford.

Franks, J., C. Mayer and L. Renneboog (1997) 'Capital Structure, Ownership and Board Restructuring in Poorly Performing Companies', mimeo, Said Business School, University of Oxford.

Freese, C. (1995) *Die Privatisierungstätigkeit der Treuhandanstalt: Strategien und Verfahren der Privatisierung in der Systemtransformation*, Frankfurt/M.: Campus.

Freinkman, L. (1995) 'Financial–industrial groups in Russia: emergence of large diversified privatised companies', *Communist Economies and Economic Transformation* 7 (1): 51–66.

Friedman, E. and S. Johnson (1996) 'Complementarities in economic reform', *Economics of Transition* 4 (2): 319–29.

Fries, S. M. (1995) 'Enterprise restructuring and control in transition economies', *Economics of Transition* 3 (1): 115–21.

Frydman, R. and A. Rapaczynski (1994) *Privatization in Eastern Europe: Is the State Withering Away?* London, Budapest and New York: CEU Press.

Frydman, R. and A. Rapaczynski (1997) 'Corporate governance and the political effects of privatisation', in Salvatore Zecchini (ed.), *Lessons from the Economic Transition. Central and Eastern Europe in the 1990s*, Dordrecht and Boston: Kluwer, 263–74.

Frydman, R., C. W. Gray and A. Rapaczynski (eds) (1996) *Corporate Governance in Central Europe and Russia*, Budapest, London and New York: CEU Press.

Frydman R., C. W. Gray, M. Hessel and A. Rapaczynski (1997) 'Private ownership and corporate performance: evidence from transition economies', Working Paper No. 26, EBRD, London.

Frydman, R., A. Rapaczynski, E. Phelps and A. Shleifer (1993) 'Needed mechanisms of corporate governance and finance in Eastern Europe', *Economics of Transition* 1 (2): 171–207

Gaddy, C. and B. W. Ickes (1998) 'To restructure or not to restructure: informal activities and enterprise behavior in transition', mimeo.

Gates, S., P. Milgrom and J. Roberts (1996) 'Complementarities in the transition from socialism: a firm-level analysis', in J. McMillan and B. Naughton (eds), *Reforming Asian Socialism. The Growth of Market Institutions*, Ann Arbor: University of Michigan Press, 17–37.

Gavrilenkov, E. (1998) 'Case study of restructuring: Russia', Economic Commission for Europe Spring Seminar on Enterprise and Bank Restructuring in the Transition Economies, Geneva: UN.

Gesell, R. and T. Jost (1997) 'The Polish state enterprise system: an impediment to transformation?', Discussion Paper No. 12/97, Frankfurt Institute for Transformation Studies, Frankfurt (O).

Gesell, R., K. Müller and D. Süß (1998) 'Social security reform and privatization in Poland: parallel projects or integrated agenda?', Discussion Paper No. 8/98, Frankfurt Institute for Transformation Studies, Frankfurt (O).

Grabher, G. (1995) 'The elegance of incoherence: economic transformation in East Germany and Hungary', in E. J. Dittrich, G. Schmidt and R. Whitley (eds), *Industrial Transformation in Europe*, London: Sage, 33–53.

Grabher, G. and D. Stark (1997) 'Organizing diversity: evolutionary theory, network analysis and post-socialism', in G. Grabher and D. Stark (eds), *Restructuring Networks in Post-Socialism: Legacies, Linkages, and Localities*, Oxford: Oxford University Press, 1–32.

Granovetter, M. (1985) 'Economic action and social structure: a theory of embeddedness', *American Journal of Sociology* 91 (3): 481–510.

Granovetter, M. (1995) 'Coase revisited: business groups in the modern economy', *Industrial and Corporate Change* 4: 93–130.

Gray, C. W. (1996) 'In search of owners: privatization and corporate governance in transition economies', *World Bank Research Observer* 11 (2): 179–97.

Gray, C. W. and R. Hanson (1993) 'Corporate governance in Central and Eastern Europe: lessons from advanced market economies', Policy Research Working Paper No. 1182, World Bank, Washington, DC.

Gray, C. W. and A. Holle (1996) 'Bank-led restructuring in Poland: the conciliation process in action', *Economics of Transition* 4 (2): 349–70.

Griffiths, J. (1998a) 'Suppliers: neighbours make for good relations', and 'Components: carmakers open Pandora's box', *Financial Times*, 23 February.

Griffiths, J. (1998b) 'Ford: Production Crisis Worsens', *Financial Times*, 17 June.

Grosfeld, I. and J. F. Nivet (1997) 'Wage and investment behaviour in transition: evidence from a Polish panel data set', Discussion Paper No. 1726, CEPR, London.

Grosfeld, I. and G. Roland (1995) 'Defensive and strategic restructuring in Central European enterprises', Discussion Paper No. 1135, CEPR, London.

Grossman, S. and O. Hart (1980) 'Takeover bids, the free rider problem and the theory of the corporation', *Bell Journal of Economics* 11 (1): 42–64.

Grossman, S. J. and O. Hart (1986) 'The costs and benefits of ownership: a theory of vertical and lateral integration', *Journal of Political Economy* 94 (4): 691–719.

Håkansson, H. (1982) *International Marketing and Purchasing of Industrial Goods: An Interaction Approach*, New York: Wiley.

Håkansson, H. (1989) *Corporate Technological Behaviour: Cooperations and Networks*, London: Routledge.

Håkansson, H. and J. Johanson (1993) 'The network as a governance structure: interfirm cooperation beyond markets and hierarchies', in G. Grabher (ed.), *The Embedded Firm: On the Socioeconomics of Industrial Networks*, London: Routledge, 35–51.

Hall, B. and D. Weinstein (1996) 'The myth of the patient Japanese', Working Paper No. 5818, NBER, Cambridge, Mass.

Hamel, G. and C. K. Prahalad (1989) 'Collaborate with your competitors – and win', *Harvard Business Review* 67 (1): 133–9.

Harris, M. and A. Raviv (1991) 'The theory of capital structure', *Journal of Finance* 46 (1): 297–355.

Hart, O. (1995) *Firms, Contracts and the Financial Structure*, Oxford: Clarendon Press.

Hau, H. (1998) 'Privatization under political interference', *European Economic Review* 42(7): 1177–1202.

Havas, A. (1997) 'Foreign direct investment and intra-industry trade: The case of the automotive industry in Central Europe', in David Dyker (ed.), *The Technology of Transition*, Budapest, London and New York: CEU Press.

Havlik, P. (1996) 'Exchange rates, competitiveness and labour costs in Central and Eastern Europe', WIIW Research Report No. 231, Vienna Institute for International Economic Studies (WIIW), Vienna.

Hayek, F. (1937) 'Economics and knowledge', *Economica* 17 (1): 33–54.

Hayek, F. (1967) 'The results of human action but not of human design', in *Studies in Philosophy, Politics and Economics*, Chicago: University of Chicago Press, 96–105.

Hayek, F. A. (1978) 'Competition as a discovery process', in *New Studies in Philosophy, Politics, Economics and the History of Ideas*, Chicago: University of Chicago Press, 179–190.

Hennart, J.-F. (1993) 'Explaining the swollen middle: why most transactions are a mix of market and hierarchy', *Organization Science* 4 (4): 529–47.

Herrmann-Pillath, C. (1994) 'China's transition to the market: a paradox of transformation and its institutionalist solution', in H.-J. Wagener (ed.), *The Political Economy of Transformation*, Heidelberg: Physica, 209–41.

Hillion, P. and D. Young (1996) 'The Czechoslovak privatization auction: an empirical investigation', Social Science Working Paper No. 921, California Institute of Technology.

Hingorani, A., K. Lehn and A. Makhija (1997) 'Investor behavior in mass privatization: the case of the Czech voucher scheme', *Journal of Financial Economics* 44 (3): 349–96.

Hoch, R. (1991) 'Changing formation and privatisation', *Acta Oeconomica* 43 (3–4): 263–80.

Hodgson, G. (1988) *Economics and Institutions: A Manifesto for a Modern Institutional Economics*, Cambridge, UK: Polity Press.

Holmström, B. and J. Tirole (1993) 'Market liquidity and performance monitoring', *Journal of Political Economy* 101 (4): 678–709.

Honohan, P. and D. Vittas (1996) 'Bank regulation and the network paradigm: policy implications for developing and transition economies', Policy Research Working Paper No. 1631, World Bank, Washington, DC.

Hoshi, T., A. Kashyap and D. Scharfstein (1990) 'Bank monitoring and investment', in R. G. Hubbard (ed.), *Asymmetric Information, Corporate Finance and Investment*, Chicago: University of Chicago Press, 105–26.

Hunya, G. and J. Stankovsky (1997) 'WIIW-WIFO database. Foreign direct investment in Central and East European Countries and the Former Soviet Union', Vienna: Vienna Institute for International Economic Studies (WIIW) and Austrian Institute of Economic Research (WIFO).

Jasinski, P. and G. Yarrow (1996) 'Privatization: an overview of the issues', in G. Yarrow and P. Jasinski (eds), *Privatization*, London: Routledge, vol. 1, 1–46.

Jensen, M. (1986) 'Agency costs of free cash flow, corporate finance and takeovers', *American Economic Review. Papers and Proceedings* 76: 323–9.

Jensen M. and W. Meckling (1976) 'Theory of the firm: managerial behavior, agency costs and ownership structure', *Journal of Financial Economics* 3: 305–60.

Jensen, M. and J. L. Zimmermann (1985) 'Management compensation and the managerial labor market', *Journal of Accounting and Economics* 7: 3–9.

Jermakowicz, W. (1996) 'Models of mass privatisation', in B. Błaszczyk and R. Woodward (eds), *Privatization in Post-Communist Countries*, Warsaw: CASE, vol. 2, 7–36.

Johanson, J. and L. -G. Mattson (1987) 'Interorganizational relations in industrial systems: a network approach compared with the transactional approach', *International Studies of Management and Organization* 18: 34–48.

Johnson, W. B., R. P. Magee, N. J. Nagarajan and H. Newman (1985) 'An analysis of the stock price reaction to sudden executive deaths: implication for the managerial labor market', *Journal of Accounting and Economics* 7: 151–74.

Jones, D. and T. Kato (1996) 'The determinants of chief executive compensation in transitional economies: evidence from Bulgaria', *Labour Economics* 3: 319–36.

Kaplan, S. (1994a) 'Top executives, turnover and firms performance in Germany', *Journal of Law, Economics and Organization* 10 (1): 142–59.

Kaplan, S. (1994b) 'Top executive rewards and firm performance: a comparison of Japan and the United States', *Journal of Political Economy* 102 (3): 510–46.

Kaplan, S. (1997) 'Corporate governance and corporate performance', in K. Hopt and E. Wymeersch (eds), *Comparative Corporate Governance*, Berlin: de Gruyter, 195–210.

Kemmler, M. (1994) *Die Entstehung der Treuhandanstalt: Von der Wahrung zur Privatisierung des DDR-Volkseigentums*, Frankfurt/M.: Campus.

Keren, M. (1973) 'The new economic system in the GDR: an obituary', *Soviet Studies* 24 (4): 554–87.

Keren, M. (1993) 'On the (im)possibility of market socialism', *Eastern Economic Journal* 19 (3): 333–44.

Keren, M. (1997) 'From hierarchy to markets: an evolutionary perspective of the transformation process', in H. Brezinski and M. Fritsch (eds), *The Emergence and Evolution of Markets*, Cheltenham: Elgar, 40–54.

Kirman, A. (1997) 'The economy as an evolving network', *Journal of Evolutionary Economics* 7 (4): 339–53.

Koenig, T. and R. Gogel (1981) 'Interlocking corporate directorships as a social network', *American Journal of Economics and Sociology* 40 (1): 37–50.

Kogut, B. (1996) 'Direct investment, experimentation, and corporate governance in transition economies', in R. Frydman, C. W. Gray and A. Rapaczynski (eds), *Corporate Governance in Central Europe and Russia. Vol.1: Banks, Funds, and Foreign Investors*, Budapest, London and New York: CEU Press, 293–332.

Kole, S. (1997) 'The complexity of compensation contracts', *Journal of Financial Economics* 43 (1): 79–104.

Kole, S. and K. Lehn (1997) 'Deregulation, the evolution of governance structure and survival', *American Economic Review. Papers and Proceedings* 87: 421–5.

Kornai, J. (1986) 'The soft budget constraint', *Kyklos* 39 (1): 3–30.

Kornai, J. (1990) *The Road to a Free Economy: Shifting from a Socialist System. The Example of Hungary*, New York and London: Norton.

Kornai, J. (1992) *The Socialist System: The Political Economy of Communism*, Princeton, NJ: Princeton University Press.

Kornai, J. (1994) 'Transformational recession: the main causes', *Journal of Comparative Economics* 19 (1): 39–63.

Kotrba, J. and J. Svejnar (1994) 'Rapid and multifaceted privatization: experience of the Czech and Slovak Republics', *MOCT-MOST* 4 (2): 147–85.

Kotz, D. (1978) *Bank Control of Large Corporations in the United States*, Berkeley: University of California Press.

Kowalczyk, B. (1997) 'The role of Polish national investment funds in restructuring privatized companies', Advanced Studies Working Paper No. 315, Kiel Institute of World Economics, Kiel.

Kreps, D. M. (1990) 'Corporate culture and economic theory', in J. Alt and K. Shepsle (eds), *Perspectives on Positive Political Economy*, Cambridge, UK: Cambridge University Press, 90–143.

Krug, B. (1997) 'Privatization in China: something to learn from?', in H. Giersch (ed.), *Privatization at the End of the Century*, Berlin, Heidelberg and New York: Springer, 269–93.

Kubin, J. and Z. Tůma (1997) 'Fiscal impact of privatization and fiscal policy', in M. Mejstřík (ed.), *The Privatization Process in East–Central Europe: Evolutionary Process of Czech Privatization*, Dordrecht, Boston and London: Kluwer, 125–44.

La Porta, R., F. Lopez-de-Silanes, A. Shleifer and R. Vishny (1998) 'Law and finance', *Journal of Political Economy* **106** (6): 1113–55.

Lagemann, B., W. Friedrich *et al.* (1994) *Aufbau mittelständischer Strukturen in Polen, Ungarn, der Tschechischen Republik und der Slowakischen Republik*, Essen: RWI.

Lastovicka R., A. Marcincin and M. Mejstřík (1995) 'Corporate governance and share prices in voucher-privatized companies', in J. Svejnar (ed.), *The Czech Republic and Economic Transition in Eastern Europe*. San Diego: Academic Press, 199–209.

Lavigne, M. (1995) *The Economics of Transition: From Socialist Economy to Market Economy*, Basingstoke: Macmillan.

Levine, R. (1997) 'Financial development and economic growth', *Journal of Economic Literature* **35** (2): 688–726.

Levinthal, D. A. and M. Fichman (1988) 'Dynamics of interorganizational attachments: auditor–client relationships', *Administrative Science Quarterly* **33** (3): 345–69.

Liefert, W. M. (1993) 'Distribution problems in the food economy of the former Soviet Union', in *The Soviet Union in Transition*, Washington, DC: US Congressional Publication.

Liska, T. (1988) *Ökonosztát* (An economic model), Budapest: Közgazdasági és Jogi Könyvkiadó.

Lizal, L. and J. Svejnar (1998) 'Enterprise investment during the transition: evidence from Czech panel data', Discussion Paper No. 1835, CEPR, London.

Lizal, L., M. Singer and J. Svejnar (1997) 'Enterprise breakups and performance during the transition', Discussion Paper No. 1757, CEPR, London.

Lizondo, S. (1990) 'Foreign direct investment', Working Paper WP/90/63, IMF, Washington, DC.

Long M. and I. Rutkowska (1995) 'The role of commercial banks in enterprise restructuring in Central and Eastern Europe', Policy Research Working Paper No. 1423, World Bank, Washington DC.

Lorentzen, J., H. P. Møllgaard and M. Rojec (1998) 'Globalisation in emerging markets: does foreign capital in Central Europe promote innovation?', Working Paper No. 1/98, Institut for Nationaløkonomi, Copenhagen: Copenhagen Business School.

Lucke, B. (1995) 'Die Privatisierungspolitik der Treuhandanstalt: Eine ökonometrische Analyse', *Zeitschrift für Wirtschafts- und Sozialwissenschaften* 115 (2) 393–428.

Lundvall, B.-A. (1993) 'Explaining interfirm cooperation and innovation: limits of the transaction-cost approach', in G. Grabher (ed.), *The Embedded Firm: On the Socioeconomics of Industrial Networks*, London: Routledge, 52–64.

MacMillan, K. and D. Farmer (1979) 'Redefining the boundaries of the firm', *Journal of Industrial Economics* 27 (3): 277–85.

Mahnkopf, B. (1994) 'Markt, Hierarchie und soziale Beziehungen', in N. Beckenbach and W. v. Treeck (eds), *Umbrüche gesellschaftlicher Arbeit*, Göttingen: Schwarz, 65–84.

Major, I. (1994) 'The constraints on privatization in Hungary: insufficient demand or inelastic supply?', *MOCT-MOST* 4 (2): 107–45.

Malinvaud, E., J.-C. Milleron and A. K. Sen (eds) (1998) *Development Strategy and Management of the Market Economy, Vol. 1*, Oxford and New York: Clarendon Press.

Malinvaud, E., and R. Sabot (eds) (1997) *Development Strategy and Management of the Market Economy Vol. 2*, Oxford and New York: Clarendon Press.

Marcincin, A. and S. van Wijnbergen (1997) 'The impact of Czech privatization methods on enterprise performance incorporating initial selection bias correction', Discussion Paper No. 97/4, CERT, Edinburgh.

Marris, R. (1964) *The Economic Theory of Managerial Capitalism*, Glencoe, Illinois: Free Press of Glencoe.

Marshall, A. (1938) *Principles of Economics*, London: Macmillan.

Maskin, E. (1992) 'Auctions and privatization' in H. Siebert (ed.), *Privatization*, Tübingen: Mohr, 115–36.

Matesová, J. and R. Seda (1994) 'Financial markets in the Czech Republic as a means of corporate governance in voucher privatized companies', Working Paper No. 62, CERGE, Prague.

Matolcsy, G. (1990) 'Defending the case of the spontaneous reform of ownership', *Acta Oeconomica* 42 (1–2): 1–22.

Mattson, L.-G. (1995) 'Firms, "megaorganizations" and markets: a network view', *Journal of Institutional and Theoretical Economics* 151 (4): 760–66.

Mayer, C. (1990) 'Financial systems, corporate finance and economic development', in R. G. Hubbard (ed.), *Asymmetric Information, Corporate Finance and Investment*, Chicago: University of Chicago Press, 307–32.

Mayer, C. (1998) 'Financial systems and corporate governance', *Journal of Institutional and Theoretical Economics* 154 (1): 144–65.

Mayntz, R. (1993) 'Modernization and the logic of interorganizational networks', in J. Child, M. Crozier and R. Mayntz (eds), *Societal Change Between Market and Organization*, Aldershot: Avebury, 3–18.

McAfee, R. P. and J. McMillan (1987) 'Auctions and bidding' *Journal of Economic Literature*, 25: 699–738.

McConnell, J. and H. Servaes (1990) 'Additional evidence on equity ownership and corporate value', *Journal of Financial Economics* 27: 595–612.

McDermott, G. A. (1997) 'Renegotiating the ties that bind: the limits to privatization in the Czech Republic', in G. Grabher and David Stark (eds), *Restructuring Networks in Post-Socialism. Legacies, Linkages and Localities*, Oxford: Oxford University Press, 70–106.

McLeod, W. B. (1998) 'Thought or reflex? On the interaction between utility and human capital theory', mimeo.

Mertlik P. (1996) 'Czech privatization: from public ownership to public ownership in five years?', in B. Blaszczyk and R. Woodward (eds), *Privatization in Post-Communist Countries*, Warsaw: CASE, vol. 1, 103–22.

Meyer, K. (1998a) 'Enterprise Transformation and Foreign Investment in Eastern Europe.' in *Journal of East–West Business* 4 (1/2): 7–27.

Meyer, K. (1998b) 'Multinational enterprises and the emergence of markets and networks in transition economies', Working Paper No. 12, Center for East European Studies, Copenhagen Business School, Copenhagen.

Meyer, K. and I. Bjerg-Møller (1998) 'Managing deep restructuring: Danish experiences in Eastern Germany', *European Management Journal* 16 (4): 411–21.

Michailova, S. (1997) 'Inertia: organizational culture of Bulgarian industrial companies between stability and change', PhD thesis 6/97, Faculty of Economics and Business, Copenhagen Business School, Copenhagen.

Mihályi, P. (1989) *Az NSZK gazdaságpolitikája* (Economic policy in Germany), Budapest: Kossuth Könyvkiadó.

Mihályi, P. (1996a) 'Privatisation in Hungary: now comes the "hard core".' *Communist Economies and Economic Transformation* 8 (2): 205–17.

Mihályi, P. (1996b) 'Management and sale of residual state shareholdings in Hungary', *Acta Oeconomica* 48: 331–47.

Milgrom, P. and J. Roberts (1990) 'The economics of modern manufacturing: technology, strategy and organization', *American Economic Review* 80 (3): 511–28.

Ministerstwo Skarbu Państwa (Polish Ministry of the State Treasury) (1996) 'Raport o Przeksztalceniach Wlasnociowych w 1995 Roku' (Report on Ownership Changes in 1995), Warsaw: Ministerstwo Skarbu Państwa.

Ministerstwo Skarbu Państwa (Polish Ministry of the State Treasury) (1997) 'Privatization Quarterly', Warsaw: Ministerstwo Skarbu Państwa.

Ministry of Privatization (1995) 'National Investment Fund Programme. Information relating to the Universal Share Certificate', Warsaw.

Mintzberg H. (1983) *Power In and Around Organizations*, Englewood Cliffs: Prentice-Hall.

Mises, L. v. (1961) 'Markt', in E. v. Beckerath (ed.), *Handwörterbuch der Sozialwissenschaften*, Stuttgart: Gustav Fischer, 131–6.

Moerland, P. W. (1995) 'Corporate ownership and control structures: an international comparison', *Review of Industrial Organization* 10 (4): 443–64.

Mohlek, P. (1996) 'Privatisierung von Staatsunternehmen in Polen', *Osteuropa-Recht* 42 (4): 312–46.

Morck, R., A. Shleifer and R. Vishny (1988) 'Management ownership and market valuation: an empirical analysis', *Journal of Financial Economics* 20: 293–315.

Morck, R., A. Shleifer and R. Vishny (1989) 'Alternative mechanisms for corporate control', *American Economic Review* 79 (4): 842–52.

Murphy, K. (1985) 'Corporate performance and managerial remuneration: an empirical analysis', *Journal of Accounting and Economics* 7: 11–42.

Myant, M. (1997) 'Foreign direct investment and industrial restructuring in the Czech Republic', paper presented at the workshop 'Central and Eastern Europe: Institutional Change and Industrial Developments', Tannishus.

National Bank of Hungary (1996) *Annual Report*. Budapest: National Bank of Hungary.

Nishiguchi, T. (1994) *Strategic Industrial Sourcing: The Japanese Advantage*, New York: Oxford University Press.

Nishiguchi, T. and E. Anderson (1995) 'Supplier and buyer networks', in E. H. Bowman and B. Kogut (eds), *Redesigning the Firm*, Oxford: Oxford University Press, 65–84.

Nickell, S. (1996) 'Competition and corporate performance', *Journal of Political Economy* **104** (4): 724–46.

Nivet, J. F. (1997) 'La privatisation en Pologne: la terre de la grande promesse?', *Document de travail du ROSES* 5: 21.

North, D. C. (1990) *Institutions, Institutional Change and Economic Performance*, Cambridge, UK: Cambridge University Press.

Nunnenkamp, P. (1995) 'The German model of corporate governance. Basic features, critical issues and applicability to transition economies', Working Paper No. 713, Kiel Institute of World Economics, Kiel.

Nuti, D. (1995) '"Corporate governance" et actionnariat des salariés', *Economie internationale* **62**: 13–34.

OECD (1992) *Globalization of Industrial Activities. Four Case Studies: Auto Parts, Chemicals, Construction and Semiconductors*, Paris.

OECD (1995) *Trends and Policies in Privatization*, 3 (1): Paris.

OECD (1996) *Economic Survey of the Czech Republic*, Paris.

OECD (1998) *Corporate Governance: Improving Competitiveness and Access to Capital in Global Markets*, Paris.

Pennings, J. M. (1980) *Interlocking Directorates. Origins and Consequences of Connections Among Organizations' Board of Directors*, San Francisco: Jossey-Bass.

Pinto, B. and S. van Wijnbergen (1995) 'Ownership and corporate control in Poland: why state firms defied the odds', Discussion Paper No. 1273, CEPR, London.

Pistor, K. and A. Spicer (1996) 'Investment funds in mass privatization and beyond', Discussion Paper No. 565, Harvard Institute for International Development, Cambridge, Mass.

Pohl, G., R. E. Anderson, S. Claessens and S. Djankov (1997) 'Privatization and restructuring in Central and Eastern Europe', Technical Paper No. 368, World Bank, Washington, DC.

Polanyi, K. (1944) *The Great Transformation*, New York: Rinehart.

Porter, M. E. (1990) *The Competitive Advantage of Nations*, London: Macmillan.

Powell, W. W. (1996) 'Weder Markt noch Hierarchie: Netzwerkartige Organisationsformen', in P. Kenis and V. Schneider (eds), *Organisation und Netzwerk: Institutionelle Steuerung in Wirtschaft und Politik*, Frankfurt/M.: Campus, 213–71.

Price, P. (1998) 'Supply chain management in a transitional economy', Working Paper No. 6, MBA Department Almaty: Kazakhstan Institute of Management, Economics and Strategic Research (KIMEP).

Prowse, S. (1995) 'Corporate governance in an international perspective: a survey of corporate control mechanisms among large firms in the U.S., U.K., Japan and Germany', in *Financial Markets, Institutions and Instruments*, Cambridge, Mass.: Blackwell.

Pye, R. (1997) 'Foreign direct investment in Central Europe: results from a survey of major western investors', Finance Working Paper A 97/1, City University Business School, London.

Rapacki, R. (1995) 'Privatization in Poland', *Comparative Economic Studies* **37** (1): 57–75.

Richter, R. (1996) 'Die Neue Institutionenökonomik des Marktes', Lectiones Jenenses, No. 5, Max-Planck-Institut zur Erforschung von Wirtschaftssystemen, Jena.

Rizopoulos, Y. (1997) 'Socio-economic networks and economic transformation: the Russian case', *Economic Systems* **21** (4): 365–9.

Roe, M. J. (1993) 'Some differences in corporate structure in Germany, Japan and the United States', *Yale Law Journal* **102**: 1927–2003.

Rojec, M. (1997) 'The development potential of foreign direct investment in the Slovenian economy', WIIW Research Report No. 235, Vienna Institute for International Economic Studies (WIIW), Vienna.

Roland, G. (1994) 'On the speed and sequencing of privatization and restructuring', *Economic Journal* **104** (5): 1158–68.

Roland, G. and K. Sekkat (1996) 'Managerial career concerns, privatization and restructuring in transition economies', Discussion Paper No. 1363, CEPR, London.

Rosenbaum, E. (1998) 'What is a market?', Discussion Paper No. 98/1, Frankfurt Institute for Transformation Studies, Frankfurt (O).

Rugman, A. and J. d'Cruz (1997) 'The theory of the flagship firm', *European Management Journal* **15** (4): 403–12.

Rzeczpospolita (1997) 'Waniejsi akcjonariusze NFI', 8 October.

Sadowski, B., S. Rodsevic, S. Kubielas, K. Müller and A. Havas (1997) 'International co-operative agreements in Central and Eastern Europe', ACE Project Interim Report to the European Commission, mimeo, MERIT, Maastricht.

Sárközy, T. (1986) *Egy Gazdasági Szervezeti Reform Sodrában* (Reforming the Enterprises in Hungary), Budapest: Magvetõ Kiadó.

Sárközy, T. (1996) 'Grundzüge des neuen ungarischen Privatisierungsgesetzes', *Osteuropa-Recht* **42** (1): 1–17.

Saunders, A. (1994) 'Banking and commerce: An overview of the public policy issues', *Journal of Banking and Finance* **18**: 231–54.

Schaffer, M. (1997) 'Do Firms in Transition have Soft Budget Constraints? A Reconsideration of Concepts and Evidence', mimeo, Heriot-Watt University, Edinburgh.

Schaffer, M., A. Bevan and R. Mochrie (1998) 'Enterprise and bank restructuring: progress, problems and policies', Economic Commission for Europe Spring Seminar on Enterprise and Bank Restructuring in the Transition Economies, Geneva: UN.

Schmidt, K. (1997) 'The political economy of mass privatization and the risk of expropriation', Discussion Paper No. 1542, CEPR, London.

Schmidt, K. and M. Schnitzer (1997) 'Methods of privatization: auctions, bargaining and giveaways', in H. Giersch (ed.), *Privatization at the End of the Century*. Berlin: Springer, 97–133.

Schmidt, K.-D. (1994) 'Treuhandanstalt and investment acquisitions: how to ensure that contracts are kept?', Working Paper No. 632, Kiel Institute of World Economics, Kiel.

Schmidt, K.-D. (1996) 'Privatisation strategies', in W. Fischer, H. Hax and H. K. Schneider (eds), *Treuhandanstalt: The Impossible Challenge*, Berlin: Akademie-Verlag, 211–40.

Schumpeter, J. (1943) *Capitalism, Socialism and Democracy*, London: Allen & Unwin.

Sedaitis, J. B. (1997) 'Network dynamics of new firm formation: developing Russian commodity markets', G. Grabher and D. Stark (eds), in *Restructuring Networks in Post-Socialism: Legacies, Linkages and Localities*, Oxford: Oxford University Press, 137–57.

Sereghyová, J. (1995) 'Dichotomy between expectations causing enterprises in Central European countries in transition to seek foreign capital participations', in *Joint Ventures in Transformation Countries in the Context of Overall Investment Strategies of their Partners*, ACE Research project, Barcelona: Grup d'Anàlisi de las Transició Econòmica, 49–98.

Serra, E., C. Buch and T. Nienaber (1997) 'The Role of Banks. Evidence from Germany and the U.S.', Institute of World Economics, Working Paper No. 802, Kiel.

Shleifer, A. and R. Vishny (1997) 'A survey of corporate governance', *Journal of Finance* 52 (2): 737–83.

Siegmund, U. (1997a) 'Was privatization in Eastern Germany a special case? Some lessons from the Treuhand', Working Paper Nr. 85, University of Michigan Business School, William Davidson Institute, Ann Arbor.

Siegmund, U. (1997b) 'Comment on the methods of privatization: politico-economic and historical issues', in H. Giersch (ed.), *Privatization at the End of the Century*, Berlin, Heidelberg and New York: Springer, 135–43.

Siegmund, U. (1998) 'Die Treuhand 1990/91: Spezialfall, Privatisierungsmonopol und Staatsversagen?', Diskussionsbeitrag Nr. 87, Universität der Bundeswehr, Institut für Wirtschaftspolitik, Hamburg.

Siegmund, U. (1999) *Privatisierungspolitik in Ostdeutschland: Eine politökonomische Analyse*, forthcoming.

Simmel, G. (1903) 'Soziologie der Konkurrenz', *Neue Deutsche Rundschau* 14: 1009–23.

Simon, H. A. (1986) 'Rationality in economics and psychology', *Journal of Business* 59: 209–24.

Sinn, H. -W. and G. Sinn (1992) *Jumpstart: The Economic Unification of Germany*, Cambridge, Mass.: MIT Press.

Smith, M. (1996) 'Shareholder activism by institutional investors: Evidence from CalPERS', *Journal of Finance* 51 (1): 227–52.

Snehota, I. (1993) 'Market as network and the nature of the market process', in D. Deo (ed.), *Advances in International Marketing*, Greenwich, CT: JAI Press, 31–41.

Soós, K. (1990) 'Privatisation, dogma-free self-management and ownership reform', *Eastern European Economics* 28 (4): 53–70.

Sorge, A. (1993) 'Arbeit, Organisation und Arbeitsbeziehungen in Ostdeutschland', *Berliner Journal für Soziologie* 4 (4): 549–67.

Soskice, D. (1994) 'Advanced economies in open world markets and comparative institutional advantages: patterns of business coordination, national institutional frameworks and company product market innovation strategies', mimeo, Social Science Research Centre Berlin.

*Spiegel* (1997) 'Provision für das Netzwerk' *51* (8): 82–7.

Stark, D. (1992) 'Path dependence and privatisation strategies in East Central Europe', *East European Politics and Societies* 6 (1): 17–54.

Stark, D. (1996a) 'Networks of Assets, Chains of Debt: Recombinant Property in Hungary', in R. Frydman, C. W. Gray and A. Rapaczynski (eds), *Corporate Governance in Central Europe and Russia. Vol. 2: Insiders and the State*, Budapest, London and New York: CEU Press, 109–50.

Stark, D. (1996b) 'Recombinant property in Eastern European capitalism', *American Journal of Sociology* **101** (4): 993–1027.

Steinherr, A. (1993) 'An innovatory package for financial sector reforms in Eastern European countries', *Journal of Banking and Finance* **17**: 1033–57.

Steinherr, A. and P. Gilbert (1994) 'Six proposals in search of financial sector reform in Eastern Europe', *MOCT-MOST* **4** (1): 101–14.

Stiglitz, J. (1992) 'The design of financial systems for the newly emerging democracies of Eastern Europe', in C. Clague and G. Rausser (eds), *The Emergence of Market Economies in Eastern Europe*, Cambridge, Mass. and Oxford: Blackwell, 161–85.

*Süddeutsche Zeitung* (1998a) 'Zulieferer verursacht bei Ford-Werken 100 Millionen DM Umsatzausfall', 18 June.

*Süddeutsche Zeitung* (1998b) 'Kiekert will sich mit Ford einigen', 24 June.

Süß, D. (1997) 'Conflicting aims of privatization', in M. Sławińska (ed.), *From Plan to Market*, Pozna: Akademia Ekonomiczna w Poznaniu, 97–108.

Swaan, W. (1997) 'Knowledge, transaction costs and the creation of markets in post-socialist economies', in H. Brezinski and M. Fritsch (eds), *The Emergence and Evolution of Markets*, Cheltenham: Elgar, 115–32.

Szalai, E. (1982) 'The new stage of reform process in Hungary and the large enterprises', *Acta Oeconomica* **34**: 25–46.

Szalai, E. (1990) 'See-saw: the economic mechanisms and large-company interests', *Acta Oeconomica* **42**: 101–36.

Szanyi, M. (1998) 'The role of foreign direct investment in restructuring and modernizing transition economies: an overview of literature on Hungary', WIIW Research Report No. 244, Vienna Institute for International Economic Studies, Vienna, 28–59.

Sztompka, P. (1993) 'Civilizational incompetence: the trap of post-communist societies', *Zeitschrift für Soziologie* **22** (2): 85–95.

Tardos, M. (1972) 'A gazdasági verseny problémái hazánkban' (The problems of economic competition in Hungary), *Közgazdasági Szemle* (2).

Teubal, M. and E. Zuscovitch (1994) 'Demand revealing and knowledge differentiation through network evolution', in B. Johansson, C. Karlsson and L. Westin (eds), *Patterns of a Network Economy*, Heidelberg: Springer, 15–31.

Teubner, G. (1992) 'Die vielköpfige Hydra – Netzwerke als kollektive Akteure höherer Ordnung', in W. Krohn and G. Küppers (eds), *Emergenz und Selbstorganisation*, Frankfurt/M. : Suhrkamp, 189–216.

Thieme, J. (1995) 'The legal structure of the national investment funds', in W. Quaisser, R. Woodward and B. Baszczyk (eds), *Privatization in Poland and East Germany: A Comparison*, Working Paper No. 180, Osteuropa-Institut Munich, 265–87.

Thornton, J. and N. Mikheeva (1996) 'The strategies of foreign and foreign-assisted firms in the Russian Far East: alternatives to missing infrastructure', *Comparative Economic Studies* **38** (4): 85–120.

TLG (1996) *Zahlen, Daten, Fakten*, Berlin: Treuhand-Liegenschaftsgesellschaft.

Topkis, D. (1978) 'Minimizing a submodular function on a lattice', *Operations Research* 26 (2): 305–21.

Treasury of the Republic of Poland (1998) 'Role of the State Treasury as a NIF Shareholder', mimeo, Warsaw.

Treuhand (1991a) *Handbuch Privatisierung*, Berlin: Treuhand.

Treuhand (1991b) *Monatsbericht März*, Berlin: Treuhand.

Treuhand (1994a) *Dokumentation 1990–1994*, 15 vols, Berlin: Treuhand.

Treuhand (1994b) *Final Report of the Treuhandanstalt as of Dec. 31, 1994*, Berlin: BVS.

U-Ausschuß (1994) 'Bericht des 2. Untersuchungsausschusses Treuhandanstalt', in Treuhand (ed.), *Dokumentation 1990–1994*, Berlin, vol. 13, 342–992; vol. 14, 10–513.

Udell, G. and P. Wachtel (1995) 'Financial system design for formerly planned economies', *Financial Markets, Institutions and Instruments* 4 (2): 1–59.

Ulrich, P. (1987) *Transformation der ökonomischen Vernunft*, Berne and Stuttgart: Haupt.

Ulrich, R. (1995) *Das Ungewißheitsproblem bei Unternehmensbewertungen in den neuen Bundesländern*, Munich: VVF.

UNCTAD (1997) *World Investment Report 1997*, New York and Geneva: United Nations.

UNECE (1996) *Economic Survey of Europe in 1995–1996*, Geneva: United Nations Economic Commission for Europe.

van Tulder, R. and W. Ruigrok (1997) 'European cross-national production networks in the auto industry: Eastern Europe as the low end of European car complexes', mimeo, Rotterdam and St. Gallen.

van Wijnbergen, S. (1994) 'On the role of banks in enterprise restructuring: the Polish example', Discussion Paper No. 898, CEPR, London.

van Wijnbergen, S. and A. Marcincin (1995) 'Voucher privatization, corporate control and the cost of capital: an analysis of the Czech privatization programme', Discussion Paper No. 1215, CERP, London.

Vaubel, R. (1992) 'Comment on Holger Schmieding, "Alternative approaches to privatization: some notes on the debate"', in H. Siebert (ed.), *Privatization*, Tübingen, Mohr, 112–14.

Vickers, J. and G. Yarrow (1991) 'Economic perspectives on privatization', *Journal of Economic Perspectives* 5 (2): 111–32.

Wagener, H. -J. (1996) 'What type of capitalism is produced by privatization?', in B. Dallago and L. Mittone (eds), *Economic Institutions, Markets and Competition*, Cheltenham: Elgar, 90–110.

Wagener, H. -J. (1997) 'Privateigentum und Unternehmenskontrolle in Transformationswirtschaften', in D. Cassel (ed.), *Institutionelle Probleme der Systemtransformation*, Berlin: Duncker & Humblot, 165–88.

Wasserman, S. and K. Faust (1994) *Social Network Analysis*, Cambridge, UK: Cambridge University Press.

Weimar, R. (1993) *Treuhandgesetz: Kommentar*, Stuttgart: Kohlhammer.

Weisbach, M. (1988) 'Outside directors and CEO turnover', *Journal of Financial Economics* 20: 431–60.

Weitzman, M. L. (1993) 'Economic transformation: can theory help?', *European Economic Review* 37 (2–3): 549–55.

White, M. (1996) 'The costs of corporate bankruptcy', in J. Bhandhari and L. A. Weiss (eds), *Corporate Bankruptcy. Economic and Legal Perspectives*, Cambridge, UK: Cambridge University Press, 467–500.

Williamson, O. (1985) *The Economic Institutions of Capitalism: Firms, Markets, Relational Contracting*, New York: Free Press.

Williamson, O. (1991) 'Comparative economic organization: The analysis of discrete structural alternatives', *Administrative Science Quarterly* 36 (2): 269–96.

Winiecki, J. (1995) 'Polish mass privatisation programme: the unloved child in a suspect family', in *Mass Privatisation: An Initial Assessment*, Paris: OECD, 47–60.

Wolff, E. (1996) 'The productivity slowdown: the culprit at last? Follow up on Hulten and Wolff', *American Economic Review* 86 (5): 1239–52.

World Bank (1996a) *World Development Report 1996: From Plan to Market*, New York: Oxford University Press.

World Bank (1996b) *Bureaucrats in Business*, Washington, DC.

Zeckhauser, R. and J. Pound (1990) 'Are large shareholders effective monitors?', in R. G. Hubbard (ed.), *Asymmetric Information, Corporate Finance and Investment*, Chicago: University of Chicago Press, 149–80.

Zemanovicová, D. and L. Zitnanská (1996), *Comparative Report of Bankruptcy Regulation: The Czech Republic & Slovakia*, Bratislava: Center for Economic Development.

# Name Index

# Subject Index

Note: page numbers in **bold** type refer to illustrative figures or tables.